OVER HERE

AND

OVER THERE:
Ilford aerodromes and airmen in the Great War

John Barfoot

Ian Henry Publications

ISBN 0 86025 845 2

The photograph on the cover
is of three advanced pupils in Sopwith Camels of 54 Training Depôt Station
in formation above some Avro and Curtiss training machines,
Fairlop aerodrome, 1918,
and is reproduced by courtesy of the Imperial War Museum

Published by
Ian Henry Publications, Ltd.
20 Park Drive, Romford, Essex RM1 4LH
and printed by
Interprint, Ltd.
Malta

PREFACE

Not since the riotous celebrations following the relief of the British garrison at Ladysmith during the Boer war, had the good people of Ilford in the county of Essex witnessed such goings on.

A locomotive on the sidings at Goodmayes ceased shunting to add yet another train whistle to a rising crescendo of factory hooters and ships' sirens along the Thames that accompanied the wildly cheering population of London and the suburbs.

Senior citizens of Ilford still recall vividly the early hours of Sunday, 3rd September, 1916, when the first German airship fell in flames on England.

Unlike the previous abandonment of British reserve sixteen years earlier, no attempts were made to light bonfires in the streets, as other `Zepps' with engines silenced may have been concealed in the clouds.

Lieutenant William Leefe-Robinson of No.39HD Squadron had pursued the `Zepp" illuminated by searchlights above the northern outskirts of London, before emptying three drums of incendiary and explosive bullets into the enormous underbelly of the raider.

The resulting fireball illuminated London and the Hertfordshire countryside as the blazing wreck of the German army airship fell out of the sky.

Overnight Leefe Robinson became the hero of the nation and the most famous pilot in the Royal Flying Corps. Subsequent public adulation of this gallant airman, who flew from Suttons Farm aerodrome, assured Leefe Robinson and Hornchurch their rightful place in history.

In consquence, two sister Essex aerodromes, Hainault Farm, Ilford, and North Weald Basset, also manned by No.39HD Squadron during the autumn of 1916, have remained in the shadow of the airship and his aerodrome.

Some eighty years have elapsed since the armistice ended the war to end all wars; however, better late than never, here is the account of Ilford airmen who also flew and fought over here and over there during the Great War of 1914-1918.

John Barfoot,
Romford,
Essex.
1998

ACKNOWLEDGEMENTS

My sincere thank you to the late Stanley Apling and his family, the late Basil Amps (Ilford Recorder), John E Barfoot, Chaz Bowyer (C&C), Leslie Bills, Rev V C Brown (All Saints, Chigwell) Peter Chapman (C&C), Muriel Cobb, Peter Craig (nephew of Lieut G R Craig, MC), Michael Crowther, Ian Dowling (Redbridge Library), Ken Feline (C&C), Norman Franks (C&C), George Gower, Barry Gray (C&C), the late Peter Gray (C&C), Pamela Hart (Hainault factory estate), Jeffery Harvey (C&C), Walter Hearn (nephew of Lieut C H Trotter MC), John Heathcott (RAF Museum), Trevor Henshaw (C&C), Sqd Ldr H M Horscroft (No.44 Squadron Association), K M Hunter (RAF Museum), Peter Jackson (Redbridge Library), Paul Leaman (C&C), Stuart Leslie (C&C), the late Cecil Lewis (the last survivor of No.44 Squadron, who flew from Hainault Farm aerodrome), Bert Lockwood (I&DHS), PC Jim Mitchell, Edward Mills (ex-Sgt No.44 Squadron), the late Bill Morgan (C&C), Eric Munday (C&C), Merle Olmsted (C&C), Harry Parr (C&C), Sheila and Colin Ross, Arthur Scarborough, Vic Sheppard (C&C), Lawrie Short (ICHS), Nell Smith, Bill Stock (Ilford Recorder), Mark Sweetingham (Ilford Recorder), Bill Thomas (C&C), Rev Michael Trodden (St Peter's, Aldborough Hatch), the late Douglas Whetton (C&C), Ted Wiles (ex-RNAS), Norman Wright.

Plus the helpful unknown staff, not acknowledged above of

The Ilford Recorder (past and present), Imperial War Museum, Public Records Office, Redbridge Public Library (local history room), Royal Air Force Museum (Research and Information Dept)

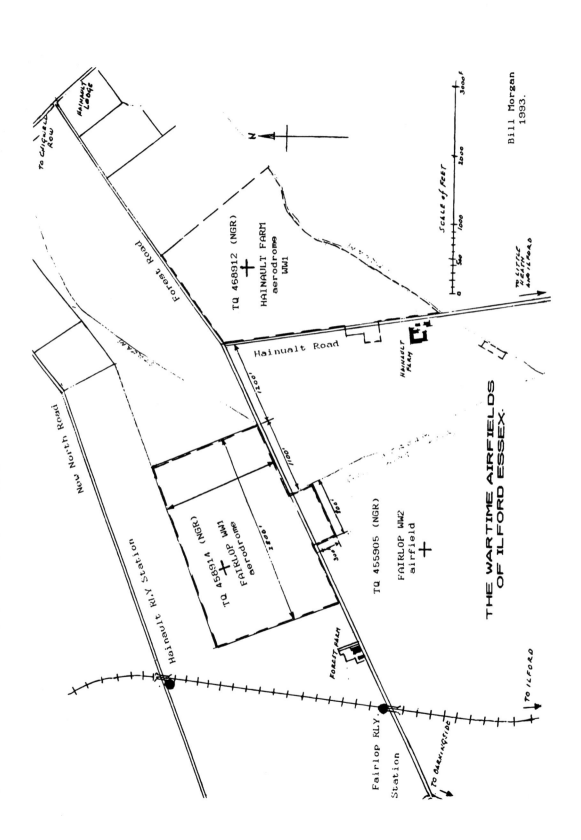

THE WARTIME AIRFIELDS
OF ILFORD ESSEX.

Bill Morgan
1993.

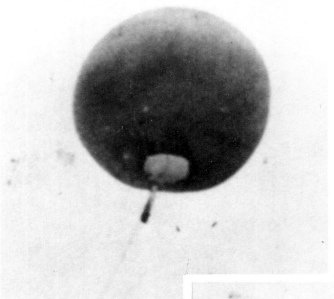

Elsa Spencer above
Gordon Fields just before
her parachute descent at the
1914 Whitsun carnival
(*Stanley Apling*)

Bentfield Charles Hucks
prepares to take off in his Blériot
monoplane from Loxford Park,
Ilford, in August, 1913
(*Stanley Apling*)

1914

The Great War of 1914 came to Ilford following the finest August Bank Holiday weather in living memory; brilliant sunshine had made light of the war clouds looming across the English Channel. On Bank Holiday Monday townsfolk availed themselves of the parks and recreation grounds. Brass band music, provided by the Council in the major parks, was much appreciated by all and the boating on the lakes in South and Valentines Parks continued all day. The young men of the Ilford 3rd XI battled it out with the Little Heath and Goodmayes 2nd XI on a cricket pitch in Valentines Park. That evening, the 'Hip' - the popular Ilford Hippodrome - played to a packed house with the revue *All French*; after the show the audience over-flowed on to the pavements of Ilford Broadway, enjoying the cool night air and the final hours of an England at peace.

The outbreak of war with Germany on Tuesday, 4th August, did not concern local farmers and Health Authorities as much as the continuing heat wave. Farmers prayed for rain; there had been little since March, many crops had been ruined and the harvest would be poor. Doctors were concerned about the effect on health the prolonged hot weather would have. Posters were on display in Ilford warning of the dangers, particularly to infants. Insects trapped on sticky fly papers suspended from kitchen ceilings buzzed incessantly. Many of the late Victorian houses built just off Ilford Lane had deep coal cellars where milk and perishable foods were stored in the cool cupboards away from the mice.

Within days of Britain's entry into the war, Ilford suffered the first of many hardships to follow - 80 men, Special Transport Reservists, were called up from the Seven King's omnibus garage, and 25 buses

had to be cut from routes in the area. Long suffering local farmers had vehicles confiscated to transport baggage of the 4th Battalion Essex Regiment, as they marched off to war along Green Lane from the Territorial Army depôt on Gordon Fields.

In happier days Gordon Fields had been the host to many local carnivals and sporting events. At the 1914 Whitsun Fête the popular and intrepid balloonist Captain Spencer returned to Ilford and allowed his equally intrepid wife to make a parachute descent. The balloon carried the courageous lady aloft from Gordon Fields, suspended by her parachute harness. By the time sufficient height had been attained, a slight breeze had wafted Mrs Spencer across the playing fields, causing her to alight upon the roof of a house in nearby Golf Road. Ladders were hurriedly obtained and many hands helped the shaken but uninjured lady to safety.

Ilford schoolboy, Stanley Apling, living with his family in Thorold Road, also enjoyed the town's Whitsun festivities. Photography being one of his hobbies, he captured the image of Mrs Spencer carried aloft by balloon with his camera.

Even more thrilling for Stanley had been visit of the famous Essex aviator, Bentfield Charles Hucks, and his Blériot monoplane to give demonstration flights from local parks the year before. He had become interested in aviation when the French aviator, Louis Blériot, made newspaper headlines with the first powered flight across the English Channel in a monoplane of his own design on 25th July, 1909. It was in 1913 that the Blériot Xl-2 owned by B C Hucks became the first aeroplane seen at close quarters by many Ilfordians, including young Stanley, who photographed Hucks and his flying machine at rest in Loxford Park. B C Hucks, the first English aviator to intentionally loop the loop, was booked to return to Barking Park on 20th

August to demonstrate his flying skills.

The splendid summer weather provided ideal flying weather, not only for Hucks' monoplane, but for the thriving Ilford Model Aeroplane Club, of which the very busy airman found the time to be Patron.

After the German invasion of Belgium bringing a hitherto reluctant Britain into the war, B C Hucks immediately cancelled his flying displays, to volunteer his services and aeroplanes to the Royal Flying Corps.

Despite strong rumours circulating that it would all be over by Christmas, bar the shouting, a fear existed in the town that the war would increase unemployment. The local firm of Harrison & Gibson urged customers to have their furniture recovered, as they were anxious to keep their workforce employed for the duration.

A small, well-trained British Expeditionary Force embarked for Flanders, led by veterans of the Boer War, their only fear being the large armies of their allies, France and Russia, would bring the war to a swift end, before they could get into action. On Friday, 14th August, the B.E.F were reinforced by the arrival of men and machines of the fledgling Royal Flying Corps, a mere two years old. Lacking experience and equipment the `Cavalry of the Air' were expected to scout ahead of the victorious advance of what the German High Command called `The Contemptible Little Army' of the British. Generals and `old sweats' alike were sceptical and amused by the mixed collection of fragile wood and fabric flying machines that the military aviators brought to the battlefield.

Four squadrons of the Royal Flying Corps were on active service in France when the Zeppelin menace that the people of Ilford had been so frequently warned of in pre-war sabre rattling days became a reality.

Reports in the dailies of Zeppelins throwing bombs on the city of Antwerp on 24th August, resulted in many sightings over England during the following weeks. Most curious had been of a Zeppelin hiding among the hills of Cumberland by day, only venturing out after dark.

2nd Lieut B C Hucks received orders to patrol the area in one of his own Blériot monoplanes, now carrying service number 619 either side of the rudder. The same machine had been destined to thrill the crowds at Barking Park had it not been for the war.

There were many similar reports involving Zeppelins, of flashing lights, and mysterious strangers speaking German. During October, 26 German nationals were rounded up in Ilford and Barking to be interned for the duration. The people of England were unaware that the RFC had just two complete squadrons left in Britain - and they were for training purposes.

Ilford mustered 225 Special Constables; Goodmayes and Chadwell Heath supplied a further 40. Their duties included enforcing wartime lighting restrictions and, with the recent drought in mind, patrolling the farmland to the north and east of the town, in case the expected Zeppelin raiders were to drop incendiary devices.

December arrived with still no sign of Zeppelins crossing the North Sea. In France a ring of high angle anti-balloon guns and searchlights surrounded Paris to defend the population from an expected aerial attack.

The proprietors of the Premier Picture Palace in Ilford High Road now allowed members of the armed services admission at half price. Throughout the war, all four of the town's picture palaces, along with the Ilford Hippodrome, would be popular with the many service personnel billeted in the area. An indoor roller skating rink near Ilford Police Station had to close later in the war, as the premises were required for urgent war work.

Ilford Special Constables on parade, 1915. Sub-Inspector H W A Apling is nearest the camera (*Stanley Apling*)

This Handley Page Type E monoplane made the first heavier-than-air flight across London from Fairlop to Brooklands, via the Thames, 27th July, 1912

Preparations for Ilford's first wartime Christmas were under way, with gifts for Tommy in the trenches a number one priority, when the newspapers released censored details of a hit and run breakfast-time bombardment by battle cruisers of the Imperial German Navy. The undefended coastal towns of Scarborough, Whitby and Hartlepool suffered many civilian casualties. Had there been any doubts that Germany would wage war on British civilians they were dispelled even before the first bomb-carrying Zeppelin droned through the night sky of England.

Throughout that autumn, Ilford had become accustomed to the sounds of war, due to the incessant popping of musketry from the Rainham rifle ranges during daylight hours and the dull thuds of artillery at practice further down the River Thames.

Distant gunfire heard in the near deserted streets of the town just after noon on Christmas Day aroused little interest and no alarm. The people of Ilford were not aware that a lone German seaplane, intent on raiding London, was responsible for the gunners' Yuletide activity. Oberleutnant Stephan Prondzynski and his observer, flying a single engined Friedrichshafen floatplane, crossed the Kent coast at 12.20 hrs. The day before they had carried out a surprise raid on Dover, shattering the peace of Christmas Eve by dropping a small bomb, shattering a few windows.

The German airmen would have been in sight of the suburbs of London as they flew up the Thames despite the misty conditions prevailing, when at 4,000 ft above Erith, they were confronted by one of the few modern aeroplanes that the Royal Flying Corps had airworthy in Britain. Machine-gun fire from the front cockpit of the Vickers Gunbus forced the unarmed German crew to abort the first attempted air-raid on London. 2nd Lieut Montagu Chidson chased the German back down the river - his observer, Corporal Martin, continued firing until the belt-fed Maxim suffered a serious stoppage in the breach that the observer could not clear in the air. Before the enemy seaplane recrossed the coast two bombs were released, exploding in open fields at Cliffe. Returning to Joyce Green aerodrome, the Vickers Gunbus came under fire from over-enthusiastic gunners at Purfleet and damaged the undercart landing in the white ground mist.

It had been a stroke of luck for the British defences that the first enemy aeroplane attempting to raid London had encountered the machine gun carrying Gunbus - no doubt it misled the enemy about the true strength of Britain's air defence. Exaggerated eye witness accounts of British and German machines locked in combat during the raid were reported.

By coincidence both pilots engaged in that historic encounter survived the war. In February, 1915, the Royal Navy rescued Prondzynski and his observer from the North Sea, after they had carryied out a night bombing raid on Essex. A few days later, on the first day of March, Montagu Chidson also became a prisoner of war whilst serving with No.16 Squadron in France, when he and his observer were shot down behind enemy lines by anti-aircraft fire.

The enemy aviators who attempted to raid the capital of the British Empire on Christmas Day, would have dropped their explosive missiles upon the vast area of

London docks. Not only were the docks a prime target, but the Kaiser, contrary to propaganda in Britain, had forbidden the bombing the city itself, home of his cousin, King George V.

As the year drew to close, the advance of the Imperial German war machine through Belgium had placed London within the range of Zeppelins and pressure mounted upon the reluctant Emperor to allow airship raids on Britain. In the Fatherland many minds, civil and military, were convinced that bombing London by Zeppelins would force Britain to sue for peace.

The rigid airships of Count Ferdinand von Zeppelin had won admiration in pre-war days by carrying hundreds of passengers in safety and style hitherto unheard of. There had been successful but small non-rigid airships constructed by Britain and her future allies, but they did not match the size, range, duration or payload of the German creation.

Alarmed by von Zeppelin's success, Britain, as early as 1908 - the year that saw the first British aeroplane make a powered hop - commissioned a 512 feet copy of the German dirigible to be constructed at a Vickers shipyard. Grossly overweight HM Airship No 1, unofficially and optimistically named *Mayfly*, had to be modified so often, that finally, on leaving its floating shed for more tests in September, 1911, the weakened framework, caught by cross winds, twisted, buckled and collapsed on to the water: it was the first of a series of disasters destined to plague rigid airships made in Britain.

Airborne at the turn of the century, before the Wright brothers' tiny biplane, the ageing pioneer von Zeppelin had combined internal combustion engines with a giant fabric covered lattice work cylinder, fabricated from ultra-lightweight alloy girders The flying cigar owed its buoyancy to a vast amount of hydrogen contained in separate cells along its interior. Had it not been for the discovery of 'inflammable air' (hydrogen) by the English chemist, Henry Cavendish, in 1776, the first war in the air would have been a different story. As it transpired, the hydrogen that made flight possible for the large airships also proved to be their Achilles heel when used as weapons in time of war. New Year's Eve arrived in Ilford with still no sign of the bomb dropping Zeppelins that had been expected months earlier.

The war had nearly been over by Christmas, but fortunately the German Army had been fought to a standstill, occupying a large area of France and almost all of Belgium. Reports of an unofficial truce that had taken place on Christmas Eve between the opposing British and German troops on the Western Front made cheerful reading in the dailies, but the High Command on both sides did not allow it to happen again.

No.1 Squadron
Note: RAF Squadron badges were not officially adopted until the mid 1920s, but are included here for interest

7

1915

The New Year began tragically, with a railway accident at Ilford, when the 7.06 morning express from Clacton collided with a local train from Gidea Park just outside Ilford station: ten people were killed and thirty more injured in the disaster. Soldiers of the Essex Regiment assisted railway staff to free the trapped and injured.

On 10th January, the German Emperor approved the bombing of England, but not London, by the Zeppelin fleet. Desperate raids by airmen of the Royal Naval Air Service on Zeppelin sheds in the closing weeks of 1914 had helped to convince the Kaiser to commit his airships to raids before they were all destroyed on the ground. Anxiously, the Imperial Navy studied weather forecasts, for they did not want to allow Army airships to beat them to England. Three Naval Zeppelins set out on Tuesday, 19th January: weather conditions were still far from ideal for crossing the North Sea, as many of the 16 officers and men on board each ship were carried in open gondola type cars exposed to the elements. Still ninety miles from the English coast, L6 suffering from engine trouble and, weighed down by a coating of ice, returned to base at Nordholz. Her two sister ships, with a lethal load of pear-shaped high explosive and tarred rope bound incendiary bombs, were forced off course from their intended industrial targets along the River Humber by strong head-winds. The deep drone of Zeppelin motors was heard for the first time in the night skies of England, and bombs fell on Great Yarmouth, King's Lynn and villages in Norfolk. As the drone of the raiders faded out to sea, four civilians had been killed and 16 injured in the county that had not been the intended target. Two Home Defence aeroplanes managed to get airborne, braving the squally blackness, but without visual contact with ground signals, it was at best a token gesture by the RFC. In the event both of the primitive night fighters crash landed in the dark, fortunately the brave crews escaped without serious injury.

News that the long awaited Zeppelin raid on Britain had taken place, along with reports of even larger machines already under construction in Germany, added to the post Christmas mid-winter gloom over the town.

Very few had seen the two airships over Norfolk, and on the following morning people of Snettisham gathered outside their church arguing whether the raiders had been Zeppelins or aeroplanes, when a lady, determined to have the last word remarked, "All I can say is it was the biggest sausage I ever saw in my life."

The loss of both L3 and L4 during winter storms on 17th February was a disaster for the German Naval Airship Division, expected to carry out important reconnaissance missions for the Navy whilst endeavouring to build up a fleet of aerial cruisers to bomb Britain.

Gale force winds across the North Sea made it impossible for the crew of Naval Zeppelin L8 to reach Britain on the night of 26th February: her disappointed crew had expected to be decorated with Iron Crosses, as all the crew members of the two Norfolk raiders had been.

On 4th March Naval Zeppelin L8 again set course for England, via the

A Henry Farman F27 of 'A' Flight No. 2 Wing, in which Sub-Lt Jameson and Flt-Lt C A Maitland-Heriot were shot down and captured

Wilfred Chalmers Jameson, RNVR
(*Ilford War Memorial Gazette*)

Belgian coast. Descending to less than a thousand feet to check the exact position of his craft, the unfortunate commander crossed the Belgian lines in error. Concentrated Belgian small arms fire so seriously damaged the gas cells of the airship that the raid had to be abandoned. Despite frantic efforts by the crew, L8 crashed to complete destruction whilst trying to return to Düsseldorf in the early hours of 5th March.

Wilfred Chalmers Jameson, a Royal Naval Volunteer Reservist, of Woodlands Road, Ilford, had been called to active service within days of Britain's entry into the war. In October, 1914, he was with the Royal Naval Division in Belgium. After the fall of Antwerp, he made his way to neutral Holland. On 1st January, 1915, Jameson attempted to escape from the Internment Camp at Groningen, but was recaptured. At the end of March, Jameson again escaped and, after an exciting ten days, succeeded in returning to England. Later in the year, Wilfred Jameson obtained a commission in the Royal Naval Air Service. In February, 1917, whilst serving in the Ægean area, Sub-Lt Jameson's aeroplane was forced down behind Turkish lines. He escaped from a PoW camp at Afron Kara Hissar in Turkey on the 8th September, 1918, remaining at liberty until his recapture on the 15th September. Attempting yet another escape from the Turks, Jameson was wounded and carried off by armed brigands, never to be seen again. The Admiralty later certified his death on or about 15th September.

Imperial Navy Zeppelin L9, on a reconnaissance mission over the North Sea on Wednesday, 14th April, 1915, made the most of an improvement in the weather to carry out the second airship raid on England. Having got permission by the wireless, Kptlt Heinrich Mathy set course for the Tyneside. Crossing the blacked out coastline at 19.45 hr, all the high explosive bombs released from the internal bomb bay fell on open country, although some of the incendiaries hit property in Wallsend. One woman and a child were injured in the attack.

Three Naval Zeppelins that visited the East Coast the following night were also thwarted by the lighting restrictions. Unsure of their exact positions, random bombs were released on Maldon and Lowestoft, injuring one person. Two RNAS machines from Yarmouth were aloft during the raid without seeing the Zeppelins. Both aeroplanes later returned safely to their station with the aid of petrol flares being lit at intervals along the landing strip. An RNAS machine from Whitley Bay that had searched in vain the night before, during the raid on Wallsend, had also made a safe landing with the aid of improvised landing flares, in spite of what had been described as exceptionally dark conditions in the area.

Along the Western Front, friend and foe alike, bogged down in the spring mud of no-man's-land, were calling upon the young airmen and their flying machines that had once amused, to perform an ever increasing range of duties, over and beyond the enemy lines.

A very low level bombing raid, carried out at 300 ft, on an important railway line just west of Courtrai, won the first Victoria Cross awarded to a British airman. Although mortally wounded by small arms fire, Lieut. W B Rhodes-Moorhouse returned to his own aerodrome to report the success of his mission on Friday, 16th April, 1915.

Attempting to break the stalemate on the Western Front, the German Army released a cloud of yellow/green chlorine gas, to be carried by the wind towards the allied trenches at Ypres on Thursday, 22nd April. Newspapers in Britain retorted with a barrage of `Hun' barbarism, but, as the war progressed, the allies also resorted to the use of poison gas.

German Army airships, transferred from their bases in Rhineland to occupied Belgium and France the previous month, were now ready to fly to England. The first, LZ38, crossed the East Anglian coast at midnight on 29/30th April, dropping bombs on Ipswich and Bury St Edmunds. There were no casualties during the two hours the raider cruised above Norfolk and Suffolk. Thick mist prevented Home Defence machines from flying, until long after the Zeppelin had departed.

A telegram received from Dover at 18.00 hrs Monday evening, 3rd May, advised the Matron of the Ilford Emergency Hospital that wounded servicemen would be arriving that night. The first intake of wounded to be cared for at Ilford included Canadian soldiers, who arrived at Newbury Park railway station just before midnight, to be transfered to the nearby hospital by ambulances. The men had left Boulogne at 16.00 hrs. that afternoon.

The powerful beat of Zeppelin motors echoed across the Thames Estuary in the early hours of Monday, 10th May, as Army airship LZ38 criss-crossed the Thames seeking targets. Bombs fell on Southend; one person died of injuries and two more were wounded in this second raid by the LZ38. Ten RNAS aeroplanes, airborne from five aerodromes between Chingford, Essex, to Yarmouth, Norfolk, had been unable to detect the giant bombing machine. When daylight arrived, a weighted streamer used to drop messages from aircraft was picked up from the sands at Canvey Island. The streamer pouch contained an engraved calling card from Hauptmann Eric Linnarz, who commanded LZ38: on the back of the card he had written, "You English! We have come and will come again soon, to kill or cure! German."

An observation balloon company had to be borrowed from the French Army, to assist the British artillery at the battle of Aubers Ridge. German and French kite balloon observers suspended beneath the gas bags in wicker work baskets with powerful binoculars, reported by telephone via the cable from the ground every enemy movement and ranged the otherwise blind artillery on distant targets. One hundred and three RFC aeroplanes with large red white and blue cockade roundels painted on fuselage and mainplanes played their part in the battle. The French method of identifying warplanes had been adopted, with one subtle difference, the British machines had a blue outer ring.

The loss of two officers of No.4 Squadron, shot down by British small arms fire on 26th October, 1914, after several RFC/RNAS aircraft had been the recipients of `friendly' fire, confirmed the fact that the Union Flag adopted by the British, appeared at distance to be enemy insignia due to the prominence of the red cross.

January had been the delivery date promised to the German Naval Airship Service of a new type of bomber, known as the Zeppelin Type P, 536 feet in length. Although four months late, the Imperial Nay welcomed the new ships that could attain speeds of almost 60 mph, thanks to four 210 hp six-cylinder Maybach motors. Designated L10 to L19 by the Navy, the new ships, with a range of 1,336 miles, would be able to bomb London from Naval bases in Germany.

True to his word, the commander of Army Zeppelin LZ38 did return, bombing Ramsgate and Dover during the early hours of Monday, 17th May. LZ38 was pursued out to sea by an RNAS pilot flying an Avro 504B, until the airship escaped through the clouds. Alerted by the Admiralty, RNAS pilots from Dunkirk and Furnes on the French coast were on the wing to trap the returning raider and encountered another Army Zeppelin instead - LZ39 returning from an aborted raid upon Calais just before 04.00 hrs. Two RNAS Nieuport type 12 machines, one armed with a Lewis machine-gun, the other with a .45 Martin-Henry carbine and incendiary bullets, attacked the LZ39 just visible in the soft glow of the approaching dawn. Unperturbed by the Nieuports, the LZ39 released water ballast, opened throttles and easily outclimbed them.

Ten minutes later Flt Lieut A W Bigsworth, piloting Avro 504B No 1009, encountered the airship at 10,000 feet above Ostend in occupied Belgium. Coaxing the Avro biplane 200 feet above the Zeppelin, Bigsworth released all four 20 pound Hales bombs from a rack beneath the narrow fuselage of his machine. In spite of heavy German anti-aircraft fire and with no other weaponry on board to finish off LZ39, he remained to watch the damaged smoking monster descend towards Evère with dead and wounded crew members on board. At long last, after months of frustration, the Royal Naval Air Service had encountered and inflicted serious damage on an airborne Zeppelin.

It had been feared that the riots taking place in east London, following the torpedoing of the Cunard liner, *Lusitania*, without warning on Friday, 7th May, would spread to Ilford. Serious anti-German rioting had taken place at nearby Manor Park during Tuesday, 11th, and Wednesday, 12th May, 1915. Shops in the area with German sounding names were vandalised and looted. Forewarned, the Ilford police and specials were out in force Wednesday evening when a crowd gathered on Ilford Hill opposite Mr Zissell's bakery; windows were smashed by missiles, but the police dispersed the rioters, assisted by a sudden downpour of rain. The single torpedo released by Kptlt Walter Schweizer, in command of the U20, would have far reaching consequences for Imperial Germany. Within twenty minutes, the ocean liner sank beneath the waves and 1,201 men, women and children, including 100 American nationals, drowned: the *Lusitania* incident began a chain of events that would eventually bring America into the war alongside the Allies. Among the distressed *Lusitania* survivors had been pretty blonde Elsie Hardy, a resident of the Ilford lane.

An American journalist in Paris in the spring of 1915, overheard a conversation in a boulevard café, that reflected the increase in aerial activity along the Western Front. 'Oh that Garros!' (Roland Garros a concert pianist who had become a renowned pre-war airman) 'Five enemy machines he has destroyed, that Garros is an ace.' Unaware that a leading sportsman or athlete in France would be called an ace, the journalist referred to Garros in a despatch to New York as an 'ace' for shooting down five enemy aeroplanes. The word 'ace' came into common use during the war, to describe an allied airman with five or more enemy machines credited to him.

Roland Garros' reign as top scoring fighter pilot was short-lived, engine failure forced his Morane monoplane down behind enemy lines. Upon inspecting their prize the Germans discovered that the French machine carried a machine-gun that fired forward through the propeller arc via crude but effective hardened steel deflectors. The Fokker factory were soon fitting forward firing machine-guns to their monoplanes with a major improvement, they had rejected the idea of bullets striking the armoured propeller blades, inventing instead a mechanical device, worked by camshaft and levers allowing the machine-gun to fire between the revolving blades. Thanks to the Fokker interrupter gear, German fighter pilots now had the advantage over their opponents in the ever-increasing aerial battles above the trenches.

On the home front the long expected Zeppelin raid on London began at about 23.00 hrs on Monday, 31st May, 1915.

Having carried out a second raid on Southend on the night of Wednesday, 26th, a confident Huptmn Linnarz, again in command of the Army Zeppelin LZ38, crossed the Thames estuary at 22.35 hrs. The airship was reported flying high over Billericay, and 15 minutes later the craft droned over Walthamstow. 16 Alkham Road, Stoke Newington, had the dubious distinction of being the first house in London to be hit by a German bomb. In all the LZ38 dropped 90 incendiaries and 30 small explosive bombs between Stepney and Leytonstone. Casualties were 7 killed; the first fatality of the raid being three-and-a-half-year-old Elsie Leggatt of Cowper Road, Stoke Newington: 32 people were injured. 15 RNAS machines from six

aerodromes carried out defensive patrols; only one pilot, flying an obsolete Blériot mono-plane, caught a glimpse of the Zeppelin in the moonlight, but engine failure forced him to abandon the chase to alight safely on the mud flats at Leigh-on-Sea.

The Royal Naval Air Service lost a champion with the resignation of Winston Churchill, First Lord of the Admiralty, in May, 1915, following the ill-fated Dardanelles expedition. Churchill had recommended the invasion of the Gallipoli Peninsula as a legitimate war gamble. Winston Churchill whilst First Sea Lord, also advocated Royal Naval aircraft not only to protect Britain, but also stationed machines on the Continent to bomb Zeppelins when most vulnerable - in their sheds. Flying from improvised flying fields in Belgium, RNAS pilots launched several daring raids in the autumn of 1914 that resulted in the destruction of a new German Army Zeppelin in its Düsseldorf shed on 8th October, 1914. Returning from the successful bombing of the Z9 (LZ25), thereby delaying part of the German Army plan to terrorise Britain, the tiny Sopwith Tabloid biplane No 168, piloted by Flight Lieutenant Reggie Marix, ran out of fuel and the plucky aviator covered the remainder of his return journey to his field on the outskirts of Antwerp by sharing a railway carriage crowded with Belgian refugees and by pedal cycle.

As First Sea Lord, Winston Churchill, in order to appease public outrage following the bombardment without warning of Durham and Yorkshire coastal towns by German battle cruisers on the morning of 16th December, 1914, wrote publicly to the Mayor of Scarborough, sharing the disappointment that the sea-borne raiders had escaped the pursuing Royal Navy. The letter contained the following sentence, 'Whatever feats of arms the

German Navy may hereafter perform, the stigma of the baby-killers of Scarborough will brand its officers and men while sailors sail the sea.'

After the Zeppelin attacks on England in 1915, resulting in the deaths of women and children, the accolade of 'baby-killers' had been passed on to German airship crews by the British press. Girls at an Ilford Lane factory, incensed by wartime propaganda, refused to return to work after lunch break until the management had assured them that no German nationals were employed by the company. The expected rise in Ilford's unemployed due to the war had not materialised. There had been a small increase in the number of women employed, but the setting up of a special Ministry of Munitions in May, 1915, following the scandal of serious shell shortages at the front, opened up endless opportunities and unemployment became non-existent in the town for the duration of the war. The second battle of Ypres raged throughout May, 1915, advancing the enemy front line almost three miles before grinding to a halt. 5,469 Canadians and 3,888 Indians were among the total of 59,275 British casualties sustained defending 'Wipers'.

Following the German Army winning the race to bomb London, the Imperial Navy ordered that newly commissioned P Type Zeppelins were to be used for raids on England, leaving older craft to carry on fleet reconnaissance duties.

On Friday afternoon, 4th June, rising gently from Nordholz Naval airship base at 13.20 hrs amid cheers from the envious 130 ground crewmen and a host of well wishers, L10, under the command of Kptlt Klaus Hirsch, set course for Britain. Skirting the islands off the Dutch coast, lest British agents telegraph warnings of the intended raid, the droning L10

approached Shoeburyness at 22.15 hrs with two 220lb, twenty 110lb and 90 incendiary bombs, destined for London. Fortunately, her commander mistook his landfall for Lowestoft and, with just a few hours of darkness at his disposal, he decided to bomb Harwich instead. Circling the mouth of the Thames, L10 then proceeded up the river dropping bombs on 'Harwich naval base', in reality Gravesend in Kent. The military hospital, in peace time the Gravesend Yacht Club, was gutted by incendiary bombs; casualties were light, only eight injured with less than £9,000 worth of damage.

The first Schutte-Lanz airship, a wooden framed rival, mistaken by the Home Defences for a Zeppelin, made its debut over England, planning to attack Hull, but, after releasing three bombs on open countryside, Kptlt Fritz Boemack abandoned the raid in the face of strong headwinds, returning SL3 to Nordholz with the remainder of the bomb load. Four RNAS and two RFC aeroplanes were airborne without sighting the raiders.

When David Lloyd George was appointed Minister of Munitions in June, 1915, he faced a daunting task; German factories produced 250,000 high explosive shells a day. British output a mere 700!

One Naval and three Army Zeppelins set out across the North Sea towards England on Sunday, 6th June, with Naval Zeppelin L9 ordered to bomb London if possible. In the event the daring Hptmn Linnarz had to return LZ38 to base, plagued with engine troubles, and both LZ37 and LZ39 aborted their missions. Kptlt Heinrich Mathy, destined to become most famous Zeppelin commander of the war and idol of the German nation, decided to bomb Hull, due to the fine clear night and promise of an early dawn making overland flight to London very risky. Casualties were heavy; 24 killed and 40 injured. The next day rioters smashed and looted many shops in Yorkshire bearing German-sounding names.

Ever alert and in possession of the German airship codes, British Naval Intelligence intercepted wireless signals from LZ37 and LZ39 returning to base in Belgium, aborting their planned raid on England due to fog over the Channel. No.1 (RNAS) Squadron at St Pol were told by direct telephone line from the Admiralty. Despite the ground mist over the aerodrome, two large single engined bombers were already being prepared for a raid on Zeppelin sheds on the far side of Brussels. Following the exploits of No.1 (RNAS) Squadron during the early hours of Monday, 7th June, the Royal Naval Air Service would acquire the reputation of being Rather Naughty After Sunset.

Flt Lieut John Philip Wilson, followed by Sub-Lieut John Stanley Hills, each flying French built Farman F27 pushers, took off from St Pol at 00.45 hrs. Without observer/navigators the machines were able to lift a trio of 65 pound bombs apiece. The pilots had to rely on compass and such landmarks visible through the patchy ground mist to cross occupied Belgium to find the Army Zeppelin sheds at Evère on the far side of Brussels. Meanwhile, two French built Morane-Saulnier high wing monoplanes, in service with No.1 (RNAS) Squadron, were armed with bombs and their 80 hp Gnome rotary engines primed for flight on an

advanced landing ground at Furnes. Shortly after 02.00 hrs, whilst circling at 2,000 ft above Evère trying to locate the Zeppelin sheds, the 53 ft span pusher of Flt Lieut Wilson attracted the attention of a searchlight, reaching for his pocket torch, the pilot satisfied the Germans with short flashes in reply and the beam disappeared. Fifteen minutes later still searching and keeping a lookout for the second Farman, Wilson discerned the huge airship sheds through the swirling mist below. The second of his three bombs caused a terrific explosion. Attracted to the target by the anti-aircraft defences, now frantically firing, as Wilson set course for home, Hills had to climb to 5,000 ft before making his attack. As the British airmen departed they had the satisfaction of seeing the sky behind them lit by eruptions of white hot flames confirming that a hydrogen filled Zeppelin occupied the shed. The RNAS had delivered their own calling cards on Hauptmann Eric Linnarz and the London-bombing Zeppelin LZ38. Both pilots were awarded the Distinguished Service Cross for a most successful night bombing raid on a military target. However, the torching of an airborne 'Zepp' within the hour eclipsed even this fine feat of arms

Airborne fifteen minutes after Wilson and Hills, the Morane monoplanes suffered a set back, Flt Sub-Lieut Rose became lost after the lighting on his instrument panel failed. Although he made a safe descent behind allied lines, his nose heavy bomb laden craft flipped over on to its back. The second Morane, piloted by Flt Sub-Lieut R A J Warneford, climbed through the mist over Dixmunde to catch sight of a distant Zeppelin reflected in the moonlight; it was LZ37 flying serenely homeward at 10,000 feet. Warneford had the reputation of a daredevil - his commanding officer knew it would only be a matter of time before the young aviator covered himself with glory or killed himself in the attempt.

Stalking the monstrous craft for 45 minutes, the Morane swooped in for the kill to be met by a hail of bullets from the not-so-relaxed machine-gunners on top of the airship. Having lost the element of surprise, Warneford banked away to play a cat and mouse game. For reasons that will never be explained, Oberleutnant Otto von der Haegen, the airship commander, did not order the release of ballast to allow LZ37 to out-climb the enemy, but turned following the monoplane, enabling his machine gunners to continue firing, until Warneford out-distanced the slower Zeppelin. Ten minutes later and one thousand feet above, Warneford cautiously approached his prey, switched off his engine and dived on LZ37, descending slowly towards its base. Above the broad back of the giant war machine he began releasing the six 20lb bombs clamped to the Moranes undercarriage. As Warneford toggled the last missile free, the first exploded, tossing the Morane onto its back, fortunately for the pilot, the fragile wire braced wing did not collapse. Endeavouring to regain control of the machine Warneford had no time to watch the blazing Zeppelin fall, the bulk of the debris, with the unfortunate crew members, fell on to a convent in the district of Ghent. Two nuns and a child perished in the inferno; one member of

the Zeppelin crew survived the ordeal with severe burns. Unable to restart the 80 hp Gnome engine, Warneford had no option but to land in enemy occupied territory. The mist that had caused concern during his descent, proved to be a blessing in disguise; as he repaired a broken fuel connection he heard German cavalry passing by unseen. With just enough fuel to recross the allied lines, Warneford landed on the coast, only to be captured by French troops as a spy. A phone call to St Pol produced apologies, a bottle of cognac and gasoline for the faithful Morane to return him to his aerodrome, where he received a telegram from Buckingham Palace the following day, conferring upon him the Victoria Cross for his gallantry.

The Germans tried to keep the destruction of the Zeppelins a secret without success, cartloads of twisted aluminium girders were loaded on to dozens of railway trucks returning to the Fatherland. Aluminium Zepp rings became fashionable among the women of occupied Belgium. A small section of aluminum from the wreckage of LZ37, that had been the first Zeppelin to bomb London, mysteriously found its way on to the desk of the ex-First Lord of the Admiralty, Winston Churchill, vindicating his plan to station RNAS aeroplanes on the Belgian coast. Many an army drill instructor eyeing the latest intake of recruits uttered, 'Thank Gawd we've got a Navy', not knowing how apt those words had been during the first airship raids on the British Isles.

Demands upon the Royal Flying Corps by the army overseas made it impossible for the service to provide an organised air defence. The pilots of the Royal Navy had acquitted themselves magnificently in the opening moves of the German plan to destroy London by fire, burning three of the monstrous war machines in the first year of the war, allowing just one Zeppelin to reach London.

However, the Royal Navy was finding the burden of home defence, in particular the city of London thirty odd miles from the coast and at most risk, growing more difficult as the U-Boat campaign increased. The reluctant War Office came under increasing pressure to assume responsibility for the air defence of the United Kingdom, creating moves that would eventually see the formation of two aerodromes at Ilford during the war.

Free balloons were seen occasionally drifting across Ilford, with RNAS officers training as observation balloon and Blimp (small non-rigid airship) crew. On Saturday, 24th July three balloons were observed passing over Ilford in stormy conditions, one occupant appeared to be in difficulties and threw out a quantity of ballast to no avail, the balloon continued to descend, brushing St John's Church, Seven Kings, before landing on open land nearby. The occupant, a naval officer, was unhurt. A second balloon fell on a house in Romford, knocking off a chimney pot.

Twenty-one RNAS machines (ten different types) hunted four Zeppelins that crossed the coast on the night of Monday, 9th August, without being able to get to grips with the raiders. Three aircraft crashed on landing, one pilot, Flt Sub-Lieut R Lord, dying later of his injuries.

For numerous reasons the raid by four of the latest Naval Zeppelins on the 9/10th August, proved to be a failure.

London, the intended target, remained untouched, whilst some good shooting by anti-aircraft guns at Dover forced L12, with rent hydrogen bags, to alight on the sea near Zeebrugge. Flt Lieut D K Johnston of the RNAS was killed attempting to bomb the crippled Zeppelin whilst under tow to Ostend.

London again had been the intended target, as four Naval Zeppelins set out on the night of Thursday, 12th August, but engine failure returned L9 and L13 to base early. L11 flew above Kent without releasing bombs, before flying out to sea, whilst L10, thwarted by headwinds en route for London, bombed the Harwich area, killing seven people and injuring twenty three. RNAS machines, hampered by mist, rain and engine troubles, searched in vain for the elusive giants

Five nights later, in clear starlit conditions, the commander of Naval Zeppelin L10 bombed the Wanstead area in mistake for central London, killing ten people and injuring another forty eight.

Four Zeppelins had left their bases in Germany with orders to bomb London on Tuesday, 17th August. Again beset by engine trouble, two airships returned without crossing the English coast. L11 bombed Ashford and nearby villages in Kent, claiming to have attacked the Woolwich Arsenal. Oberleutnant Friedrich Wenke had brought his craft to within six miles of the City to drop ten of his missiles on the open ground of the Wanstead Flats, after leaving a trail of destruction through Walthamstow, Leyton and Leytonstone. Wenke reported that his craft had bombed an area between Blackfriars and London Bridge, much to

Alfred de Bathe Brandon

the jubilation of the German press, whose readers passionately believed in the Zeppelin as a war winning machine, predicting that Britain would have to sue for peace, rather than have her capital destroyed by aerial bombardment.

The following day, wild rumours were circulating in rural Essex that Zeppelins had inflicted much damage on Ilford, Stratford, Leyton, and Blackheath. Again, the RNAS had risen to the occasion, but made no contact with the raiders. Flt Sub-Lieut C D Morrison suffered severe burns to his hands and face when the 20lb Hale's bombs racked beneath his Caudron biplane detonated as the machine touched down on the Chelmsford night landing ground at the end of his patrol.

A sign of the times - to replace men volunteering for the armed services, two postwomen were employed in Ilford at the end of August; by the end of the year, twelve conductresses also manned Ilford omnibuses.

Alfred de Bathe Brandon, who was to serve at Hainault Farm aerodrome, had been born in Wellington, New Zealand in 1841, and had been educated in England, later to read law at Trinity College, Cambridge, before being called to the bar at London's Middle Temple in 1906. Returning to New Zealand, he joined the family law practice in Wellington. With Britain's entry into the war Brandon wanted to enlist, but had been dissuaded by his partners, who, like so many in 1914, were convinced the war would be over in a matter of weeks. Brandon finally secured his release from the family business and sailed for England at the end of April, 1915, to become a pilot in the Royal Naval Air Service. Having

travelled halfway around the world at his own expense, he wasted no time on arrival in applying to the Admiralty for a commission, who, in turn, rejected him, as he was over age for pilot training. A fellow New Zealander, serving with the RNAS at Chingford, suggested to Brandon that several civilian flying instructors were still giving lessons at Hendon aerodrome, the Mecca of London pre-war aviation, and the Royal Navy would accept him as an experienced aviator, even at the ripe old age of thirty-one. A two guinea flip in a Grahame-White Box Kite that lasted for three minutes convinced Brandon that he had to become a pilot and he promptly enrolled for a £75 course at the Hall School of Flying at Hendon.

At four o'clock the following morning, before the wind rose, Brandon reported to his instructor, Mr Hill. The school bus, a 30 hp Caudron biplane, was ready and waiting for him. It did not take long to explain the few controls the machine possessed, although it took Brandon a while to master the Anzani engine as, like many air cooled engines of the period, it had no throttle, the engine speed being reduced by 'blipping' the ignition switch off and on. The Hall School of Flying did not own a dual control machine, so Brandon had to manoeuvre the small Caudron on the ground, until Mr Hill became satisfied with his performance and allowed him to become airborne. Brandon, piloting a larger 40 hp Caudron biplane, qualified for his pilot's licence on 17th October, 1915, and volunteered for the Royal Flying Corps, who were desperately trying to organise Home Defence squadrons to enable the Royal

Naval Air Service to concentrate on the increasing menace to allied shipping posed by the growing German U-Boat fleet.

By the time Brandon had qualified for his pilot's licence, the Zeppelin raids on England - London in particular - had reached crisis proportions. The War Office, which had been reluctantly committed to assume the responsibility for the air defence of Britain from the Admiralty, were now under immense pressure from government and outraged public opinion following the serious Zeppelin raids that autumn.

Three Imperial Army ships had set out from their sheds in occupied Belgium on Tuesday, 7th September; two of them raided London, fortunately LZ74 dropped all but one of her deadly cargo of incendiary and explosive bombs on a nursery at Cheshunt shattering a sea of glass in the greenhouses and damaging two cottages. The remaining bomb, an incendiary device, fell near Fenchurch Street Station. London may have escaped the full bomb load of LZ74, but the wooden framed SL2 commanded by the experienced Hptmn Richard von Wobeser attacked the Millwall Docks and surrounding area, inflicting 18 fatal casualties and injuring a further 28 civilians. The third Army airship, LZ77, obviously lost, meandered above Suffolk after crossing the coast, released a few bombs and flew out to sea.

The following night it was the turn of Naval Zeppelins in a contemptuous attack on London. Kptlt Heinrich Mathy, commanding L13, made the most of the exceptionally good visibility above the city to select his targets, releasing 45 incendiary and 13 H.E bombs, including one 660 lb missile that fell upon Bartholomew Close, killing two and injuring three civilians. As Mathy, in L13, enhanced his reputation above London, L9 carried out a bombing raid on Skinningrove, whilst L14 bombed East Dereham, Norfolk, thinking it to be Norwich. Total casualties inflicted by the three Naval Zeppelins that night were 26 killed, 94 injured; the majority of them being victims of Mathy's L13, including the hapless occupants of two London omnibuses blasted by falling bombs. MURDER BY ZEPPELIN newspaper head-lines, following the bombing of London by Kptlt Mathy, did little to calm the fear of the dreaded 'Zepps' that appeared to be oblivious to the motley collection of guns and searchlights defending the City and what, people demanded to know, were the Royal Flying Corps doing? The RNAS had flown 7 patrols in search of the raiders without seeing the elusive giant airships.

The unfortunate pilot of B.E.2c 990, Flt Sub-Lieut G W Hilliard, attempting to land at Bacton, died instantly when his anti-Zeppelin bombs exploded on touch down at the end of his patrol.

A B.E.2c biplane of the Royal Flying Corps had taken off from Writtle to inter-cept an Army Zeppelin intending to bomb London on the night of 11th September. LZ77, a new ship, had made her first flight on on 4th August. Her commander, Hptmn. Horn, bombed the black expanse of open countryside at North Weald in mistake for London. Lieut Morrison, the pilot of an RFC machine that had been ordered to an emergency landing ground on the outskirts of Chelmsford with great urgency two days earlier, reported at the end of his search for LZ77, that there would be little chance of intercepting a `Zepp', unless it had been illuminated by searchlights. Two RNAS machines had also patrolled from nearby Chelmsford without sighting the raider.

The following night an RNAS aeroplane again endeavoured, without success, to find an elusive Army Zeppelin, lost above blacked out East Anglia, where the bomb load of LZ74, destined for London, had been scattered - again without casualties or damage to property.

Lord Kitchener, Secretary of State for War, having seen the air raid on London on 8th September, immediately ordered Sir David Henderson, the Director-General of Military Aviation, to re-organise the virtually non-existent Home Defence provided by the Royal Flying Corps.

Thunderstorms and headwinds foiled two of the three Imperial Navy Zeppelins that set out from Germany with orders to bomb London on 13/14th September. L13, under the command of the fearless Kptlt Mathy, with full bomb racks, again destined for the capital, received damage from an anti-aircraft shell above Harwich, forcing him to jettison his cargo and recross the North Sea for repairs in the safety of the huge shed code-named `Hannibal' at Hage.

A combination of poor navigation on the part of the Zeppelin crews, unsuitable weather conditions, plus a few well placed anti-aircraft shells, had saved London from much of the intended death and destruction. However, despite the splendid endeavours of the Royal Naval Air Service to destroy the Zeppelins on the continent,

the raids on Britain were increasing and Intelligence reports of even larger airships under construction gave cause for grave concern. The approaching longer nights of mid-October that would be ideal for `Zepp' raids on London added to the urgency of the situation. Spurred on by Lord Kitchener and the population of London who demanded to know, "What are you going to do about these airship raids?" The War Office were forced to draw on men and machines from RFC training squadrons in the U K.

As early in the war as October, 1914, the Royal Naval Air Service had earmarked Hainault Farm, on the edge of Ilford, as a Day Landing Ground for future development, but passed the 60 acre site over to the Royal Flying Corps in February, 1915, for Home Defence duties. Although the well-drained land at Hainault Farm, surrounded by open countryside in all directions and within a two mile radius of Hainault, Fairlop and Goodmayes railway stations, would have been an ideal aerodrome, the RFC - short of men and machines - were unable to man the site until October, 1915.

The War Office, in an attempt to meet the demands of Lord Kitchener, robbed Peter to pay Paul; pilots under training for squadrons overseas were detached from their units in a bid to form a ring of aeroplanes around London to defend the City against the Zeppelin raids expected during the moonless nights of October. Hainault Farm, also known locally as J T Poulter's Farm, became `Landing Ground Three': a temporary aerodrome to house two Home Defence aircraft during the emergency. These, along with two more

Hainault Farm Aerodrome from the east. The farmhouse is on the extreme left across Hainault Road; WD pattern aeroplane sheds are on the right, with Sopwith Camels in front of them; the bell tents were replaced by permanent buildings after the formation of No.44 Squadron in July, 1917 (*G S Leslie*)

No.14 Squadron

22

machines at Landing Ground II (Suttons Farm, Hornchurch), would supplement established aerodromes at Joyce Green and Northolt. Unlike the Royal Artillery, who were unable to produce a cordon of anti-aircraft guns and searchlights around London in a matter of days, the 5th Wing of the RFC were able to provide a few token aeroplanes to appease the demands.

On Sunday morning, 3rd October, 1915, military transport collected portable canvas hangers, 16 twenty-pound bombs, four underwing racks, two gallon cans of petrol and oil, with stores and rations for ten days from Romford railway station, to be divided between the two Essex farms at Hornchurch and Ilford. As dusk fell on Hainault Farm, the RFC personnel were able to relax, it had been a busy day, two R.E.5 hangers had been erected across the road from the empty farmhouse, where the officers were to be billeted.

Just before mid-day on Monday, 4th October, air mechanics, who had arrived at Hainault Farm by road, heard the sound of an approaching aeroplane. A large white canvas T, laid out in front of the portable hangers, indicated that he had permission to land to Lieut E W Powell, flying in from No.23 Squadron at Gosport. It would be four days later that Landing Ground III received the second aeroplane, when 2nd Lieut F H Jenkins of No.14 Squadron flew in via Suttons Farm. Looking over his bare room at the empty Ilford farmhouse he must have envied the two Hornchurch pilots, who were billeted in comfort at the White Hart Hotel.

The arrival of the small contingent of RFC personnel, in their distinctive field service caps and khaki 'maternity jackets' at Hainault Farm, had not gone unnoticed. Although the telephone was a luxury many Ilford households could not afford, news of aeroplanes at Hainault Farm spread through the flourishing town grapevine. Arthur Scarborough of Chester Road, Seven Kings, recalls that the novelty of seeing aeroplanes on the ground tempted schoolboys to play truant, lest the 'airybuzzers' departed as swiftly as they had arrived. At school the next day, young Arthur and friends received 'six of the best' from the Headmaster's cane for truancy.

The original plan for the temporary landing grounds at Hainault and Suttons Farms had been to cover the south-east approach to London for nine nights until 12th October. As the Zeppelin raids had not materialised the would-be Zeppelin fighters were being recalled to their training squadrons for posting abroad. Reports from Naval Intelligence of activity at German Zeppelin bases, indicating that a bombing raid was imminent, decided the War Office to continue occupying the emergency landing grounds for a few more days. Lieut Edward Powell, who had brought the first B.E.2c biplane into Hainault Farm a few days earlier, had already been recalled to Gosport, and had to be replaced hurriedly by 2nd Lieut C E Wardle from No.14 Squadron.

Fog began to creep across Hainault Farm on the evening of Wednesday, 13th October. For Jenkins and Wardle, the duty pilots, it was difficult to believe that the remote farmhouse, almost empty apart from camp beds, a folding table and chairs was on the fringe of a modern town; at least they consoled themselves with the fact that Hainault Farm again had two aeroplanes equipped with night flying instruments, armed ready for immediate action. 2nd Lieut J C Slessor, delivering a replacement B.E.2c to Suttons Farm, had been seriously delayed by fog, but managed to land his machine there late in the afternoon.

Just after 17.00 hrs the telephone on the bare wooden table in the 'office' at Hainault Farm rang, echoing around the room, the cheerful voice of Colonel Warner at the War Office, informing them that 'Zepps' were on their way and to take air raid action. Within minutes the once dark and silent field, across the road from the farmhouse, resounded with the sound of men's voices and the roar of aero engines being warmed up.

The Imperial German Navy had launched five Zeppelins against England. In ideal weather conditions they were to inflict 71 fatal casualties, injure 128 and cause in excess of £80,000-worth of damage to property during the night. The first of the raiders crossed the Norfolk coast at 18.15 hrs; L11, the last Zeppelin to make landfall at 20.30 hrs, bombed open fields at Coltishall, after coming under fire from mobile anti-aircraft guns, and flew out to sea; her commander reported bombing West Ham and Woolwich. Kptlt Heinrich Mathy, the experienced commander of L13, dropped the last of his bomb load on Woolwich, having regained his bearings, after becoming lost above the mist-shrouded countryside of East Anglia en route for London. Fatally for 15 soldiers at a military camp near Dover, L14, also lost, released four bombs, hitting Shorncliffe Barracks, before wandering off to bomb Tunbridge Wells and Croydon. It was the bombing of London's theatreland that provoked the biggest outcry of indignation following the raid. Twenty-three year old Kptlt Joachim Breithaupt, commander of L15, one of the new P class Zeppelins, arrived over the suburbs just before 21.30 hrs. The flight to the capital had not been without incident for the Zeppelin. Above Broxbourne at 6,000 feet, L15 suddenly came under fire from a mobile anti-aircraft gun. Breithaupt retaliated with four bombs, three of which fell close enough to blow a gun crew off their feet and damage two of their motor vehicles. Constantly changing course to confuse the defences, L15 finally approached London with her motors silenced, drifting with the prevailing wind. Wartime restrictions had dimmed the exterior lights of London's theatreland, but inside it was business as usual, with servicemen home on leave making the most of their precious few hours with loved ones. The Gaiety in the Aldwych, packed to capacity with an unsuspecting audience enjoying the revue, *Tonight's the Night*, were about to be brought back to reality with a bang. High above the dimmed out metropolis, mechanics on board L15 re-started the four powerful 240 hp Maybach motors, alerting the City below to the danger. Searchlights were uncovered, which found and illuminated the raider about to commence its bombing run. One of the first missiles fell opposite the Gaiety theatre, killing one person and injuring three, including the Gaiety's call-boy, wounded by 22 bomb splinters.

Intense activity at Hainault Farm following the order to take air raid action subsided, one hour passed, then another, with still no indication if an airship had crossed the coast. At long last, the telephone rang again - a Zeppelin reported flying over Thetford, heading towards London. Five minutes later, at 20.00 hrs, 2nd Lieut Jenkins waved the chocks away, opened the throttle of the 90 hp engine and roared across the stubble of Hainault Farm. The rumble of wire spoked wheels straining against rubber cord shock absorbers ceased, as guided by a line of cans filled with burning petrol soaked cotton waste, the B.E.2c became airborne. Climbing steadily with engine running smoothly, Jenkins had time to collect his wits, it had all happened so suddenly. What he did not know was that he had become the first Home Defence pilot to take off to intercept the raiders. Looking back he could still see the L formed by the makeshift flare path of Hainault Farm, flickering through the ground mist. Jenkins had been lucky; at Northolt aerodrome, across the dimmed out sprawling mass of London, visibility was so bad that airmen setting out the flare path became lost. At Suttons Farm there had been no time, since Slessor had landed a few hours earlier, to fit bomb racks and install cockpit lighting to his new machine, but he had successfully argued 2nd Lieut Yates into handing over his serviceable machine for the expected air raid. Unable to get airborne at 20.00 hrs, because of dense fog at Hornchurch, Slessor could do little but wait.

Aloft in the clear air at 8,000 ft, Jenkins levelled his machine off and started to patrol in a wide circle between Hainault Farm and London. Suspected gun fire to the north elongated the patrol area for a few minutes until, satisfying himself, the pilot returned to his lonely vigil over east London. There had been no sign of the coloured rockets that would indicate the whereabouts and direction of a 'Zepp' as arranged. Reluctantly Jenkins, running low on fuel, began to seek the searchlights at Chigwell Row and Becontree Heath that were to guide him back to Hainault Farm. At fog bound Suttons Farm, landing flares were lit to help the machine that had been airborne from Landing Ground III. Anxious ground crew at Hainault heard Jenkins' aeroplane returning, his altitude less than 100 feet. He could just discern the flare path and, conscious of the bombs racked beneath his lower wings, he throttled back to land.

Misjudging his distance from the row of flickering landing flares, the under-carriage of Jenkins' machine crashed through a hedge. The engine cut as the propeller shattered, ripping up a barbed wire fence and bringing the aeroplane to a halt.

As the shaken, but unhurt, Jenkins was being helped back to the primitive comfort of the farmhouse, L15 began a trail of death and destruction from the West End to Cable Street, Stepney. Of the 30 bombs released by Breithaupt, the second, landing in busy Wellington Street, off the Strand, caused the most casualties; 17 killed, 21 injured. Caught in the glare of searchlights at 11,000 feet, the Zeppelin droned on, with anti-aircraft shells bursting angrily below, well out of range. The number of guns and search-lights in action against L15 took the crew by surprise and a well placed farewell shot from a mobile Naval anti-aircraft gun exploded too close for comfort.

Turning north from the river to avoid the Woolwich Arsenal defences, the great ship flew over Hackney, Leyton and, within minutes, came under fire again from guns at Loughton, Kelvedon Hatch and Hainault Farm.

The ground mist had cleared sufficiently and, with the sound of the mobile 13 pounder across the field banging away above the roar of his engine, 2nd Lieut Wardle took off, knowing he had no chance of overtaking the Zeppelin overhead. Had his intended patrol not been delayed by fog he would have had enough altitude to intercept the fleeing Germans. When Wardle reached 8,000 ft, he had long lost sight of the enemy bombing machine and commenced to patrol the area allotted to Landing Ground III. Apart from a damaged aeroplane and a little gunfire observed to the east, he would have nothing to report on returning to Hainault Farm an hour and a half later. Leaning over the low cut side of the open cockpit in a concentrated effort to see the flares as the mist rolled back across the landing ground, Wardle stalled the B.E., luckily low enough to escape serious injury. 2nd Lieut Slessor, who had managed to get airborne from Hornchurch at 21.40 hrs, had reached 2,000 ft, when he observed L15 high to the east. He gave chase for a few minutes, until losing the Zeppelin among the clouds. On his return, Suttons Farm was again fog bound and, blinded by a searchlight intended to help his descent, the pilot nosed over in a turnip field.

Two RFC pilots from Joyce Green aerodrome had become airborne during the London Zeppelin raid on the night of Wednesday, 13th October, but both were plagued with engine trouble. At Northolt aerodrome the frustrated airmen waited in vain for the fog to clear and not one Naval flyer had taken off, despite the unseen raiders being heard flying above RNAS aerodromes.

The following morning, as the clearing up operation across London slowly began, the full extent of the casualties were realised. Fortunately, the four packed West End theatres damaged by the L15 during the raid had escaped direct hits, or the casualty list would have been far more horrific. Woolwich barracks and Arsenal, a legitimate military target, had suffered casualties during the attack by Mathy's L13 that could also have been far worse.

Ilfordians heard the sound of RFC machines searching for the enemy and later heard the heavier drone of Zeppelins, homeward bound from London. Although the few Home Defence pilots airborne during the raid were unable to get to grips with the enemy, their glowing exhaust stacks were seen by Zeppelin crews, already concerned about the increase of guns and searchlights around London. The crew of Breithaupt's silently drifting L15 claimed to have seen and heard no less then four enemy flyers searching for them, although the German press hailed the strike against London as a great victory. It would be months before the Zeppelins returned to the City.

In the aftermath of 13th October raid, angry meetings were held, further fuelled by the news of the execution by the Germans of nurse Edith Cavell in occupied Belgium. 'Reprisals' were called for, speaker after speaker condemning the Government for its failure to protect London, and calling for a fleet of large aeroplanes capable of bombing Germany under the direct control of a Ministry of the Air. Police had to escort an RFC vehicle and trailer through a mob of angry Londoners in the Mile End Road, as 2nd Lieut J C Slessor returned from the Royal Aircraft Factory at Farnborough with a replacement lower wing, undercarriage struts etc, needed to repair the damaged B.E.2c at Suttons Farm, Hornchurch. In spite of the furore, the War Office admitted that the inexperienced RFC pilots had acquitted themselves well in the circumstances.

Fog that hampered Britain's airmen during 13th October raid also delayed the raider's homecoming the next morning. The commander of L15 found a tethered balloon above a shrouded Nordholz. Unlike aeroplanes, lighter-than-air ships could remain aloft until fog dispersed. Although the Zeppelin had almost exhausted her supply of benzine, Breithaupt, by running on one motor, managed to circle the marker for a further two hours, until the fuel ran out and he was faced with the choice of drifting out to sea or valving gas and descending slowly into the murk. It took the ground crew an hour to find the slightly damaged L15, before walking her three miles back to her great shed.

At Hainault and Suttons Farms, the damaged aeroplanes were repaired and flown back to their respective squadrons, the canvas hangers were dismantled and, as quickly as they had arrived, the Royal Flying Corps evacuated the sites.

One thing had been made clear to the War Office. Although the display of fire-power around London had bluffed the Zeppelin crews, many of the guns in action were unsuitable. A few converted 13 pdr field guns mounted upon flat backed lorries and a French 75mm auto-canon on trial had the range and showed promise. It had also become apparent that more searchlights were required.

During November a small detachment of Royal Engineers arrived at the tramcar depôt in Ley Street, Ilford, with two 120cm searchlights. Ilford tramcars 14 and 16 were converted at the depôt to carry a searchlight upon the open upper deck, part of which had been protected by a steel shelter for the crew, on the lower deck all the windows were boarded over. For the rest of the war, the mobile searchlights were a familiar sight at dusk, rattling off in opposite directions from Ley Street depôt, to take up post by Chadwell Heath and Barkingside police stations.

As the people of Ilford looked forward to the second Christmas of the war, the mood of the town has been described as 'not merry, but bright and happy nevertheless'. During Christmas week the shopkeepers in High Road and Cranbrook Road shared in the prosperity brought about by the abundant war work in and around the town. Church attendance on Christmas morning was affected by the inclement weather, however every effort was made to ensure the children in the Barnardo cottages, the Belgian guests - refugees - at Valentines mansion, and 24 wounded soldiers at the Ilford Emergency Hospital, who were joined by six civilian patients, enjoyed a real old fashioned Christmas dinner.

The Lyceum Theatre, a casualty of the Zeppelin raid on 13th October re-opened to the public on Boxing Day, Monday, 27th December, 1915. One familiar landmark, however, would be missing; an elderly orange seller, who had occupied her corner pitch by the theatre for years had been killed in the bombing.

1916

1916 arrived to find the people of Ilford determined to 'Keep The Home Fires Burning'; community spirit had never been higher. During the first week of January, local members of the Soldiers' and Sailors' Families' Association invited 500 wives, widowed mothers, and children to Ilford Town Hall, for a buffet and an evening of entertainments. The highlight for many present had been the unexpected arrival of a soldier home on leave from the trenches. There were cheers and tears as his wife, one of the guests, hurried across the crowded hall to greet her husband.

January saw the introduction of compulsory military service in Britain, not a popular move with the patriotic press, who had scored on the propaganda front by claiming British volunteers were better fighting men than the enemy conscripts.

Landing Ground III at Hainault Farm did not remaine free of military personnel for long. By 31st January, canvas hangers had been re-erected, housing two B.E.2c machines from No.17 Reserve Aeroplane Squadron at Beddington (Croydon). Hainault Farm became a link in the improved Home Defence plans for London. The detached men and machines were now part of No.19 Reserve Aeroplane Squadron, commanded by Major T C R Higgins.

A three month respite from Zeppelin activity over England, partially due to the severe weather during the winter of 1915-16, had provided the War Office time to begin the re-organisation to take over the air defence of Britain from the Admiralty. Germany resumed the bombing of England early in January with a series of hit and run daylight raids against Dover and Folkestone. Flying singly or in pairs, German Naval seaplane raids placed a burden on the Royal Naval Air Service, who were still committed to coastal defence. German hopes of terrorising British civilians with Zeppelin bombing raids were given a boost when the Imperial Navy commissioned five new P class ships. In the Fatherland news of the resumption of Zeppelin raids was eagerly awaited, as the Royal Navy blockade hit not only German war production, but on the home front food was scarce.

On the evening of Monday, 31st January, the shout of, "the Zepps are coming", echoed across Hainault Farm. Nine Imperial Navy Zeppelins were flying the North Sea through rain and snow: unbeknown to the War Office their target would be the ill-defended Midlands. It had been nearly two weeks since Peter Strasser, the energetic commanding officer of the Navy Airship Division, had convinced not only Vizeadmiral Scheer, but the majority of the Imperial High Seas Fleet Command, to resume Zeppelin raids. Crossing the Norfolk coast at intervals, the noisy monsters eluded Royal Naval Air Service pilots from North Denes aerodrome, Great Yarmouth, patrolling the wintry night. Although the intended targets - Liverpool and Manchester - remained untouched, the `Zepps' cruised above the blacked-out Midlands hour after hour dropping 309 high explosive and incendiary bombs at random. One Home Defence aeroplane aloft from Castle Bromwich during the raid, inspecting Birmingham's black-out from the air, saw nothing of the Zeppelins and crashed on landing in mist. For the re-organised Home Defences the latest air raid proved to be a disaster - 183 civilians killed and injured, two RFC pilots killed in accidents, and six aeroplanes wrecked.

Hainault and Suttons Farm pilots patrolled for a raid on London that never materialised. Lieut R S Maxwell, at Ilford, was ordered into the air at 19.40 hrs; clearing the cloud base at 8,500 ft, he continued climbing to his allotted height at 10,000 ft. Apart from a strange light - probably the exhaust glow of another patrolling B E that he chased for a few minutes before it vanished into the clouds - Maxwell would have little to report.

Reginald Stewart Maxwell, 'George' to his fellow officers, had no difficulty in locating the flarepath of Hainault Farm at the end of his patrol an hour and fifty minutes later. Throttling back the 90 hp engine at 250 ft, as he levelled the machine out, Maxwell realised that something was wrong and opened up again; just too late his propeller and undercarriage shattered with a spine jarring crash. Fortunately, the bombs attached to B.E 2c 2087 failed to detonate or a third RFC pilot would have been killed that night. An investigation later revealed the altimeter of the Hainault Farm machine, checked before take-off, still indicated 200 ft when Maxwell flew his biplane into the ground to be shaken, but uninjured.

Major R S Maxwell DFC MC also survived two tours of duty in France and ended his WW1 career as the C O of No. 54 Squadron RAF, with nine enemy aircraft to his credit.

Lieut Steele discovered another faulty altimeter fitted to the one Hornchurch machine patrolling on the last night of January. Although aware of approaching the flare path on his return, he had the misfortune to overshoot the runway.

Instrument failure also dogged the second machine taking off at 21.00 hrs from Hainault. A few seconds after B.E.2c 2087 lifted from the ground, the cockpit lighting failed; barely airborne the engine began misfiring. Colliding with a tarpaulined haystack, the B E crashed into a barbed wire fence and nosed over. Clambering down from the cockpit, as flames threatening to engulf the oil soaked fabric, Lieut C P Court struggled out of his leather coat to smother the fire with it, saving the aeroplane from becoming a complete write-off.

Three quarters of an hour later Lieut Jowett, running low on fuel at the end of a patrol from No 17 R A Squadron at Hendon, saw the welcome sight of the Hainault Farm flares twinkling below. A green Very light in answer to his own gave him the all-clear to land without mishap.

Once again, two Ilford pilots had been fortunate to escape serious injury; not so fortunate were the two experienced pilots killed, as nine RFC and three RNAS home defence aeroplanes crashed during the alert. Not one of the twenty-two pilots, aloft to intercept the raiders, was able to report a definite sighting of a Zeppelin.

The German Navy, however, was to lose one of the latest airships in service, with all 16 officers and men of her crew in the aftermath of the raid. Although experiencing trouble with three engines, L19 remained above East Anglia and the

Midlands for nine hours, dropping bombs on Burton-on-Trent and the suburbs of Birmingham. Engine trouble further delayed the homeward flight of L19, and at 17.00 hrs the low flying Zeppelin, obviously in difficulties, came under small arms fire from the Dutch Army garrison on the neutral island of Ameland. The damaged airship, with gas cells peppered by bullets, was carried westward by the prevailing wind and fell into the sea during the early hours of Wednesday, 2nd February. At 07.30 hrs the sight of a British trawler heading towards them raised hope for the fatigued airship men clinging to the wreck. Kptlt Otto Loewe begged the trawler skipper to save his crew from certain death, but, outnumbered two to one by the Germans, the skipper of the *King Stephen* refused to take the risk of allowing them to board his tiny craft, and left them to drown in the icy waters of the North Sea.

On 9th February, the *Frankfurter Zeitung* pilloried the Bishop of London, who had publicly condoned abandoning the `Baby Killers' to their fate.

By no means a desk-bound leader, Korvettenkapitan Peter Strasser, fürher of Imperial Navy Airships, accompanied Kptlt von Buttlar aboard L11 during the 31st January raid. Hampered by mist and fog, and unable to locate a military target during four hours over enemy territory, Strasser conferred with von Buttlar before returning to base at Nordholz, with a two ton bomb load intact The fact that German Zeppelins roamed unchallenged at will throughout the night did little to allay the fear of the dreaded `Zepp'.

A bad case of jitters developed on the night of 10th February, when a false alarm at Scarborough instigated a total black-out and disruption of rail traffic all over the Midlands, causing a serious loss of munition production and distribution. Earlier in the day, the War Committee that met to discuss the problems facing the Royal Flying Corps engaged on home defence, decided that special squadrons would have to be formed to combat the Zeppelin menace. One step in the right direction had already been taken on the day after the fiasco of the Midland raid, Major T C R Higgins, C O of No 19 R A Squadron at Hounslow, had been ordered to take command of all the aerodromes surrounding London.

On 16th February, Field Marshall Lord French, on behalf of the War Office, assumed the responsibility for the defence of London - it would not be long before all of Britain's air defences came under his control.

Teething trouble with a number of the new HSLu engines, fitted to Navy Zeppelins, necessitated their removal and return to the Maybach works, along with crew members, who were instructed by factory technicians how to maintain the powerful motors - it also gave England a few weeks respite.

The L19 had brought the total of Imperial Navy Zeppelin losses since the outbreak of war to seven; the Army had ten airships destroyed during the same period and were about squander another upon a clear moonlight night raid.

Four Zeppelins, in support of the massive assault on Verdun launched on Monday, 21st February, bombed railroad junctions bringing French reinforcements to the front. The LZ77 fell in flames with the loss of all her crew, after receiving a direct hit from anti-aircraft fire. It would be two months before the German Army, with a critical battle on its hands in France, was able to spare airships for raids against England, in spite of the clamour from the press.

Hefty fines, up to a maximum of £5, were commonplace for the people of Ilford convicted for failing to comply with the wartime lighting restrictions in force.

In March, 1916, members of the Ilford Appeal Tribunal sat at the Town Hall to deal with the problems facing unmarried men brought about by the introduction of the Military Service Act.

A little ditty sung at the Town Hall by an eleven year old lad during the January party for servicemen's families had remained popular with children, going to and from school -

'The moon shines bright on Charlie Chaplin,
His boots are cracking, for the want of blacking,
And his little baggy trousers they'll want mending,
Before we send him to the Dardanelles."

Vying with 'Tipperary', 'Rule Britannia' and 'Who's your lady friend?', 'Charlie's boots', sang to the tune of 'Red wing', over and over again, by the Town Hall revellers had been the hit of the evening, in spite of the concern over local casualties in the failed Dardanelles campaign.

Determined to prove the superiority of rigid airships over the aeroplane, the Imperial Navy launched L11 and L14 from snow-covered Nordholz to attend L13, that had been marched from the shelter of the huge `Hannibal' shed at Hage The commanders of the `elderly' ships, still powered by four 210 hp engines, were under orders to target Royal

Navy bases in the north of England. Buffeted by 50 mph gusts and lashed by blinding snow, the trio abandoned their attempt to bomb Navy dockyards at Rosyth. Instead, Hull became the recipient of most of the bombs dropped, suffering majority of the casualties during the raid - 18 killed, 52 injured.

Driven further south than intended, L13, once again commanded by Kptlt Heinrich Mathy, placed the aerodromes around London on alert by reaching the Thames Estuary, before setting course for home. It had been a minor victory for the German airmen and their giant powered balloons. Heavy snow grounded all Home Defence aeroplanes deployed by the Royal Flying Corps. Alerted by anti-aircraft fire directed at the L13, Flt Sub-Lieut Wyllie of the Royal Naval Air Service managed to get airborne from Eastchurch. Too late to catch the high flying raider, he returned safely to thaw out at the tortoise stove in the Mess.

Across the Channel where weather conditions were marginally better, no less than 14 aeroplanes attempted to head off the returning snow-laden Zeppelins. Snow-blinded and frozen in open cockpits, once again young RFC pilots risked their lives in vain as the elusive Zeppelins and their crews escaped to raid another night.

2nd Lieut Alfred de Bathe Brandon reported for duty at Hainault Farm in the third week of March. Although he had qualified as a civilian aviator the previous 17th October and at once volunteered for a commission in the Royal Flying Corps, he had to wait another six frustrating weeks, until a telegram finally arrived with orders to report to No.11 R.Q.

Squadron at Northolt.

During February, Brandon and 2nd Lieut R Kilpatrick Muir were posted to Salisbury Plain for advanced training and were awarded their RFC wings on the 26th of the month. Just two flights made at dusk had entitled both men enough night flying experience to be posted to aerodromes in Essex as night fighting pilots.

Tragedy marred the flying career of 2nd Lieut Muir within days. Sunday, 12th March, began with the pleasure of a visit to the Suttons Farm by his proud parents and ended in horror as the B.E.2c, piloted by Muir with his father as passenger in the front cockpit, side-slipped and crashed. The older man died instantly; after receiving first aid, the injured and grief-stricken airman was taken to the Military Hospital at Romford.

On the evening of 31st March, Brandon, with just thirty hours flying experience in his log book, sat waiting in the farmhouse on standby during the dark of the moon. As on previous `Zepp', raids the warning of raiders crossing the coast 'phoned through from the War Office prompted activity among the handful of airmen at Hainault Farm. 24 well-greased Ranken darts were carefully inserted into the tubes of a purpose-made box fitted to Brandon's machine, which would enable him to release the explosive and phosphorus missiles in batches of three at the turn of a handle. A memorandum would be issued to Brandon in two weeks time instructing him how to best make use of the latest anti-Zeppelin missiles. As a back-up to the untried Ranken darts, the B.E.2c had been fitted with an RL

tube, designed early in the war by the Royal Laboratory at Woolwich. 10 lb incendiary bombs had to be loaded into the RL tube by hand, in order to complete an electric circuit needed to ignite the missile as it fell clear of the biplane. Brandon's machine carried no H.E. bombs that had been used with success by the RNAS in destroying an airborne Zeppelin, as several RFC pilots had been killed in accidents that involved the 20 lb Hale bomb, later to be replaced with the more reliable Cooper bomb. The Ranken and RL carcass incendiary bombs were about to be tested in action by the Ilford pilot and found wanting.

Waiting for the call to arms in Essex on a Friday evening in March, Brandon had time to reflect that it had been less than a year since he had set out by steamship from New Zealand, intending to join the Royal Naval Air Service. That year had been incident-packed.

Refused a commission in the RNAS, he paid for his own flying lessons as a civilian, qualifying as a pilot at Hendon two weeks after Hainault Farm became Landing Ground No 3 in October, 1915. Following his commission in the Royal Flying Corps, the weeks became a blur of instruction on military etiquette, aero engines, rigging, morse code and solo cross-country flying, culminating in the award of his RFC brevet on the 26th February, 1916. Two flights in a B E 2c at dusk, ended his training to qualify as a Home Defence pilot and detachment to No.19 R A Squadron at Hainault Farm.

Combined forces of ten Imperial Army and Navy Zeppelins, loaded with 25 tons of bombs, set course for England on the afternoon of 31st March. Two of the seven Navy ships were forced to return to base; the crew of L9 managed to save their fragile craft from destruction, after a detached bracing wire wrapped around a propeller shaft, winching the gondola up towards the hull. Slashing through the gangway and control cables running the length of the ship, the 18 ft diameter walnut and mahogany propeller shattered, one blade ripping a large hole in No 11 gas cell. Only the cool courage of the crew saved the airship from falling into the sea.

Although Zeppelin commanders no longer signalled their departure, as on previous raids, British Intelligence had alerted the War Office to the impending air-raid. The first droned over the coast, by Southwold, under cover of darkness at 19.45 hrs; Joachim Breithaupt, L15's commander, intended to bomb Woolwich Arsenal, 110 miles away. Suffolk villagers ran from their cottages and hid in the hedgerows as the noisy unseen terror of the night approached, accompanied by barking dogs. Infant Phillip Cotten, snatched from his warm cot, shivered in his mother's arms, as they sheltered alongside the open fields. In later years, Phillip lived in Ilford until his death at an early age. Never robust, he blamed `Zepp' nights as the cause of his ill-health.

Another Zeppelin was heard at 20.00 hrs; L13, with Mathy in command, was heading for the New Explosive Works at Stowmarket. At 21.45 hrs he was over the target and under fire from an anti-aircraft battery. Twelve bombs released did little damage, apart from shattering windows; returning for a second bombing run, L13 came under fire again and two gas cells,

rent by shell splinters spewed out hydrogen, forcing Mathy to jettison the remaining bombs and return to Germany at full speed.

L15, en route for Woolwich, encountered 2nd Lieut Claude Ridley of No.19 R A Squadron from Joyce Green, who had a brief skirmish with the airship, before losing it in the dark. The target area was clearly visible on the far side of the glistening Thames, when the airship, illuminated by five searchlights, came under heavy anti-aircraft fire. Desperate measures were needed to escape the much improved outer London defences, and Breithaupt ordered all bombs to be released, in an effort to gain altitude rapidly. Rainham Marshes absorbed the bombs in vain, as L15 was badly damaged, two 3 inch shells bursting alongside, with compliments from the sweating gunners below.

Over Hainault Farm Brandon breathed a sigh of relief, he had a fear of the air-cooled engine cutting out on take off. He recalled the words of his night flying instructor Lieut Collins who had insisted that, "It isn't as bad as they say it is," and found to his satisfaction visibility improving as the machine gained altitude. Brandon had flown twice at dusk during training, and now, airborne at night for the first time, could easily discern the dimmed-out city and suburbs in contrast to the dark open countryside and the black shadow of Hainault Forest 6,000 ft below. Suddenly searchlights were uncovered, sweeping to and fro; one beam faltered and remained almost motionless - other beams intersected to form an inverted cone, illuminating a silver pencil floating above the Thames pointing towards London. The excitement of flying at night was forgotten as Brandon set off in pursuit of the `Zepp'. Orange fireballs twinkled around the airship as ground defences opened fire.

Alarmed by the barrage, Breithaupt ordered the helmsman to steer the damaged L15 north-east towards Brentwood, to escape London's outer defences. Making use of cloud cover, the experienced Kapitanleutnant eluded the few beams searching the night sky above rural Essex, as he appraised the damage reports reaching the control car. Three of the ship's 15 gas cells were destroyed. Although the craft had climbed rapidly when freed from the weight of 20 high explosive and 24 incendiary bombs destined for Woolwich Arsenal, it now began losing height as riggers desperately climbed the spiders web of bracing wired aluminium lattice work, seeking and patching the gas cells punctured by shell splinters.

"Flieger!": the warning was quickly passed through the airship; the lights of an English flyer in pursuit had been observed from the rear gondola. Brandon doggedly continued the chase, in spite of losing sight of the elusive giant, until a solitary searchlight held her just long enough for him to close within striking distance. Climbing to get his machine above the Zeppelin, Brandon watched fascinated as the airship grew ever larger as he approached, so much so, he was heavy handed on the stick and only just saved the B.E. from a stall that would have wasted valuable altitude required to attack the monster.

Overtaking L15 in a climbing turn, Brandon crossed the enormous bow of the Zeppelin at about 400 feet, to be greeted by a belt-fed Maxim machine gun mounted on top of the ship. Over the broad back of the giant war machine, Brandon cranked the first batch of Ranken incendiary darts out of their carrier.

Above the noise of Zeppelin motors, spluttering machine-gun fire and his own engine roar, the Ilford pilot thought he heard the explosive darts detonate. In his combat report, on file at the Imperial War Museum, Brandon stated, "I continued and circled in front of the Zeppelin and turned around to get to its rear, on going past there was a tremendous amount of machine-gun firing going on. At this point I switched off my lights and continued in my direction for two or three hundred yards and then turned and got in direct line with the Zeppelin. I was then about five hundred feet above it; I closed the throttle and volplaned towards the Zeppelin. The nose of my machine was pointed about a quarter way from the rear I then got out an incendiary bomb and, trying to get it into the tube, I had to take my eyes off the Zeppelin. On looking up again I was astonished to find that in a very few seconds I would have passed the Zeppelin, so I quickly placed the incendiary bomb in my lap and let off No.2 and No.3 lots of darts. I did not hear any reports from these, I concluded that the Zeppelin was, in reality, coming towards me, so I opened up the engine again and turned completely round and followed a southerly course, continuing for some considerable time, as I thought the

Zeppelin had got a good start. In the meantime I turned on my lights again and I was at 8,000 feet. I cruised around at 8,000 feet for some time and saw nothing and then dropped to 6,000 feet and cruised around for some considerable time without also seeing any sign of the Zeppelin."

The crew of the airship survived the daring attack by the lone flyer, due to the fact that the Home Defence machine carried none of the explosive bombs RNAS pilots used with success against Zeppelins over Belgium. Had Brandon been allowed to carry Hale bombs, no doubt Ilford would have long since named a road in his memory. Hand over hand Breithaupt climbed the 60 ft cat ladder up through the blacked out interior of L15, reeking with escaping hydrogen gas, to reach the 'Storks Nest' above. The machine-gunners reported the flieger dropped bombs on to the ship, but did not know if further damage had been done.

Brandon, low on fuel, was eventually forced to give up the hunt for the elusive Zeppelin and descend through the clouds to search for a friendly flarepath. At 23.10 hrs he made a shaky landing, breaking a wing skid and flare bracket, the far side of the Thames on the NLG at Farningham in Kent; his first true night flight concluded.

Repairs to Brandon's B.E.2c were minimal and he returned to Hainault Farm the following morning, when the damaged brackets were replaced and fabric patches doped over the bullet holes in the flying surfaces of the machine. Unlike previous sorties from Hainault Farm, Brandon had not been let down by defective instruments; thanks to the ground crew his machine had behaved perfectly. His courage more than compensated for his lack of night flying and combat experience, only the ineffective weapons at his disposal had saved the crew of L15 from a fiery end.

Eluding the enemy flyer did not put an end to Breithaupt's problem; the once proud airship, now with gas cells no. 11 and 16 completely empty, and cells no. 9 and 12 spewing out the hydrogen needed to keep his huge craft airborne, he would need all his experience to reach the safety of occupied Belgium. Overboard went the maxim machine-guns, ammunition belts and anything not required to keep the Zeppelin in flight. Following a message requesting assistance between the Thames and Ostend, the wireless set went over-side. Log book and documents useful to the enemy were bound by wire inside the small cupboard that served as a stool for the wireless operator and dumped in the Thames. As a last resource to remain airborne, fuel for the return flight had been jettisoned in vain.

At 00.15 hrs on 1st April, Zeppelin L15, once pride of the Imperial German Navy, the bomber of London theatreland, now a floundering monster in its death throes, fell with a broken back 500 ft into the sea. All but one of the 17 man crew were rescued by a destroyer of the Royal Navy, but attempts to salvage the monster failed and L15 sank beneath the waves off Westgate on Sea. HMS *Vulture* landed the prisoners at Chatham. Breithaupt, aware that his crew, subjected to wartime propaganda, were expecting to be shot for the murder of civilians, faced his captors and claimed full responsibility as the commander of L15 for the bombing. A Zeppelin had been brought down by the combined efforts of searchlights, guns and aeroplanes. Special gold medallions presented by the Lord Mayor of London were awarded to 353 officers and men, who had been in action with the London anti-aircraft units. The Military Crosses awarded to Brandon and 2nd Lieut C A Ridley, flying from Joyce Green, who had witnessed the Ilford pilot attacking L15, whilst trying to climb to his assistance, proved at long last the Royal Flying Corps were doing something about the 'Zepps'.

Easter Monday, 1916, heralded an improvement in the weather and daylight aeroplane reconnaissance flights along the coast; six German Naval airships droned across the North Sea, their target London. Two older Zeppelins, also airborne, were to assist German battle cruisers on their way to another hit and run raid on the English coast. Planned to coincide with armed rebellion in Dublin and the declaration of an Irish Republic, Germany hoped that a double blow on England would boost the morale of the rebels.

No. 39 Squadron, standing by for the call "take air-raid action", had fitted some of their B.E.2c biplanes with an upward firing machine gun, now being made available to the new squadron. The light-weight drum-fed lewis machine gun had proved itself with the RFC in France, where, with the aid of the stripped down Lewis mounted to clear the propeller arc, the Fokker monoplanes, with a synchronised Maxim gun, could be engaged on equal terms.

A strong south by south-west wind again saved London; Kvtkpt Peter Strasser, commander of the Naval Airship Division accompanying L21, aborted the attack on the enemy capital shortly after making landfall; he did not intend to risk his crews tonight, larger more powerful Zeppelins were under construction in the Fatherland. London would have to wait until more favourable weather conditions. Rain and mist prevented the Zeppelins finding suitable targets in East Anglia, the only fatal casualty of the raid occurred when a poor woman died of shock as 45 bombs fell around the village of Dilham in Norfolk. Lowestoft came under a six minute bombardment by German battle cruisers just after 04.00 hrs on Tuesday, 25th April, four people were killed on shore, another twelve were injured.

The elderly Zeppelin L9, carrying out a low reconnaissance for the fleet, had a narrow escape when two RNAS machines from Great Yarmouth carrying Ranken darts dived on to the vulnerable airship. Only the skilful handling by the crew and the erratic fall of the lightweight missiles saved L9, chased 25 miles out to sea by the Naval airmen in their B.E.2c biplanes. If the pilots of No 39 Squadron were disappointed that the 'Zepps' had not come within range of their night and early morning patrols, they would not have long to wait. As they slumbered on their camp beds, five Zeppelins of the Imperial German Army were being prepared for an assault on London that night.

Few Ilfordians about their business on the evening of Tuesday, 25th April, paused to give tramcar No.16, crewed by 'Tommies', a second glance as it juddered along the rails set

A B.E2c of No.35 Reserve school (*Colin Ross*)

Avro 504K biplane of No.189 Training Squadron (*Colin Ross*)

into the High Road en route for Chadwell Heath. The locals had become accustomed to the two military trams that rattled out of the Ley Street depôt at dusk, carrying a 1200m. searchlight on the open upper deck. Although Ilford electric trams had been painted green and cream for the last six months, cars No 14 and 16 still sported the earlier red livery as worn when they had been requisitioned by the War Office in November, 1915. Tramcar No 14 had arrived to take up position by Barkingside terminus a little earlier than No 16, as it came to rest at the Chadwell Heath terminus. Both mobile searchlights - part of 2 rings of lights now surrounding London - would receive instructions via nearby police station telephones in the event of a raid.

Four of the five Army Zeppelins prepared earlier in the day for a raid on London crossed the coast; LZ26 returned to base with mechanical problems. A fine night with a light south east wind, ideal for the Home Defences, no doubt influenced some of the Army airshipmen to proceed with caution. Whilst LZ87 dropped bombs in Deal harbour at 21.55 hrs, heavy anti-aircraft fire drove the Zeppelin along the coast, until, drawing parallel with Ramsgate, her commander flew out to sea. Hauptmann Linnarz, in LZ97 - the replacement for his London bombing LZ38 destroyed by the RNAS - crossed the Blackwater at 22.00 hrs. Over-flying a blacked-out Chelmsford, LZ97 turned south-west towards London, sowing 47 incendiary bombs between Fyfield and Chipping Ongar, as searchlights coned the enemy airship in a blaze of light.

Imperial Army Zeppelin commanders were not noted for their navigational prowess; even the experienced Linnarz had mistaken the River Roding for the Thames. Assuming his craft to be above London, Linnarz ordered the release of 12 explosive bombs that fell between Forest Farm and Aldborough Hatch, shattering cottage windows near Fairlop railway station. Exposed in the unwanted glare of searchlights, LZ97 came under machine-gun fire from nightfighters. Turning to escape, Linnarz dropped an explosive bomb on Newbury Park. 2nd Lieut W L Robinson and Capt Arthur Harris had made the first attacks on enemy aircraft by the recently formed No.39 Squadron, both men were destined to become famous - but not tonight.

Bomb load almost exhausted, Zeppelin LZ97 climbed away from 2nd Lieut William Leefe Robinson; his makeshift B.E.2c had been within range of the monstrous flying machine long enough to fire 20 rounds, in spite of no less than five stoppages to clear on the new gun. On his return to Suttons Farm Robinson made a vow, at the next encounter 'it would be either the Zepp or me'. His Flight Commander, Capt Arthur T Harris, suffered similar frustration, as his single Lewis jammed twice after firing a few rounds. Above Seven Kings, coned in searchlights, the anxious Zeppelin crew were relieved as Linnarz ordered the release of water ballast and full ahead on a homeward course. Two small bombs fell between Goodmayes and Chadwell Heath, as the fleeing Zeppelin vanished into the clouds. Luckily, the owners of a wooden cottage, destroyed by the bombs, were visiting family in Ilford. 2nd Lieut A de B Brandon and 2nd Lieut C T Black, airborne from Hainault Farm, saw LZ97, but were unable to climb above 8,000 ft in their B.E. biplanes. Frustrated Hounslow pilots, beset with engine trouble, also saw the Zeppelin held in searchlight beams above Ilford. At least one of the two B.E aeroplanes that fired on LZ97 carried the very latest in a long line of anti-'Zepp' missiles. Brock explosive bullets, soon No 39 Squadron will be issued incendiary and explosive ammunition in quantity. The problem with the Lewis Gun jamming, though frustrating for the pilots, would be overcome by carefully checking each round being loaded into the drum.

Once again a Zeppelin raid upon London had proved a failure. Sister ship LZ93 crossed the Essex coast at 22.30 hrs, flying a figure eight, dropping bombs in the Harwich area, before heading out to sea 15 minutes later. LZ88 made landfall above Herne Bay at 00.30 hrs and, skirting Canterbury, flew north-east, dropping bombs between Preston and Westgate, unseen by patrolling aircraft of RNAS Westgate, before departing the Kent coast at 01.35 hrs.

One person had been injured in the Army Airship raid and damage to property minimal, the only justification apart from the rise in morale on the German home front following extravagant claims of damage wrought, had to be the large number of guns, equipment, aircraft, trained military and naval personnel, required to man the air defences of Britain, to the detriment of the armed forces fighting overseas.

No.39 Squadron took to the air again as Army Zeppelin LZ93 returned the next night to bomb London, engine trouble forced her commander to drop bombs into the sea off Deal and limp home.

The encounter with an enemy airship by pilots of No.39 HDS on the night of Tuesday, 25th April, highlighted the improved state of London's aerial defences at this period, although two machines from A Flt Hounslow suffered engine trouble, they both made a successful emergency landing with the aid of Chingford and Joyce Green flare paths. Criticism of the layout of flares at Ilford by Capt Harris, echoed by other 39 Squadron flyers, had not bothered the two pilots of C Flt returning safely to Hainault Farm. With the aid of searchlights, the raider had been exposed and put to flight by airmen of B Flt from Suttons Farm. Mysterious flashing lights from the ground were thought by the patrolling airmen to be signals guiding the Zeppelin towards the Woolwich Arsenal.

At Ilford the vigilant Special Constables enforced the black-out with such vigour that residents were forced to complain that the severe lighting restrictions increased burglary in the town. There were also complaints in the local press regarding the use of bad language by soldiers returning home on leave from the trenches, and wartime vocabulary spawned by the BEF in Flanders also began to infiltrate the home front. Shortage of labour brought about by conscription was highlighted, as the people of Ilford were requested to collect their own bread and release more men for the front. To cheer the townsfolk, nightly living in the shadow of the Zeppelin, H E Bulley advertised patriotic songs on sale at his shop on Ilford Hill, with the proud boast, 'English-made records only stocked'.

Eight Naval and one Army Zeppelin rose from their sheds on 2nd May in a combined raid upon northern England

and Scotland. Fortunately for the over-stretched northern Home Defence squadrons, bad weather intervened, restricting fatal casualties to nine and thirty injured. Blown off course returning to Germany, Naval Zeppelin L20 crash-landed out of fuel into a Norwegian fjord; six of the crew were repatriated, the remaining ten interned. Two days later the Imperial Navy suffered the loss of L7, sent to reconnoitre a flotilla of ships, including seaplane carriers, attempting to raid the Tondern Zeppelin base. Hit by anti-aircraft fire from two British cruisers, *Galatea* and *Phaeton*, L7 fell into the sea off Horns' Reef, where seven survivors of the eighteen man crew were rescued by Royal Navy submariners aboard E31.

In retaliation for RNAS night raids on aerodromes in occupied Belgium, seven German seaplanes carried out a moonlight bombing raid on the Dover area in the early hours of Saturday, 20th May, killing one person and injuring two more.

An attack by airmen upon the `Zepp' above Seven Kings boosted morale in the town, but as luck would have it, Romford, in the path of the Zeppelin, had been spared the horror of a monster sized hydrogen inferno falling upon it.

On 30th May, the Imperial Naval Airship Division commissioned L30, the first of the long awaited six engined R class Zeppelins at Nordholz. This impressive flying machine, a little over 644 ft overall, matched the mighty battle cruisers of the Royal Navy in length. Nicknamed `The Super-Zeppelin' by British Naval Intelligence this, and sister ships under construction, would soon be carrying 2½ ton bomb loads to England.

The scattered flights of No 39 HD Squadron awaited the return of the `Zepps' with increasing confidence; night patrols were becoming routine with training and practice all sixteen RFC machines hunting Zeppelin raiders on the night of 25th April had landed safely, including the two emergencies on strange flarepaths by No. 39 HDS pilots. This indicated the rapid progress in techniques, compared with the raid of 31st January, when eleven of fifteen Home Defence machines crashed, killing three pilots and injuring a fourth.

The open unused front cockpits of No. 39 Squadron B.E.2c's were faired over with aluminium sheet or thin plywood as available. This simple conversion eliminated a little drag on their biplanes. Far from convinced that the Lewis machine gun, with the untried incendiary ammunition being issued, would be the answer to the Zeppelin menace, the War Office arranged for a launch to tow targets in the Thames estuary to enable pilots to practice dropping Ranken darts; a heavier 5 lb version would replace the 1 lb missile in use.

Fortunately for the men of No.39 HDS and the ever increasing number of British night flyers, the Holt magnesium flare had become part of the standard equipment on night flying aeroplanes. In the event of a forced night landing in open country without the aid of a flarepath, the Holt flares attached to the underside of each lower wingtip proved a life saver. Ignited by an electrical switch from inside the open cockpit, the magnesium flared with such brilliance for 60 seconds that pilots found it easier in practice to look over the opposite wing as they attempted to land. Parachutes were in use, saving lives of observation balloon crews both sides of the lines in France, but they would not be issued to British airmen during the Great War. A number of German and Austrian pilots were saved from certain death by parachutes in 1918.

On the last day of May, 1916, British and German fleets fought the battle of Jutland, both sides claiming victory. The bare facts are that the Royal Navy suffered 6,097 fatal casualties and 510 wounded, with the loss of 14 ships. German casualties amounted to 2,551 men killed and 507 wounded, losing 11 ships.

Weakness had been exposed in the design of Royal Navy battle-cruisers, prompting Admiral David Beatty to remark, 'There seems to be something wrong with our bloody ships today'. He would later be responsible for the refitting of the fleet, but the Germans never again challenged the might of the Royal Navy.

Able Seaman John Nicol Kirkpatrick of 32 Sylvan Road, Ilford, who died of wounds received on board HMS *Chester* during the battle of Jutland, was buried with full Naval Honours at Ilford on Monday, 12th June. A ninety man contingent of the Royal Naval Reserve, with their band, followed the Union Jack covered coffin on an open hearse by way of Ley Street, Ilford Broadway and High Road, lined with Boy Scouts, to St Mary's Church. Along the route the Band played the 'Dead March' and crowds of reverent townsfolk paid their respects; later at the church volleys were fired over the grave of the 23 year old seaman and finally trumpeters sounded 'The Last Post'.

Another local seaman killed in action on board HMS *Chester* had been buried in a common grave at Grimsby, but, as the exploits of 16 year old John Travers Cornwell became

known to the press, his body was exhumed and on Saturday, 29th July, Londoners turned out in their thousands to watch his funeral cortège, including many local dignitaries *en route* for Manor Park Cemetery; the occasion has been described as almost Victorian in splendour. Because of his youth, Jack Cornwell became the hero of Jutland and was awarded the Victoria Cross posthumously. Later, a brass plate to commemorate him was placed on the wall of his old school in Walton Road, Manor Park.

Thursday, 30th September, was called 'Jack Cornwell Day' in elementary schools and seven million children paid a penny each for a stamp bearing his portrait. Eli Cornwell, his father, in peace time a local tram driver, serving as a private in the Royal Defence Corps, died on 25th October, and was buried with his son at Manor Park. Jack Cornwell's mother Lily attended Buckingham Palace to receive her son's Victoria Cross from King George on Thursday, 16th November, 1916; her second son, Arthur, died in action on the Western Front in August, 1918.

The magazine *Sphere*, published on 29th April, a month before the Battle of Jutland, pointed out that Zeppelins were at their best scouting for the battle-fleet. Illustrations in the article compared the visual range of a Zeppelin, flying at a mere 1,000 ft equalled 40 miles, with the approximate 16 miles radius from the fire control platform of a battleship. It was not until 04.00 hrs the following morning a powerful wireless-carrying Zeppelin sighted the British fleet, by then the battle of Jutland had been fought and the Imperial German Navy was in retreat. The long awaited confrontation of British and German battle fleets had resulted in the 'victorious' battle of Jutland; now people looked forward to the expected big push by the Army in France.

No.39 HD Squadron came under the

command of Major W C Mansfield on Tuesday, 13th June, and 2nd Lieut Alfred de B Brandon became the commander of C Flight at Hainault Farm.

Ilford Roller Skating Rink closed its doors to the public for the duration of the war. The corrugated sheet iron covered building had been taken over by Oakley Ltd of Westminster and renamed the Ilford Aeroplane Works, for the repair and installation of aero engines. In the spring of 1917 the Ilford Aeroplane Works, subcontracting work from the Sopwith Aviation Company, commenced work on 25 Sopwith Triplanes; three of the machines were completed before the order was cancelled due to the Triplane becoming obsolete as a front line fighter. One Sopwith triplane built at Ilford has survived the passage of time; N5912 can now be seen among the collection of WW1 aeroplanes currently on display at the Royal Air Force Museum, Hendon.

Above the lines in France, a new breed of British scouts, the fighter planes of the Great War, were meeting the Fokker monoplanes on equal terms. Oberleutnant Max Immelmann, Germany's idolised leading ace with 15 victories, was killed in action with an FE2b pusher biplane of No.25 Squadron on Sunday, 18th June. German propaganda, having woven the legend of Immelmann, the invincible 'Eagle of Lille', went to great lengths to prove he had not been downed by British airmen, but had died in a crash following the break up of his Fokker monoplane in mid-air during the fight.

Eluding allied scout patrols the following day, the crew of a high flying reconnaissance machine, confirmed reports of a massive build up of men and equipment behind the British lines on the Somme

Following a break-through by German infantry using phosgene gas on the French front, the BEF were urged to commence at once the big push planned for the British-held Somme front to ease the pressure on the French army at Fleury. In response to the plea from his Ally, General Douglas Haig unleashed a thunderous bombardment on 24th June that continued for days, although the planned offensive could not begin for another week. Hour after hour the low rumble of distant gunfire could be heard in Ilford as British and French artillery pounded German front line trenches; at outlying villages in Essex rumour spread that another big naval battle raged on the North Sea.

On Monday, 26th June, the Ilford Hippodrome featured a revue called *The Big Push*, as the heavy artillery barrage in preparation for the big push continued along the 16 mile Somme front.

Royal Flying Corps machines, including the ubiquitous but obsolete BE2c biplanes, were flying under the low clouds ranging the fall of shells for the artillery, despite bad weather blamed on the non-stop thunder of heavy guns.

On Thursday, 29th June, the crew of a No.8 Squadron BE2c, busy spotting for the gunners, were attacked by a Fokker, wounding the pilot 2nd Lieut Charles Thomas Vaisey who lost consciousness; his observer, 2nd Lieut. Charles Pickthorne, clambered from the front cockpit and managed to fly the machine back across the lines to land safely on their aerodrome. The cool-headed observer of Endsleigh Gardens, Ilford, had also managed to buzz a message with the Morse key requesting a doctor to tend his wounded comrade on their return.

At 0730 hrs on Saturday, 1st July, after a week of continuous bombardment, over half a million British and French infantry followed their officers over the top. By the end of the worst day in the long history of the British Army, 19,000 thousand British soldiers were dead; the French, who had employed heavier artillery to destroy the deep dugouts sheltering German machine-gun crews, were able to recapture some ground.

Among the British wounded during the first day of the Somme battle, had been 21-year-old Lance Corporal Arthur Latreille of 5 Kingswood Road, Goodmayes. With both legs smashed by German machine-gun fire, he had been stretchered back to 'Blighty' - but succumbed to his serious wounds at Reading Hospital on Sunday, 9th July. His family and friends filled All Saints Church at Goodmayes for his funeral service on Saturday, 15th July.

War work on the home front also took its toll, 21 year old Sidney Lee of 66 Buntingbridge Road, met an untimely end on Sunday, 8th July. Reservist Sidney was employed at Woolwich Arsenal inserting detonators into hand grenades for Major A H Taylor to test-throw from inside splinter proof sand bagged butts. His last words were, 'This cap is very stiff, sir,' followed almost immediately by an explosion; a verdict of accidental death was returned at the inquest.

Carpenter and joiner, Ernest Ashmole, of 1 Thorold Road, Ilford, suffered serious injuries sustained when a wooden hanger he was assisting to erect at Fairlop aerodrome collapsed. The inscription upon his headstone, just inside the main gates of St Mary's Church, reads 'CIVILIAN ERNEST ASHMOLE, 16TH AUGUST, 1916, AGED 43. HIS DEATH WAS THE RESULT OF AN ACCIDENT AT FAIRLOP AERODROME ON JULY 19TH 1916'. The unfortunate carpenter had become the first fatal casualty of Fairlop aerodrome manned by Royal Naval Air Service personnel.

Fairlop had been chosen as a Flight Sub-Station to the expanding RNAS flying school at Chingford in the spring of 1916; no doubt pre-war aviation activities at the Ilford playing fields influenced the choice. Although 15 feet lower than Hainault Farm, the well-drained playing fields were an excellent choice for an aerodrome, compared with Hainault Farm, where more than one RFC pilot recalled the mud in his memoirs.

In pre-war days, the first aeroplane flight across London had commenced from Fairlop, when Edward Petre in a Handley-Page monoplane flew to Brooklands, via the Thames in 50 minutes on 27th July, 1912. Frederick Handley-Page (1885-1962), an astute business man as well as a trained engineer, rented a shed at Barking Creekmouth, a mile from the Dagenham Experimental Ground, opened on 5th February, 1909, with the aid of subscriptions from fellow members of The Aeronautical Society. Handley-Page made the generous donation of six pounds one shilling and proceeded to make components for fellow members lacking the necessary engineering skills, but ambitious to build a flying machines. Early the following year, unable to raise a further £400 needed for the upkeep, the Dagenham Experimental Ground ceased to exist. Handley-Page expanded his Barking works by purchasing from the Aeronautical Society three large sheds from the site, now part of the Ford Motor Company main plant at Dagenham.

The little factory at Barking Creek became the birthplace of the famous Handley-Page Aircraft Company. However, the land surrounding the site proved unsuitable for test flying and the playing fields of Fairlop were rented for this purpose. In September, 1912, Handley-Page moved his factory from Barking to larger premises at Cricklewood, close by the established aerodrome at Hendon.

The arrival of the Royal Naval Air Service at Fairlop in 1916 and the subsequent expansion of the aerodrome, also known locally as Forest Farm, just 400 yards along the road from Hainault Farm has led to confusion with the passing years - but not for Mrs Nellie Smith of Cornshaw Road, Dagenham, who recalls her childhood days as little Nellie Fogg, playing with friends in the goods yard at Hainault Railway station, just to the north-west of Forest Farm (Fairlop) aerodrome. Her vivid memories include hearing instructions shouted above throttled back aero engines and the whine of wind in the wires as two-seat biplanes skimmed the station roof coming down to land at Fairlop. Although Fairlop would become a very busy training aerodrome due to the ever growing demand for pilots, experienced pupils still found time to return the waves of the railway children.

At Hainault Farm, along Forest Road from Fairlop aerodrome, it was business as usual for the men of C Flight No. 39HD Squadron. Captain A H Morton MC replaced Major W H C Mansfield as CO of the squadron on 27th July, the third change of command since 15th April when the Squadron had been formed.

The lull in Zeppelin raids came to an end in the early hours of Saturday, 29th July, when six 'Zepps' dropped 70 bombs on Eastern England. There were no casualties and little damage, but fog prevented Home Defence machines from playing an active role.

Seven 'Zepps' visited Eastern England two nights later with no casualties and very little damage. One RFC machine crashed in fog injuring the pilot.

One person sustained injuries in a raid by six 'Zepps' again on Eastern England during the night of Wednesday, 2nd August. A mixture of 32 RNAS and RFC machines were airborne, hunting the elusive giant war balloons. A Bristol Scout from HMS *Vindex*, a small aircraft carrier with a 64 ft long flight deck, chased and attacked Naval Zeppelin L17 with Ranken darts, without any visible damage, before ditching his machine in the sea to be rescued by a Belgian steamer.

Once again, Ranken incendiary darts had failed to destroy a Zeppelin, despite spirited attacks carried out by Naval airman Flt Lieut C T Freeman, piloting a tiny 24 ft 7 in. span Bristol Scout. With daylight hours growing shorter, No.39HD Squadron, patrolling during the recent raids on the eastern part of the country, knew it would not be long before Zeppelin commanders would be tempted to strike at London again.

During August, 1916, A Flight of No. 39HD Squadron moved from Hounslow to North Weald, approximately 7½ miles north of C.Flight at Hainault Farm. The whole Squadron now occupied fields on Essex farmland, with headquarters at Salway Lodge, Woodford Green, 4 miles from Hainault Farm and 9 miles from both North Weald Basset and Suttons Farm. 2nd Lieut J I Mackay of A Flight, now flying from North Weald, would be the only pilot from No.39HD Squadron to catch sight of Naval Zeppelin L31 that penetrated London air defences during the early hours of Friday, 25th August. Kptlt Heinrich Mathy had brought the R class Super Zeppelin L31 to London via the Kent coast, making his first raid on the capital since October the previous year. There were 9 fatal casualties and 40 injured by the bombs dropped on south east London, the searchlights and gunners along with the airmen had been hampered by the low clouds and heavy rain during the raid. The North Weald pilot had pursued the L31 for some miles, until it disappeared into the clouds and Mackay, realising that he was lost, searched the murk below for the flares of a Night Landing Ground. He eventually made a heavy landing at Burnham on Crouch, collapsing the undercarriage of his B.E. in the process.

2nd Lieut C S Ross, who had left North Weald 15 minutes prior to Mackay, put down without incident at Joyce Green after patrolling for three hours.

Two pilots of B Flight, Lieut W Leefe Robinson and 2nd Lieut F Sowrey, carried out patrols without sighting the enemy airship among the clouds and returned safely to Suttons Farm in the driving rain.

At Hainault Farm, C Flight launched B.E.2c, piloted by Lieut A D Broughton at 01.45 hrs; within minutes, blinded by mist and rain, the pilot spun the machine into the ground, escaping serious injuries.

Super Zeppelin L32 also crossed the Kent coast, but was chased out to sea by Capt J W Woodhouse of No. 50 Squadron, firing a drum and a half of incendiary bullets at long range. Two older 4 engined airships, L16 and 21, gave London a wide berth and caused minor damage in Suffolk and no casualties. Mathy had saved the raid from being a complete failure.

It would have made little difference had the people of Ilford known that 9 of the 13 Zeppelins ordered to attack England had failed in the attempt, the fact remained that once again London had been bombed.

Light cruisers and destroyers of the Royal Navy fired upon at least six Zeppelins trying to cross the North Sea. L13, Mathy's old ship, lived up to its reputation, with a lucky escape when a shell from HMS *Conquest* tore through gas cell no.8, before exploding above the Zeppelin, forcing Kptlt Prolss to jettison his bomb load and return to base for repairs. A strong headwind delayed some of the raiders who dropped their bomb loads without success on to the warships, rather than risk crossing the coast with a rising moon at 02.00 hrs.

Assurances from the War Office to calm the fears of a population, outraged that the `Baby Killers' were still able to bomb England at will after 18 months, were met with demands that something be done about the `Zepps' immediately. Members of the Air Board, meeting after the latest London air raid, had little hope to offer, except that adequate supplies of the new .303 explosive and incendiary bullets were now available for home defence aircraft.

The first day of September arrived in Ilford, coupled with the never ending casualty lists from the Somme. The sadness of tearful farewells, as service men took leave of their families, added to the depression brought about by the seemingly invincible `Zepps'.

At Hainault Farm on Saturday, 2nd September - a gloomy wet day over the county of Essex - C Flight checked and double checked their BE2c aeroplanes; it would be ideal `Zepp' weather after dark.

At B Flight Suttons Farm, Lieut W Leefe Robinson, now acting Flight Commander, rolled up his sleeves to help the ground crew remove the boxes of Ranken darts from his machine. He had used, in the parlance of the day, `a little bit of gumption'; it was against orders of course, but Robinson, a competent and experienced pilot, knew his machine had been overloaded on his previous encounter with a `Zepp' and wanted to get the best out of the `old bus' to make good use of the Lewis machine-gun and incendiary ammunition.

During the afternoon, no less than 16 giant air ships arose at intervals from nine separate bases across the North Sea in Germany. It was to have been the greatest aerial blow struck against England yet and the first time rival Imperial Army and Naval airship services combined their efforts to bomb London; it would also be the last.

The Happisburg lightship, 8 miles off the Norfolk coast, confirmed Naval Intelligence reports of an impending raid by Zeppelins on the evening of Saturday, 2nd September. The call by underwater telephone cable, relayed to the War Office, resulted in the order "Take air raid action" being issued to Home Defence squadrons and anti-aircraft units just after 21.00 hrs.

Three quarters of an hour later Naval Zeppelin L14 crossed the coast, followed at intervals during the next two hours, by more droning giants, making a scattered landfall over East Anglia.

But all was not well on board Army Zeppelin LZ97, lashed by driving rain;

her commander aborted the raid and returned to base without dropping a single bomb on enemy soil.

Naval Zeppelin L17, in the clouds above Norfolk, was also forced to abandoned the raid early by re-occurring engine trouble.

Telephonists at Air Defence HQ were receiving information of Zeppelin movements from the efficient and well-established network of railway depôts, Police stations and observer posts across East Anglia, indicating London might be a target during the raid.

At 23.00 hrs, motors shut down and silently drifting above Essex, Army Zeppelin LZ90 attempted to use an observation car lowered by steel cable to penetrate the clouds below. Fortunately the observer had not been inside the sub-cloud car for the test run, as it plunged to earth with 500 ft of steel cable, near Manningtree.

At 01.15 hrs on Sunday, 3rd September, Lieut W Leefe Robinson, aloft in B.E.2c 2693 hunting for the elusive giant Zeppelins dropping bombs from the Thames to the Humber, chased LZ98 into the clouds and lost sight of it. Robinson had been the first pilot airborne from No.39HD Squadron; three minutes later Lieut C S Ross took off from A Flight at North Weald Basset in a B.E.12 6484, followed a minute later by 2nd Lieut A de B Brandon from C Flight at Hainault Farm in B.E.2c 2090.

Clifford Ross in the 150 hp B.E.12 from North Weald cut his patrol short to make an emergency landing back at his field, but crashed, without serious injury to himself, at 01.00 hrs.

Robinson of B Flight continued his patrol between Suttons Farm and Joyce Green across the Thames. Around 02.00 hrs, although running low on fuel, he set off in pursuit of an airship caught in searchlight beams and under heavy anti-aircraft fire to the north of London. Two other machines piloted by members of No.39 Squadron were also closing the distance between them and the `Zepp'.

Hauptmann Wilhelm Schramm, commander of Imperial Army airship SL11, had been born in London 31 years earlier, but, as a professional soldier and captain of the army dirigible, he had no qualms obeying orders to bomb the city of his birth. The throb of four 240 hp Maybach engines propelling the enormous craft were first heard at 22.40 hrs among the rain clouds above the river Crouch on the Essex coast. To avoid Home Defence aerodromes on the perimeter of East London, SL11 droned over Chelmsford, then Colchester, before taking a westward course to approach London from the north. After dropping bombs between London Colney and Edmonton to gain altitude for the attack on the City, the raider became coned in searchlight beams and presented anti-aircraft gunners with an excellent target.

Unaware of the danger from falling shell fragments, many people were watching far below in the streets, back gardens and, because of the late hour, leaning out of bedroom windows clad in their night attire, willing the guns to score a direct hit on the `Zepp'.

Free from the drag and weight of bombs and incendiary darts, the B.E.2c piloted by Robinson outpaced the other two biplanes racing towards the dirigible, now gripped in searchlight beams from Finsbury and Victoria Park. Cocking his Very pistol Robinson fired a red flare, warning anti-aircraft gunners that the Royal Flying Corps were about to engage the enemy. A determined Robinson, having coaxed his machine to nearly 13,000 ft during his long patrol, dived to attack the awesome vessel from beneath with his upward firing Lewis gun clamped upon a mounting just in front of his face. As the anti-aircraft gun fire subsided, the sound of an aeroplane engine could just be heard above heavy throb of the airship; the streets below, dim in the reflected glare of searchlights, began to darken again. The growing throng of excited spectators realised that the searchlights were being covered in an effort to conceal the aeroplane from the Zeppelin's machine gunners and cries of encouragement filled the air. One elderly gentleman, unable to contain his excitement, shouted at the top of his voice, "They are going to bomb the bugger".

On board the Schutte-Lanz, temporary repairs were being carried out to ballonets punctured by shell splinters and an engine crankcase holed by anti-aircraft fire plugged with cotton waste, as Robinson zoomed under the bow in a frontal attack and opened fire.

Few of the thousands of excited civilians watching the David and Goliath drama unfolding 11,000 ft above their heads realised the irony of the situation. Fifteen German soldiers, commanded by the able and experienced Wilhelm Schramm, were about to be roasted alive in an enormous fireball, that seconds earlier had been a powerful airborne terror machine. En route for London, SL11 bombed the suburbs, injuring one woman and killing three horses, when incendiaries set fire to racing stables.

The following is an extract of the typically modest report written by Lieut William Leefe Robinson, before collapsing exhausted on to his camp bed, falling asleep immediately. "I flew 800 feet below it from bow to stern and distributed one drum along it (alternate New Brock and Pomeroy). It seemed to have no effect; I therefore moved to one side and gave it another drum distributed along its side - without apparent effect. I then got behind it (by this time I was very close - 500 feet or less below) and concentrated one drum on one part (underneath rear). I was then at a height of 11,500 feet when attacking Zeppelin. I hardly finished the drum before I saw the part fired at glow. In a few seconds the whole rear part was blazing. When the third drum was fired there were no searchlights on the Zeppelin and no anti-aircraft were firing. I quickly got out of the way of the falling, blazing Zeppelin and, being very excited, fired off a few red Very lights and dropped a parachute flare."

William Leefe Robinson had been born on the family coffee plantation in India on the 14th July, 1895. He had been educated at public school in England and five months at Sandhurst Royal Military College, followed by a commission in the Worcestershire Regiment as a second lieutenant. In March 1915, keen to see active service before the war ended, Robinson transferred to the Royal Flying Corps, to serve as an observer/gunner with No.4 Squadron in France. A shrapnel wound in the right arm, received during a dawn reconnaissance flight above Lille on the 7th May, 1915, gave Robinson a `Blighty' posting home to convalesce. At the end of June he was fit enough to commence pilot training. Five days after gaining his `wings' he joined No.19 Squadron, pioneering the art of night flying on 20th September, 1915.

Almost a year later, now an experienced flight commander, he had become the hero of the hour. With very little fuel to spare, Robinson landed at Suttons Farm at 02.45 hrs, to be carried shoulder high to the flight office by the cheering officers and men of B Flight.

In spite of a thunderstorm mid-morning a multitude of people gathered around the steaming remains of the downed `Zepp', cordoned off by military personnel. The lucky ones were rewarded with a glimpse of the handsome young airman responsible for the firework display during the night. He had been forced protesting from his camp bed by 2nd Lieut Frederick Sowrey, who wanted his friend to view the wreckage before the Intelligence chaps had it carted away for evaluation. Not that there was much to see; the charred bodies of the crew had been placed inside St Andrew's church that had narrowly escaped destruction when the blazing wreckage of the SL11 fell close by.

The first Zeppelin shot down by the Royal Flying Corps was such a morale booster to the long suffering civilian population, that the War Office decided it would be in their interest to conceal the fact that the wooden framed airship had not been constructed at the Zeppelin works. To add to the subterfuge the Schutte-Lanz airship would be given the identity of L21, a German Naval Zeppelin. Propaganda points were scored by Lord French C-in-C Home Forces, who claimed, "The large amount of wood employed in the framework is startling and would seem to point to a shortage of aluminium in Germany."

On Tuesday, 5th September, the newspaper headlines THE ZEPP V C FOR AIRMAN came as no surprise to the people of Ilford; many had witnessed the fiery end of the airship and joined in the cheering. At Hainault Farm, C Flight were elated with the success of the squadron pilot who had demonstrated that giant Zeppelins were vulnerable to incendiary bullets.

Such are the fortunes of war, that 2nd Lieut B H Hunt, airborne from Hainault Farm, also pursuing the SL11, had no idea that Robinson had attacked the monster and had closed to within 600 ft. He was about to open fire, when the airship erupted in a ball of flames.

Half a mile away, Naval Zeppelin L16, having just bombed Essendon, resulting in the deaths of the village blacksmith's two daughters, became clearly visible in the glare of the burning Army airship. Hunt saw L16, but found it impossible not to have another look at the awesome end of the doomed airship and lost sight of the fleeing Zeppelin. Half an hour later, with his night vision restored, Hunt gave chase to another Naval Zeppelin, L32, that had also seen the destruction of SL11 and was heading for

the coast at full speed, but he lost it in the clouds. Frustrated Hunt concluded his eventful patrol and landed safely back at Hainault Farm at 03.44 hrs.

On Tuesday, 12th September, 1916, again the people of Ilford heard the distant sound of a massive artillery bombardment as the third phase of the Somme battle commenced. The British Army unleashed its secret weapon, the tank, three days later. RFC machines had overflown the area in an effort to muffle the sounds of the tanks moving into position in vain; a German kite balloon observer telephoned down warnings and the element of surprise had been lost.

Above the trenches, the new German Albatros single seat fighter biplanes, with twin machine guns firing through the propeller arc, had began to wrest the hard won dominance of the air from the Royal Flying Corps.

During an air battle on Sunday, 17th September, three out of a flight of eight F.E.2b pusher machines were forced down by Jagdstaffel 2, commanded by Haupt Oswald Boelcke. An F.E.2b of No.11 Squadron fell to the guns of a keen young pilot named von Richthofen, as his first aerial victory. Boelcke, a recipient of the Pour le Merit, Prussia's highest award for bravery with 27 confirmed victories to his credit, was the idol of Germany, vying with Kptlt Heinrich Mathy of the Zeppelins for popularity in the Fatherland: thousands of postcard portraits of the two heroes were being bought as fast as they could be printed.

In England, the Home Defence squadrons awaited the return of the Zeppelins with confidence, thanks to Lieutenant W Leefe Robinson flaming SL11.

No.39HD Squadron almost lost their

star pilot when Robinson took off from Suttons Farm on a routine night patrol on Saturday, 16th September. Barely airborne, the B.E.2c that had served Robinson so well during the early hours of 3rd September, clipped a hedgerow, nosed over into the ground and burst into flames. The pilot jumped clear and a few minutes later B.E.2c 2639 was completely destroyed by an explosion. It would have been tragedy, in more ways than one, if the handsome aviator had been killed in the accident as Leefe Robinson had become a household name and by far the best known Lieutenant in the British Army. Newspapers carried his photograph for days and the War Office turned a blind eye to the £4,000 prize money presented to Robinson as the first airman to bring a `Zepp' down in Britain. Thousands of Leefe Robinson picture postcards were appearing, to be eagerly collected by a grateful nation. The village of Hornchurch were to present their `Zepp VC' with a silver cup subscribed for by nearly 300 donations and B Flt became inundated with fan mail and invitations for Robinson.

With the utmost faith in their dapper commander, Leader of the Naval Airship Division, Freggatenkapitan Peter Strasser, the crews of 12 Zeppelins droned towards the English coast on the evening of Saturday, 23rd September. Strasser wasted no time following the horrific end of Army airship SL11, seen by some of his crews, to restate his conviction that Zeppelins were capable of destroying London and forcing Britain out of the war. He raised the morale of his men by reminding them the accident rate for

Army airships had been far higher than the Navy, and that, by carelessly operating at low altitudes, the Army lost airships to small arms fire and enemy aeroplanes.

Although Strasser had been right to criticize the military that had lost or forced to decommission 23 airships since 1914, his theory of the Zeppelins as war winning weapons were about to be disproved.

Four `super Zeppelins' were among fleet of raiders crossing the coast under cover of darkness Aware of London's much improved defences, they alone would bomb the City, leaving the less defended Midlands to the older airships.

No.39 Squadron, not yet six months old, but already the most experienced Home Defence squadron in the Royal Flying Corps, were waiting to greet the London bound raiders. Having made landfall at Foulness shortly before 23.00 hrs, Kptlt Aloys Bocker, in command of the latest R-class Zeppelin L33, eluded a pursuing RNAS B.E.2c from Eastchurch and arrived over east London. After bombing Streatham and Brixton, held in a pyramid of searchlights, L33 came under fire from the Becton and Wanstead anti-aircraft guns and received a direct hit amidships destroying hydrogen gas cells. Rapidly losing height with a damaged propeller adding to the din of racing motors, the Zeppelin could be heard crossing the outskirts of Ilford, heading towards Chelmsford. No.39 Squadron aeroplanes had seen the two large fires started by incendiaries from L33 and were hunting blind for the Zeppelin that had shaken off the dangerous caress of the searchlights.

Aboard the stricken Zeppelin, descending 800 ft per minute over enemy territory, Bocker gave orders to release the water ballast, followed by equipment, including heavy machine-guns and ammunition. Above Kelvedon Hatch, with the descent of the airship barely in check, a night fighter zoomed in for the kill. Lieut A de B Brandon, C Flight commander at Hainault Farm, has been rated by eminent aviation historians as the unluckiest home-defence pilot of the war, following his encounters with Naval Zeppelins L15 and L33.

Brandon had been ordered aloft from Hainault Farm at 23.33 hrs, no longer the novice pilot who had attacked L15 on his first true night flight. Six months later, now an experienced flight commander, he was about to engage in nocturnal combat once again with a Zeppelin above the Essex countryside.

An excerpt of Brandon's official report of his encounter with the L33, on file at the Imperial War Museum, London, reads - "At 12.12 I saw a Zeppelin in the search-lights some distance away and made for it. Very shortly after this, it escaped from the searchlights and I lost it, but I continued on and picked it up again. I went on climbing and managed with some difficulty to keep it in view, as there were no searchlights on it and my automatic pump had failed and I had to work the cocking handle of the Lewis gun. After putting on a drum of ammunition I came up behind the Zeppelin and on raising the gun jerked it out of the mounting, the gun and the yoke falling across the nacelle. I managed to replace the gun, but in the meantime had passed under and past the

Zeppelin. I turned and passed along it again, but from the bow, but we passed each other too quickly for me to take aim. On turning, I came up behind and fired a drum of ammunition. The Brock ammunition seemed to be bursting all along it, but the Zepp did not catch fire. I was using Brock, Pomeroy and sparklet. I turned again and put on a fresh drum and came up from behind and fired again. The gun jammed after about nine rounds. I now decided to get above the Zepp and went on climbing but there was a large bank of grey cloud all around the horizon and it was impossible to see the Zeppelin against it, after I had got level with the Zeppelin. I first saw the Zeppelin at 12.13 and lost it at 12.33."

The twenty minute attack by the New Zealander added to the volume of gas escaping through hundreds of rents in the remaining ballonets, compounding the problems of Bocker and his crew. Climbing about in the vast black spider's web of alloy girders and bracing wire surrounding the sagging ballonets inside the Zeppelin, the crew frantically doping and patching did not know how kind fate had been to them. Hard pushed front line squadrons were being issued with 97 round Lewis drums to spare pilots having to change the 47 round so frequently in combat with the better armed enemy. Had the Home Defence squadrons carried double drums, Brandon may have been able to have fired 106 instead of 56 rounds. Not to be out done by a jammed gun, Brandon climbed above the Zeppelin, intending to use the Le Prieur incendiary rockets attached to his outboard inter-plane struts, but once again, as with L15,

A section of the intricate alloy structure of the 644 feet length of Zeppelin L33 in the church at Little Wigborough (*Ken Feline*)

No.39 Squadron

the enormous Zeppelin had disappeared.

Losing height fast, L33 crossed the coast at West Mersea, but the odds were against the crippled airship surviving and, with no hope of gaining altitude to reach occupied Belgium, Bocker ordered the helmsman to turn back. At 01.20 hrs the vast hulk of the Zeppelin crunched to rest at Little Wigborough and the uninjured crew jumped clear. Bocker tried to destroy the grounded super Zeppelin to prevent British Intelligence from examining the latest in German technology. Members of his crew knocked on the doors of nearby cottages, shouting warnings that the airship would be set on fire. The frightened families remaining behind locked doors as Bocker set the wreck on fire with a signal flare. The ensuing blaze did not compare with the two fires the incendiaries dropped by L33 had started at an oil store and timber yard in Old Ford Road, which the London Fire Brigade was still battling to bring under control.

The terrified occupants of the cottages, a mere sixty feet from the burning Zeppelin, were safe, as most of the hydrogen had escaped. The remainder set fire to the yellow grey rubberised fabric, leaving the framework untouched.

Falling in his men, Bocker marched them off in an orderly manner, to be arrested shortly afterwards by Special Constable Edgar Nicholas on a bicycle.

Upon his return to the Flight Office at Hainault Farm, Brandon reported a second Zeppelin that he pursued after his attack upon L33. With the engine of the biplane running smoothly again and climbing steadily towards the Zeppelin

coned in searchlights above Tilbury, Brandon would have been forgiven for thinking third time lucky. Although his single Lewis gun had jammed he still had the Le Prieur rockets he had intended to fire at L33. Home Defence had not fired the French rockets in anger; however, front line pilots had been successful in flaming German observation balloons with them over the lines.

Brandon climbed to within 2,000 ft of the Zeppelin, glistening silver in the exposure of the searchlights, when suddenly he saw the Zeppelin 'being hosed with a stream of fire'. As the Zeppelin erupted into an enormous fireball, Brandon watched fascinated as it fell slowly on to the Essex countryside, before continuing his patrol and landing safely back at Hainault Farm.

Once again the people of Ilford witnessed the fiery end to a 'Zepp' and read of the capture of another complete with crew of 'Baby Killers' in the news-papers. The feared war machine, the dreaded 'Zepp', would now become the subject of 'Gas Bag' jokes, and comic postcards mocking Count von Zeppelin and the Kaiser were soon on sale in town.

The Zeppelin Brandon had watched falling in flames during the early hours of Sunday, 24th September, had been reported by telephone to the Ilford Police as being brought down on the 'Bricky', the Brickfields in the Green Lane, today known as Cricklefields. No doubt there was great relief, not to mention a red face, when later it was confirmed that the Zeppelin had fallen upon the open fields of Billericay.

2nd Lieut Frederick Sowrey had emulated his flight commander and very good friend, 'Robbie' - Lieut W Leefe Robinson - by torching a Zeppelin to the unrestrained delight of his fellow country-men watching far below. He had served with the Royal Fusiliers in France and, wounded in action, during three months convalescence in England, he applied for a transfer to the Royal Flying Corps and qualified as a pilot before his posting to No.39HD Squadron in June, 1916.

Sowrey had left Suttons Farm aerodrome, piloting B.E.2c 4112, at 23.30 hrs and climbed to 13,000 ft. Above the patchy ground mist, he found the clouds that had covered Essex for most of the day were breaking up. Suddenly, the routine, cold, boring patrol between Hainault Farm and Joyce Green aerodromes became hot pursuit, as a Zeppelin broke cloud cover to be seized and held by searchlight beams.

The following is extracted from a report written by the young pilot shortly after having put the advice of his flight commander destroyer of SL11 to good use. "At 12.45 a.m. I noticed an enemy airship in an easterly direction. I at once made in this direction and manoeuvred into a position underneath. The airship was well lighted by searchlights, but there was not a sign of any gunfire. I could distinctly see the propellers revolving and the airship was manoeuvring to avoid the searchlight beams. I fired at it. The first two drums of ammunition had apparently no effect but the third one caused the envelope to catch fire in several places; in the centre and front. All firing was traversing fire along the envelope. The drums were loaded with a mixture of Brock, Pomeroy and Tracer ammunition.

I watched the burning airship strike the ground and then proceeded to find my flares. I landed at Suttons Farm at 1.40 a.m., 24th instant".

In fact Sowrey had concentrated the last drum of ammunition 'on one spot' as advised by Robinson. He also referred to the enemy craft as an airship in his report, in case it had been a sister ship to the Schutte Lanz destroyed earlier by Robinson, and not a Zeppelin.

A cordon of men from the Manchester Regiment, surrounding the enormous aluminium skeleton of the downed Zeppelin, greeted the early arrival of souvenir hunters and sightseeing crowds at Little Wigborough. Among the first visitors were officers of Naval Intelligence searching for the code book of L33. German Naval codes had been changed since the battle of Jutland, but they searched in vain. Kptlt Aloys Bocker had disposed of the well weighted code book of the doomed craft at sea before returning to crunch to rest on Essex farmland.

British Intelligence, however, did have a virtually intact example of the latest R class super Zeppelin that enabled Britain to construct two successful non-rigid airships, R33 and R34. The R34 made aviation history in July, 1919, as the first aircraft to cross the Atlantic Ocean in both directions.

Examination of the captured super Zeppelin revealed that the Ilford pilot had punctured fuel tanks along the keel of L33 with explosive and incendiary bullets. Fortunately for the crew, the benzine did not ignite until Bocker attempted to destroy the stranded monster with the signal flare. Twenty-five miles away across the Essex countryside, Naval Intelligence officers sifting through the burnt out remains of L32 strewn over mangold fields at Snail's Hall Farm, Great Burstead, recovered the scorched but still readable German Naval code book of the ill-fated Zeppelin. The night had been a triumph for the combined efforts of the searchlight crews, anti-aircraft gunners and the two pilots of No.39HD Squadron. Lieut A de B Brandon, who earlier in the year had been awarded the MC for his part in the destruction of Naval Zeppelin L15, received a DSO for the attack upon L33. 2nd Lieut. F Sowrey also received a DSO for the single handed destruction of Zeppelin L32; neither pilot received prize monies collected by the civilian population. However, the War Office was unable to prevent the people of Hornchurch from presenting the local pilots, Frederick Sowrey and William Leefe Robinson, with engraved silver cups as a token of admiration and gratitude.

Everyone in Ilford by now, had their own 'Zepp' stories to tell, although a parachute flare dropped by L33 over Chadwell Heath was the subject of much discussion, its purpose may have been to confound local searchlight crews. The buzz of aeroplanes above the town had become common-place, as the Royal Naval Air Service increased training flights at Fairlop during the hours of daylight and the Royal Flying Corps at Hainault Farm reassured Ilfordians with the sound of their nocturnal anti-Zepp patrols.

Compared with the blood-letting taking place at the battles of the Somme and Verdun, the loss of two rigid airships and 44 trained personnel in one raid upon Britain had been acceptable to the German High Command. Two days later,

six Naval Zeppelins returned, giving the London area a wide berth, bombing the Midlands and southern England. Peter Strasser, shaken by the loss of two experienced commanders with the latest R class Zeppelins, told his commanders to use extreme caution. For the home defences, eager to come to grips with the 'Zepps' again, the raid of 25/26 September, proved to be frustrating, two RNAS airmen briefly glimpsed one of the raiders and a No.33 Squadron pilot escaped serious injury landing in fog near Sheffield, the RFC machine was badly damaged. Led by Kptlt Heinrich Mathy the six Zeppelins inflicted 43 fatal casualties and injured 31 during the raid; once again he returned to the Fatherland for a hero's welcome, but the prestige of bombing London would lure him back within range of No.39HD Squadron waiting on the fields of Essex.

On Sunday, 1st October, in line with the Daylight Saving Bill passed in May, the people of Ilford set their clocks back an hour. It was not popular with the local farmers, but was soon forgotten by the townsfolk, as No.39HD Squadron once again set the sky on fire with a blazing Zeppelin. After Sunday lunch, taking the advantage of heavy cloud and mist covering much of England, 11 Naval Zeppelins left their bases, under orders to bomb London and the Midlands. Severe icing and mechanical failures whittled the raiders down to seven. True to form, the experienced Mathy crossed the coast first at Lowestoft flying south-westwards. Escaping the clutches of searchlights this side of Chelmsford at 21.45 hrs, Mathy altered course, skirting the patrol area of

No.39HD Squadron, to approach London. The Zeppelin commander had intended to confuse the defences by zig-zagging across Hertfordshire before making his bombing run across the city. At 23.40 hrs above Cheshunt L31, caught by a sweeping searchlight beam, became coned by others in the matter of seconds. Night fighters of No.39HD Squadron raced towards the blaze of searchlights and anti-aircraft fire to do battle with the German Navy attempting to bomb London. The obsolete B.E.2c biplane, falling like autumn leaves in action over enemy lines on the Western Front, would prove yet again the vulnerability of the inflammable Zeppelins

Four aeroplanes, three from A Flight and one from C Flight, were in pursuit of Mathy. 2nd Lieut Wulstan Joseph Tempest, airborne from North Weald Bassett at 22.00 hrs, had been patrolling at 14,500 ft, when he saw L31 illuminated some fifteen miles away. Lieut L G S Payne, the C Flight pilot from Hainault Farm, handicapped by a slow climbing B.E.2c over-loaded with bombs and Rankin darts, could only watch fascinated the destruction of the aerial Goliath some 3,000 ft overhead. Tempest, flying through a barrage of ant-aircraft shells, arrived above the Zeppelin, to suffer petrol pressure pump failure - the same fault that had plagued Brandon in his attack on L33 a week earlier. On sighting the English night flyers, L31 jettisoned bombs and began climbing to escape, Tempest frantically pumping manually, dived beneath the huge belly. So close to the underside of the Zeppelin did Tempest position the B.E.2c that the machine gunners on either side of the

underslung gondolas were unable to return his fire. The following report of the destruction of the L31 is brief as indeed was the action. "Sir, I have the honour to report that on 1st October at 10 pm I left the ground on B.E.2c 4577 to patrol between Joyce Green and Hainault. Approximately at 11.40 I sighted a Zeppelin. I immediately made for her and fired one drum which took effect at once and set her on fire at about 12,700 ft. I then proceeded to North Weald to land and wrecked the machine on the aerodrome, without hurting myself, at 12.10 am." Later Tempest elaborating on the action states, "As I was firing, I noticed her to begin to go red inside like an enormous Chinese lantern and then a flame shot out of the front of her and I realised she was on fire. She then shot up about 200 feet, paused and came roaring down straight on to me before I had time to get out of the way. I nose-dived for all I was worth, with the Zeppelin tearing after me and I expected every minute to be engulfed in the flames. I put my machine into a spin and just managed to corkscrew out of the way as she shot passed me, roaring like a furnace". Tempest had put the previous experience gained by the pilots of B and C Flights to good use, by closing with the enemy he enabled the incendiary bullets to enter the inflammable gas cells of L31 before they burnt out, at such close range a single 47 round drum of mixed explosive and incendiary ammunition proved to be lethal to Zeppelin

The pride of the German Navy crashed to earth in two halves, the blazing tangled wreckage strewn across a field outside Potters Bar. To escape the blistering searing heat of the inferno, a few crew members without parachutes, managed to hurl themselves to a quick death. By the glow of the burning wreckage sizzling in the autumn drizzle, villagers found an enemy naval officer, half imbedded in the mud, breathing his last. With Kptlt Heinrich Mathy died the hope and expectation of the German people - the gas-filled monster flying machines created by Count Ferdinand von Zeppelin had failed to force Britain and her Empire out of the conflict. The greatest airship commander of the war left behind a young widow, who proudly remained Frau Hertha Mathy until her death at the age of 93, on 23rd January, 1990.

Returning to North Weald Bassett, Tempest misjudged his height in the light drizzle partially shrouding the landing flares and smashed the undercart and propeller of the B.E.2c. Still dazed, the pilot who had bruised his head on the Lewis gun in the crash, was carried shoulder high into the office of A Flight to write his brief and modest report. 2nd Lieut Wulstan J Tempest received a reprimand, not for damaging the biplane, but for having removed the boxes of Ranken darts and bomb load that enabled him to overtake the enemy craft. However, in recognition of his conspicuous gallantry in destroying an enemy airship, Tempest was awarded the DSO on October 13th.

The day before, in the escalating air war across the Channel, 15 single-engined bombers and six fighters of No.3 Wing RNAS, combined with nine bombers Groupe de Bombardment 4 of the French Air Service, and escorted by twenty-five fighters, bombed the Mauser small arms factory at Obendorf inside Germany. On October 15th, the German High Command concentrated a third of the Army Air Service along the Somme: two days later the pilots of No.8 Squadron RNAS were ordered to the Somme to reinforce the Royal Flying Corps; although still out-numbered, the German flyers had the advantage, as the British High Command continued with the policy of offensive patrols over the enemy lines with obsolete aircraft. On 28th October a flying accident robbed the German Army Air Service of their best tactician with 40 confirmed victories. For Oswald Boelcke, as with Max Immelmann, the propaganda machine stressed that Boelcke had not fallen to an English flyer and the 'Flaming Bullets' used against Mathy had been illegal.

Not all Ilfordians who witnessed the first Zeppelin falling in flames shared the feeling of relief and joy; Annie, the wife of William Jones, a building contractor, and mother of four, was such a person. Caught up in the mass hysteria of cheering and hand clapping her daughter Rosie joined in, until Annie reminded her that men were dying cruelly in the fireball and mothers losing sons. A few weeks later Rose had a chance encounter near the Ilford Broadway with an aviator from Hornchurch, who had an eye for a pretty girl, when not hunting enemy airships. When Lieut William Leefe Robinson invited Rose to have dinner with him in a few days time Rose accepted; after all, she later reminded her surprised parents, there was a war on and she was nearly seventeen. Since the destruction of the German airship, life had been a round of social engagements for Robinson, culminating with his investiture with the VC at Windsor Castle. A visit to the Gaiety theatre resulted in a standing ovation for the modest hero, who

No.24 Squadron

An Ilford rose with fond memories of a dinner date with an RFC officer in the autumn of 1916 (*Leslie Bills*)

afterwards found it uncomfortable dining at the Piccadilly Grill, his favourite restaurant, as he became the centre of attention.

Dressed in her Sunday best, with the calming influence of her elder sister Violet sitting beside her in the front parlour, Rose tried hard to conceal her excitement. For Robinson, driving through the country lanes from Suttons Farm aerodrome, the thought of a pleasant few hours in the company of a delightful, unsophisticated, young lady, was a pleasing prospect for the 21 year old pilot. Robinson's open tourer, a Vauxhall 'Prince Henry', purchased with the prize money awarded him by grateful citizens, came to rest outside the family home at 10 Clements Road. Minutes later Rose noted with satisfaction the flutter of neighbours' curtains, as the famous airman helped her into his car, closed the door, and casually vaulted into the driver's seat beside her. Resisting the temptation to wave at people she knew as the Vauxhall sped along the High Road, Rose held her favourite flower-trimmed hat in place on her head.

After visiting Cranbrook Castle, a picturesque folly in pleasant surroundings, the couple were having dinner at Jerrard's restaurant in High Road, when Rose suddenly realised all eyes were upon her and the 'Zepp VC'. Disaster struck the teenager; in a moment of panic her knife slipped, showering peas on the floor. Robinson, beckoning a nearby waiter, ordered, 'more peas for madam', then, taking her hand, he said quietly looking into her eyes, 'Don't worry, Rosie.' It was a bitter-sweet moment that the Ilford girl never forgot with the passing years. During dinner Robinson had confided that he expected to return to France soon; they never met again.

With the exception of two hit and run raids on the Kent coast by single engined aeroplanes on the 22nd and 23rd October, enemy air activity over England had been conspicuous by its absence, since the loss of Mathy and L31 at the beginning of the month. Committed to the vulnerable and costly Zeppelin raids, the head of the Imperial Naval Airship Division argued with the growing number of critics that the mere threat of Zeppelin raids forced Britain to retain men and equipment at home manning air defences.

Peter Strasser was correct - no fewer than 110 aeroplanes with 2,200 RFC personnel, plus 12,000 men on anti-aircraft duties, awaited the return of the 'Zepps'. Justifiable fear of the improved air defences round London forced the airships to seek targets in less defended areas when they eventually returned.

On Thursday, 23rd November, the Royal Flying Corps in France suffered the loss of Major Lanoe George Hawker VC, Commanding Officer of No.24 Squadron. Behind the enemy lines, running out of fuel after fighting with the latest twin gun Albatros scouts for half an hour, Hawker, flying a D.H.2 pusher scout with a maximum speed of 93 m.p.h., looped his machine, fired a short burst at his opponent and dived for the British lines. That had been the moment Manfred von Richthofen had been waiting for; zig-zagging, Hawker's machine levelled out at 100 feet above the ground with the guns of the superior Mercedes powered Albatros firing short bursts at close range from behind. Major Hawker fell with a bullet in his head, von Richthofen added a Lewis gun and serial number cut from the rudder of his eleventh victory to his growing collection of trophies of the first war in the air.

Under cover of darkness on Monday, 27th November, nine Zeppelins attempted what proved to be a further disaster for the German Navy. 2nd Lieut Ian Vernon Pyott of No.36 Squadron, patrolling in B.E.2c 2738 from Seaton Carew, emptied a drum of mixed explosive and incendiary into the vast hull of L34 that fell blazing into the sea in view of the delighted inhabitants of Hartlepool, who had suffered the German Naval bombardment just before Christmas, 1914. A second raider, L22, damaged by gunfire and harassed by night fighters, managed to limp back to base; the crew of L21, her sister ship, were not as fortunate. The skilfully handled airship eluded pursuing RFC machines from No.38 and 51 Squadrons, but the diversions had delayed the Zeppelin with fatal results.

Dawn greeted Zeppelin L21 escaping out to sea, as aeroplanes from RNAS aerodromes in the Yarmouth area swooped in for the kill. Another casualty of 'flaming bullets', the blazing Zeppelin fell into the sea at 06.42 hrs on Tuesday, 28th November. In recognition of their combined attack, resulting in the destruction of the airship and crew, Flt Sub-Lieut E L Pulling received the DSO, and Flt Lieut E Cadbury and Flt Sub Lieut G W R Fane were awarded the DSC. 2nd Lieut I V Pyott RFC also received a DSO for conspicuous gallantry and devotion to duty in connection with the destruction of L34 during the same raid. Four civilians were killed and 37 injured, with less than £13,000 worth of damage inflicted by the nine Zeppelins during their last raid on England in 1916.

The combined efforts of military and naval home defence units had destroyed two and damaged a third Zeppelin during

the night.

However, before lunch an incident occurred to set alarm bells ringing at Home Defence aerodromes surrounding London. In broad daylight at 11.50 hrs, a single engined biplane dropped six bombs without warning on central London. In the subsequent confusion the Home Defence Wing of the RFC failed to order aeroplanes aloft until 12.45 hrs. Lieut C V Kerpen of C Flight left Hainault Farm at 13.05 hrs, far too late to overtake the raider; not one of the 17 home defence pilots eventually airborne saw the daylight bomber. Rumours quickly spread that German airmen had breached the London defences by flying a captured Allied machine. In fact, it had been a daring raid planned and executed by German Naval aviators Lieut Walther Ilges and his pilot Deck Offzr Paul Brandt. Their target had been the Admiralty buildings, White-hall, though the missiles fell in Brompton Road and close to Victoria Station.

As Lieut Kerpen touched down at Hainault Farm for a belated lunch at the end of his patrol, fate overtook the German airmen in the form of engine failure. At 14.15 hrs the unfortunate crew of the L.V.G, with their 220 hp Mercedes motor silenced, were forced down near Boulogne and captured by French forces. Had the first aeroplane raid upon London in broad daylight been completely successful, it would have eroded even more the Zeppelin's credibility as a weapon of war. However, Strasser claimed that his airships frequently suffered the loss of more than one engine and still returned safely home.

Following the first daylight air raid on

London, this ominous warning of things to come appeared in *The Times*. "We have always believed that the method of raiding by aeroplanes, which are relatively cheap and elusive, has far more dangerous possibilities than the large and costly Zeppelin."

The coming year would prove this warning to be correct. Lord Asquith, who had been in office as Prime Minister since 1908, resigned on the 5th December, 1916, and David Lloyd George accepted the Premiership and hurriedly formed a new War Cabinet.

In mid-December French infantry, attacking in severe winter conditions, recaptured much of the land lost to the enemy at the battles of Verdun during the year.

Bread baked to new wartime regulations arrived for sale in the shops just before Christmas, and coal stocks in the local yards were dangerously low, with much of the railway rolling stock used to keep the home fires burning commandeered for the war effort. Potatoes were also in short supply following a poor season and they would be scarce in the coming months. However, Ilford shops had a plentiful supply of meat, poultry, cheese, dried fruits and nuts - not to mention wines and spirits available for the third festive season of the war. Ajax Co., a toyshop in High Road, displayed a working model tank in their window, advertising the latest toys for boys - toy tanks from 3s.6d. to 10s.6d each, just three months after the 'landships' had crawled across No Man's Land for the first time.

Christmas day brought snow, turning to slush and mud, at Hainault Farm, where the RFC were on standby. Enemy planes had attempted to bomb London at Christmas before, but flying conditions were no better across the North Sea.

Zeppelins attempted another raid on Thursday, 28th December, but it was another catastrophe for the Imperial Naval Airship Division. Three airships were destroyed in landing accidents, after being recalled in the face of a south westerly gale over the North Sea.

Private Alfred Saunders of Uphall Road, Ilford, home on leave from France, accompanied his two boys to Stratford Police Court: they had been apprehended in the act of kicking a full size football along Grange Road on 30th December. He was told by the Chairman that lack of parental control was responsible for the considerable number of juvenile offenses, but in this case they would be lenient and bind the defendants over in the sum of 40 shillings each for six months.

No.36 Squadron

1917

1917 saw more Ilford men volunteer for flying duties, as the war in the air extracted an ever-increasing toll of casualties and the urgent need for pilots. Lieut Arthur Newman, the first Ilford serviceman to be awarded a Military Cross by the King, volunteered for a transfer to the RFC. Arthur, who lived with his family in the Cranbrook Road, joined the 4th Essex in May, 1915, and served with his regiment in Gallipoli. It was for gallantry in rescuing a comrade, lying wounded out in No Mans Land, that he received the medal.

In January at the front, in spite of the elements, superior enemy machines began to appear in ever increasing numbers; at least 214 two gun Albatros D.I & D.II fighters were in action and D.III Vee strutted versions, with high-compression engines were to enter front line service.

A nightmare for workers employed on munitions became reality on Friday, 19th January, when massive explosions at Silvertown killed 69 and injured nearly 400, many of them women and young girls. Windows and venetian blinds in Ilford rattled with the force of the detonations, where it was first thought the `Zepps' had returned.

When weather permitted, the RFC maintained offensive patrols over enemy lines. Local airman, 2nd Lieut Charles Pickthorne, who had saved the life of his pilot the previous June whilst serving as an observer with No.8 Squadron, had since trained as a scout pilot and had been posted to No.32 Squadron, flying the now outclassed D.H.2 single seat pusher. On patrol with his flight on the 27th

January, Charles, cocooned in leather flying coat and thigh length `Fug' boots with the exposed part of his face greased with bear fat to combat the danger of frost bite in the cramped open cockpit of the little pusher scout, assisted in shooting down a two seat photographic machine over Courcelles-Achiet.

February brought the coldest weather to Ilford for 20 years and for the townsfolk an opportunity for ice skating on local ponds. Due to popular demand Valentines Park remained open until 10 pm for moonlight skating during the big freeze.

Herbert Musgrove Beck of Mayfair Avenue enlisted in 1914 at the age of 18. After two years service with the City of London Rifle Brigade, Herbert had been offered a honourable discharge owing to a foot injury, but the ex-Bancroft and Ilford County High pupil, with a promising future with the Union Castle Steamship Company, refused to be discharged from the Army and applied for a transfer to the Royal Flying Corps, where he commenced his pilot training as a Cadet at Denham in February, 1917.

The only Victoria Cross granted to an N.C.O pilot during the Great War would be posthumously awarded to Sergeant Thomas Mottershead of No.20 Squadron for saving the life of his observer/gunner, 2nd Lieut Gower, on 7th January, 1917. With his F.E.2b pusher set on fire by the enemy and engulfed in flames, the young pilot succeeded in recrossing the lines, only to die trapped in the burning wreckage on landing.

Snow covered aerodromes behind the front lines on the Western Front for most of January; ground crews draining engine

Wilfred Jameson (third from right, back row) with personnel of No.2 Wing RNAS on the island of Thasos

No.32 Squadron

oil overnight, re-warming it to start the engines for dawn patrol. The frozen ground played havoc with tailskids and the bungee rubber suspension on undercarts.

In Palestine, Macedonia, the Ægean area, Mesopotamia and East Africa, the so-called 'Side Shows' of the war, airmen faced hazards other than the enemy and the elements. Since the evacuation of the Dardanelles, the Royal Navy had maintained a constant pressure upon the Turkish coast from islands within flying range of their single engined aeroplanes, in spite of the ever present risk of engine failure over the sea, malaria and dysentery. In spring, 1916, having obtained a commission with the RNVR, Sub/Lieut Wilfred Jameson, the Ilford man who eluded capture by Germans at the fall of Antwerp whilst serving with the Naval Division, and later successfully escaped from an internment camp in Holland, joined the RNAS in the Ægean.

On January 10th, Jameson, acting as observer to F/Sub Lieut Devlin piloting a Henry Farman F.27 of No 2 Wing, successfully bombed a bridge at Kuleli Burgas, flying at 100 ft, returning with their mainplanes shot full of holes. On a previous attempt to bomb the bridge on the 13th December, with F/Sub Lieut F L Waistell piloting Henry Farman 3915, both airmen escaped injury in a landing accident at the end of the long distance raid. The charmed life that Wilfred Jameson had led over the previous six months as a Naval aviator flying unarmed photographic or bombing missions in Henry Farman pushers, with a variety of pilots, ended on Monday, 12th February. Diving out of the sun, a Fokker, flown by Ltn Emil Meinecke, shot up the Henry Farman crewed by Flt/Lieut C M Maitland Heriot and Jameson on anti-U-boat patrol from Gallipoli to Cape Helles. Forced to land in enemy territory, they were observed by the crew of another Farman F.27 to set fire to their machine, before Turkish soldiers arrived to take them prisoners of war.

In the early hours of Saturday, 17th February, No 50 Squadron, with flights stationed in and around Dover, flew patrols in search of enemy airships. Zeppelin LZ107 had been heard approaching the Kent coast before turning for home. The Army Airship Service would soon be disbanded and all airships transferred to the Imperial Navy.

The long cold winter vigil for C Flight on the bleak open aerodrome at Hainault Farm would be enlivened for an hour on Thursday, March 1st, when the alarm bells rang in daylight. Duty pilots, Capt W T F Holland and Lieut V T Normington, were airborne at 10.30 hrs, although the enemy seaplane had fled out to sea, after dropping six bombs upon Broadstairs at 0945 hrs. None of the 24 Home Defence machines scrambled saw the raider.

As winter relaxed its grip along the Western Front, the RFC increased its offensive patrols over the enemy lines. On Sunday, 4th March, seven RFC and two RNAS machines were forced down in fierce combats. One of the RFC casualties had been F.E.2b 4965, piloted by 2nd Lieut W E Jones of No 23 Squadron, who had been detailed to escort a photographic machine, with 2nd Lieut W A Golding acting as observer/gunner. The 23 year old son of an Ilford licensee, from the White Horse Hotel, Ilford Broadway, Golding had served two years with the HRC prior to transferring to the RFC in September, 1916. Five miles over the lines at 10,000 ft, the pusher biplane came under attack from two enemy fighters,

This Albatros D1, shot down behind Allied lines by 2nd Lieut Charles Pickthorne in March, 1917, let the RFC examine the Hatzke synchronising gear that allowed two machine guns a rapid rate of fire through the propeller arc (*P L Gray*)

Major Charles Pickthorne (centre, front row) Commanding Officer, No.84 Squadron, 1918

wounding Golding in the knee. Although the F.E had been badly damaged, 2nd Lieut Jones managed to land just inside the British lines; subsequently the young airman had his right leg amputated just below the knee.

Two days later Charles Pickthorne, the Ilford pilot serving in No.32 Squadron, was in combat with Albatros biplanes. Pickthorne, in D.H.2 7898, although wounded, pursued one of the Albatros D1 fighters and shot it down. On his return, he discovered two members of his flight were missing over the lines. Enemy fighters accounted for 11 more British machines the same day.

German pilots had orders not to cross the lines, in case the successful Albatros-Hetzke synchronizing system, allowing two machine guns a rapid rate of fire through the propeller arc, fell into Allied hands.

On Sunday, 11th March, the enemy increased their daily toll of RFC machines to 16. Charles Pickthorne, in D.H.2 7938 after a lengthy combat with an Albatros D1 painted with a skull and crossbones emblem, forced the machine down behind the British lines where the pilot Crown Prince Frederich of Prussia was captured along with his two gun Albatros.

Although the D.H.2 entered frontline service early in February, 1916, and was hopelessly outclassed by German fighters in the spring of 1917, it was not withdrawn from the Western Front until June. One of the hazards pilots of the agile little pusher scout faced in flight was the loss of a cylinder from the whirling 100 hp Gnome Monosoupage rotary engine, which would prove fatal were it to sever one of the pusher's fragile tail booms.

An Ilford airman, undergoing flight training with No.51 Reserve (Training) School in Kent, became a victim of a rotary engine shedding a cylinder whilst in flight. On Thursday, 15th March, 2nd Lieut Frederick Edmund Hillebrandt of Goodmayes had been airborne in an Avro 504 machine, piloted by 2nd Lieut O C Bryson, when a detached cylinder of the 80 hp Gnome rotary engine powering the Avro, tore off the horseshoe cowling of the training machine. Before the pilot could switch off the ignition, escaping petrol burst into flames. Bryson attempted to land, but the aeroplane stalled and nose dived into the ground. Both officers were rescued from the burning wreck, but 23 year old Hillebrandt succumbed to his serious burns eight days later. The unfortunate airman had flown on active service as an observer with the RFC in Salonika, after transferring from the Suffolk Regiment. Frederick Hillebrandt had been an active member of the congregation at St Paul's, Goodmayes, where a well attended service was held at his funeral at St Mary's in Ilford High Road, on Tuesday, 27th March.

The whole staff of the Ilford Aeroplane Works were entertained at the second house of the Ilford Hippodrome on Friday, 26th March. Their manager, Major Frederick Leighton, had reserved the front five rows of the circle for the occasion. He had arrived early with his wife to cordially greet his workpeople and guests and, during the entertainment, Major and Mrs Leighton passed around abundant supplies of cigars, cigarettes and packets of chocolates. The evening was much enjoyed by all the staff of the Works, which were under the control of Oakley Limited, with main offices in Regency Street, London. Since mid-

1916 the pre-war skating rink had been busy with engine installation and repairs on B.E.2c aircraft. The night out at the Hippodrome, enjoyed by the management and staff, had been partly in celebration of a recent Admiralty contract for the construction of 25 Sopwith Triplanes.

An attempt later that night by four German Naval Zeppelins to bomb London failed. Modified as height climbers, the airships were operating at 17-19,000 ft, much to the discomfort to the crews, who also found the British were jamming their wireless frequencies, preventing them from obtaining a navigation fix from the direction finding stations at Nordholz and Borkum. Drifting too far south, the fatigued crew of L39 were shot down in flames by anti-aircraft fire at Compiègne in France while trying to return to base.

In combat over the enemy lines in the spring of 1917, the Triplane with a single machine gun, had been able to meet the Albatros on almost equal terms. The climb 10 min 35 sec. to 15,000 ft and a service ceiling of 20,000 ft, the `Tripe' had so impressed German pilots that many aircraft designers were tempted to copy the triplane layout, including Anthony Fokker, whose monoplanes have been eclipsed by the shark like biplanes from the Albatros factories.

In Britain a new breed of warplanes were under construction to replace the obsolete sporting machines, with a machine gun added as an after-thought, flown by front line squadrons. In March, No.55 squadron RFC arrived in France, equipped with sturdy powerful Airco D.H.4 two seat fighter bombers, fitted with a hydraulic synchronisation gear for the forward firing machine gun, equal to that already in use by the enemy.

The urgent need to develop ever better warplanes brought about the death of Ilford airman, 2nd Lieut John Bernard Fitzsimons, on Monday, 26th March. F C Nestler, Ltd, of Westminster had manufactured aircraft components since the outbreak of war. Along with many other sub-contractors, they set up their own design office for the construction of aeroplanes as a private venture. John Fitzsimons, an instructor at a Hendon Flying School, had been employed as a test pilot for the prototype Nestler for some weeks prior to his fatal crash. On 22nd March, *Flight* magazine had paid tribute to Fitzsimons in a write-up on the experimental Nestler machine with the following comments, "In connection with this excellent performance, it should be mentioned that Messrs F Nestler (Ltd) have been fortunate in finding an experienced and very skilful pilot in Mr J B Fitzsimons, who has had over a year's flying at the front. Mr Fitzsimons took his ticket at the Ruffy-Baumann School at Hendon after a very brief period of tuition in 1915. His handling of the new Nestler `bus' is certainly spectacular, if somewhat daring and he appears to have absolute mastery of the machine." The 20 year old Ilford pilot crashed to his death a mere four days later.

The fatal crash of the experimental Nestler biplane had been viewed by a number of spectators, who saw the upper wing fabric flapping as Fitzsimons did low level aerobatics at Hendon aerodrome, just before the machine dived, under full power, through the roof of an aerodrome

John Fitzsimmons at the controls of a Caudron G111 biplane at the Ruffy-Baumann School of Flying, Hendon, 1915

John Fitzsimmons, employed by the F C Nestler Company for test flying, with his experimental Nestler Scout (*J M Bruce/G S Leslie*)

workshop - luckily unoccupied at the time. As a youth, Fitzsimons attended the Ilford County High School, where he started a model aeroplane club and later he was instrumental in the formation of the Ilford & District Model Aeroplane Club, of which the famous pre-war aviator B C Hucks, now a very busy test pilot, had been patron.

On leaving school, Fitzsimons became a clerk with the Port of London Authority, but with the outbreak of war he learned to fly and applied for a commission in the Royal Flying Corps. The funeral cortège of 2nd Lieut John Bernard Fitzsimons left from his parents' home at Endsleigh Gardens, en route for the City of London Cemetery on Friday, 6th April, 1917.

On the same day, the United States of America declared war on Germany.

There were some quite extraordinary scenes in Ilford during March brought about by the potato shortage. On Friday, 9th, a queue began to form at daybreak outside Messrs Prentis, the High Road greengrocers. The news that Ilford's premier greengrocer would be receiving several tons of potatoes in time for the weekend had spread across the town grapevine and, by opening time, the queue of hopefuls clutching baskets stretched as far as Ilford Hill. Although Mr Prentis rationed each customer to 2 pounds of potatoes, there were many Ilfordians facing the prospect of Sunday lunch without them when the supply ran out. One women with six children, who also waited their turn in the queue, managed to acquire 14 lbs during the morning - not to mention the wrath of those who went away empty handed. During the potato famine, at least one local greengrocer received a ten shilling fine for refusing to sell customers 2 pounds of potatoes without buying greens as well. The Seven Kings,

Goodmayes & District Allotment Holders' Association had been able to obtain 15 tons of seed potatoes that were sold to members as fast as they could be weighed into 14 lb bags at the Society shop on the corner of Barley Lane. A potato shortage could be overcome, but the unrestricted U-Boat warfare that commenced on the first day of February, 1917, would bring about many more shortages and hardships to the Home Front. U-boats sank 200,500 tons of British Merchant Shipping during the next four weeks: by the end of April the total had exceeded 500.000 tons a month.

The introduction of a convoy system for the protection of allied merchant ships was brought about by the loss of 373 allied ships sunk by U-boats during the month of April, 1917. Such losses could not be allowed to continue, as food stocks in Britain were perilously low.

That month became known as 'Bloody April', not because of the serious losses inflicted by the U-boats, but for the casualties incurred that month by the Royal Flying Corps in France. Although the RFC outnumbered their opposite numbers by three to one, so many of their aeroplanes were obsolete and those arriving to replace them were plagued by teething problems, such as the Bristol F2a, destined to become one of the best allied aeroplanes of the war.

Bristol Fighters of No 48 Squadron arrived in France on the morning of 18th March; it had been the first time that all 18 machines of an RFC squadron had made the Channel crossing without mishap. Returning to France at the controls of a Bristol, Captain William Leefe Robinson VC soon found out that fighting in the air had changed dramatically since his service with No. 4 Squadron in 1915. Such are the fortunes of war, the first offensive patrol over enemy lines ended in disaster for No 48 Squadron. Six Bristols, led by Flight Commander Leefe Robinson, left Bellevue aerodrome at 09.00 hrs, Thursday, 5th April, but two returned after the patrol had been attacked by five Albatros V strutters over Douai.

Leut Manfred von Richthofen accounted for two of the new English warplanes as his 35th and 36th victories, Robinson the Zeppelin VC and his observer, Lieut Edward Darian Warburton, fell to the guns of an Albatros D III, piloted by Vizefeldwebel Sebastian Festner. Too much had been expected of the 'Hero of Cuffley', who had defeated the Zeppelin menace by using a little bit of 'gumption' the previous autumn.

One of the teething problems with the Bristol Fighter had been the gun oil issued to No.48 Squadron: it froze on the exposed Lewis guns manned by the observers. Capt Leefe Robinson once again used his 'gumption' and ordered the offending oil to be wiped off the observers' guns, but the weapons seized up in action after a few rounds. Time would prove the Bristol Fighter could be flown as a single seat fighter, but time had not been on the side of No.48 Squadron, rushed to the front with a brave, but inexperienced, flight commander leading them in their untried machines across the enemy lines.

Weeks elapsed before Leefe Robinson's fiancée received a letter, via the Red Cross, confirming that he was alive and well as a prisoner of war in Germany. The RFC lost 14 machines on the day that No.

48 Squadron went to war.

The following day, 6th April, German airmen shot down 23 RFC machines: the unfortunate No.57 Squadron suffered the loss of an entire patrol of five FE2d pushers.

At home, Ilford aerodromes were swept by a snow blizzards on Good Friday, 1917.

Four of six pilots comprising C Flt at Hainault Farm had been sent to replace hard hit squadrons on the Western Front.

In rain, sleet and snow on Easter Monday, 1917, the BEF commenced the battle of Arras. The RFC lost three BE2 biplanes on low flying contact patrols with the infantry - two brought down by ground fire. The weather improved on 11th April, the RFC being able to support the infantry in force, at the cost of 14 aircraft and their crews, including three more Bristol Fighters of the unfortunate No.48 Squadron.

On Friday, 13th, as another 'Big Push' floundered in the mud, Canadian infantry recaptured Givenchy and Bailleul, whilst fierce air battles were fought overhead, almost unnoticed by the exhausted infantry occupying ex-German trenches.

Six RE8 biplanes on photographic missions over the lines failed to return to No.59 Squadron, seven vulnerable FE2 pusher biplanes of Nos 11, 25 and 57 Squadrons were among the seventeen RFC machines destroyed that Friday.

The daily sacrifice of the young airmen, ground-strafing and carrying out low level contact patrols over the snow covered battle ground, assisted the Poor Bloody Infantry advance the front line four miles and capture the Vimy Ridge.

On Monday, 16th April, French infantry went over the top along a 25 mile front. In spite of German reserves and aircraft withdrawn to the British sector, the French Army suffered heavy losses for little gain and morale began to crack.

After a rest period as an instructor in England, Capt Albert Ball, the leading fighter pilot of the RFC, returned to France with No.56 Squadron, equipped with the SE5, destined to replace the out-classed pusher and Nieuport machines. No 56 Squadron carried out their first offensive patrol on the 23rd April, and Ball downed his 32nd and 33rd victories. During 'Bloody April' RFC losses amounted to 151 aeroplanes and 316 airmen killed and missing, German losses amounted to 66 aeroplanes and 119 airmen - among the dead, Sebastian Festner, the sergeant pilot who had shot down Leefe Robinson VC.

A determined effort not to be frightened by the blacked-out streets of the town at night by the citizens of Ilford during the winter of 1916/17 encouraged the proprietors of the Premier Electric Theatre in the High Road to re-decorate and install 'the most perfect Picture Screen in existence', at the cost of over £100. An ever growing number of dances organised for wartime charities at the Town Hall and numerous venues in Ilford, prompted 'ABSOLUTELY DISGUSTED' to write to the *Ilford Guardian*, 'Is Ilford not overdoing the dancing business?'

The sadness at local Railway Stations, as tearful farewells were made to loved ones going off to war, could have easily overflowed into the increasing war weariness in the town. Fortunately for the war effort, 'ABSOLUTELY DISGUSTED' was in the minority, as Ilfordians determined to put on a brave face, and kept the bright lights burning brightly behind heavy curtains for the 'Boys' home on leave.

During the early hours of Monday, 7th May, five 22 lb bombs were dropped on North London by a single engined biplane in a hit and run raid. One civilian died, two were injured in the bombing. Offstlvtr Rudolf Klimke and Oblt Walther Leon, pilot and observer of the Albatros machine, returned safely to a German Army aerodrome near Ostend and a reprimand, as the air raid on London had not been ordered.

Although the War Office frowned upon the 'Ace' system and publicity for individual airmen, Capt Albert Ball had become well known as Britain's leading fighter pilot, thanks to American and British newspaper journalists. His death in action on the evening of Monday, 7th May, gave the German propaganda machine an opportunity to claim that the English ace had been brought down by the younger brother of Manfred von Richthofen, who had also been shot down and wounded, probably by Ball as his last and unclaimed victory.

British losses at sea and in the air peaked that April and so did British propaganda, that had raged since the sabre rattling at the out-break of war, when Kaiser Wilhelm II stated that, 'My forces would be feared as were the Huns of old'. As the German Army marched into France and Belgium headlines of 'Hun' atrocities appeared on the front pages of British newspapers; as the war escalated so did 'Hun' barbarisms until the spring of 1917, when *Daily Mail* headlines read HUN GHOULS: OIL FODDER AND DIVIDENDS FROM THE DEAD, which made even the most loyal newspaper readers begin to doubt the printed word.

Naval Zeppelins attempted to bomb London again during the early hours of

Thursday, 24th May. Six height climbers, with orders to attack the City, were frustrated by weather conditions, as were the Home defence machines hunting them. The `Zepps' were lost among the clouds above East Anglia, telephoned warnings of the approaching L42 alerted London defences, but the raider turned away at Braintree. No 39HD Squadron had five machines aloft during the raid. The two machines from A Flight at North Weald made emergency landings safely. Although 76 RNAS and RFC machines carried out patrols during the raid, only Lieut G D F Keddie of No 37HD Squadron actually saw and gave chase to L44, drifting with engine trouble among the clouds, until losing sight of it 20 minutes later. One civilian had been killed and the damage done during the four hour Zeppelin raid did not exceed £600.

London escaped damage again on Friday, 25th May, when 21 twin-engined Gotha biplanes of the Imperial Army Air Service flew the Channel in daylight, en route for the capital. As they approached Tilbury, the commander observed thick cloud cover obscuring their target and switched the attack to Folkestone. The first large scale daylight raid on England carried out by up to date well armed twin engined enemy bombers caught the Home Defence squadrons, with their obsolete B E night fighters, at a great disadvantage. In ten minutes' bombing, 95 had been killed, 195 injured and £19,405 damage inflicted upon the unsuspecting citizens of Folkestone. At least one returning raider fell into the sea after a fight with RNAS Sopwith Pups from Dunkirk. British newspapers claimed a great victory as the Home Defence machines had prevented the raiders from flying inland and, after dropping their bombs, they made off at high speed. One tabloid claimed that only half the bomber force had escaped and hoped the bomber attacks would continue, so that more might be destroyed.

The Express did not have to wait long; another attack came on the evening of Tuesday, 5th June. By then some Home Defence Flights had been issued with a few Sopwith 1½ Strutters and Armstrong Whitworth F.K 8 two seat aircraft. Among the 62, mainly obsolete, Home Defence machines flown during the raid were two B.E.12a machines from Hainault Farm, piloted by Capt W H Haynes and Capt O V Thomas. With the arrival of the Gotha bomber over England, No 39HD Squadron, defending London, had been among the first to receive pilots to bring its depleted Flights up to strength, ready for the new aerial menace threatening the capital.

During the autumn 1916, the Gotha G 11 and G.111 had proved successful in missions over both the Western and Balkan Fronts. Luckily a G.111 fell into Allied hands intact, when forced down by the French air ace, Lt George Guynemer, for his 31st victory on 8th February, 1917. Upon inspection the captured machine, spanning 77 ft 9 in, powered by two 260 hp Mercedes engines, appeared to be a fragile cumbersome opponent. However, the proof of the pudding was in the eating, a forthcoming daylight bombardment of London by a squadron of the latest Gotha bombers, the GIV. would bring about a rapid change of British policy, with the formation of an air service completely independent of the Admiralty and War Office.

On Tuesday, June 5th, Hptmn Ernst Brandenburg, the commander of Kagohl 3, warned by his weather officer of severe thunderstorms, once again resisted pressure from the High Command to bomb London, opting instead for military and naval coastal targets either side of the Thames Estuary. A formation of 22 Gothas crossed the Essex coast. Brandenburg, standing in the exposed front cockpit of the leading machine, gestured to his pilot, deafened by the roar of a 260 hp Mercedes engine within six feet of each ear, raised a flare pistol, and signalled his following squadron. Apart from a heat haze, visibility was excellent that June evening; bomb aimers adjusted vertical 3 ft long Zeiss telescopes, clicked stop watches setting the sophisticated Goerz bombsights and reached for the bomb release toggles. Twenty-six missiles were dropped on Essex soil, the majority aimed at Shoeburyness gunnery ranges. Many of the 50 kg bombs fell on open ground or failed to explode, but two Artillerymen were killed when the Gun Park received a salvo of bombs. Warned of the approaching raiders, the gunners defending Sheerness dockyard were ready and waiting; one Gotha attempting to bomb a troublesome battery from 9,000 ft was damaged and fell into the sea. Disregarding the gun fire, the remaining bombers circled Sheerness for five minutes, selecting military and naval targets. A few missiles fell on the town, killing three civilians and injuring nine; service casualties were ten killed, 25 injured. British propaganda claimed half the raiders had been destroyed, although only two out of a total of sixty-two airborne Home Defence machines had indecisive combats with the enemy aeroplanes this side of the Channel. Newspapers reported the 'Hun' raiders were soundly thrashed, they might have been had the returning bombers not met a fighter escort over the Belgian coast that engaged the pursuing RNAS machines from Dunkirk closing in for the kill.

Airmen at the Ilford aerodromes were getting accustomed to seeing German soldiers working in the fields around them. Seventy-five prisoners of war, who had been farm labourers in happier days, were billeted under armed guard at Foxburrows Farm, Chigwell Row. One of the first local farmers to apply for their services had been Mr C E Reynolds of Fencepiece Farm, Barkingside, who reasoned, "We have got to keep them, so why shouldn't they do something towards helping to keep us."

In the early hours of Thursday, 7th June, a booming sound could be heard in the town as 400 tons of high explosive tunnelled secretly by British Sappers beneath the enemy lines along the Messines Ridge, 130 miles away in France, were detonated. Following an artillery bombardment, British infantry went over the top, assisted at dawn by the Royal Flying Corps carrying out low level contact patrols and ground strafing. German losses were 25,000 against 17,000 British; 7,000 dazed and shell-shocked German prisoners were marched into captivity.

Accustomed as they were to the sound of aeroplanes and gun fire from distant ranges, German PoWs hoeing the fields on the outskirts of Ilford on Wednesday, 13th June, became excited as a large number of aeroplanes could be heard approaching from the north east. As Haupt Brandenburg led his Gotha squadron across the town towards the heart of London at 11.30 hrs, hazy conditions obscured the raiders, flying three miles high, from the anti-aircraft gunners at Hainault Farm and Chadwell Heath. A bomb fell on North Street, Barking; seven bombs released over East Ham killed four and injured thirteen civilians.

Twenty-two bomb-laden Gotha aircraft had taken off from Belgian aerodromes for the long-planned daylight raid on London. A patient man, Ernst Brandenburg had waited days for favourable winds and cloud cover. Wednesday morning would be ideal, confirmed his meteorological officer, but warned of thunderstorms during the mid-afternoon. Machines had dropped out of the loose formation crossing the North Sea plagued with engine troubles. Above Essex the gaggle of Gothas dwindled down to 14, as a further three crews waved good luck to their comrades, before flying off to carry out diversionary raids on coastal targets to confuse the defences. Although two B.E.12 machines from No.39 Squadron were engaged in firing at targets towed along the Thames, their pilots were unaware of the nearby raiders, the sounds of anti-aircraft fire and 28 Mercedes engines were lost in the slipstream of their own four bladed propellers.

Eight dockers were killed and nine injured, as two bombs fell upon the Royal Albert Docks, Silvertown, before the bombers closed up into a well rehearsed diamond shaped formation for the flight across London. The sight of so many

aeroplanes in flight together was still a novel sight, that many spectators disregarded the danger of falling shell fragments to watch. Two civilians were killed and 18 injured by debris of the anti-aircraft fire during the morning raid.

Bathed in the bright sunshine, London lay at the mercy of the German airmen high above, who had little time to admire the magnificent spectacle of the great city below. As last adjustments were made to bomb sights, gunners in rear cockpits scanned the surrounding sky for British aeroplanes, which could be seen taking off in pursuit far below as the squadron crossed Essex. Seventy-two bombs fell within a mile radius of Liverpool Street station - its glass roof, reflected in the brilliant sunshine, made an excellent target. Three bombs scored direct hits upon the railway station; 16 men were killed, including Herbert H Daniel of 7 Clarendon Gardens, Seven Kings: the 28 year old local man had been employed on the Railway.

As the bombers circled overhead dropping their lethal load, Herbert Daniel stayed calm, sending passengers to safety, via the lift, until blast from a nearby bomb tore off his left arm. Rushed to hospital in the aftermath of the raid, the unfortunate man expired from his terrible injuries. Another fatal Ilford victim of the air-raid was Mrs Olive Noakes, who lived at 63 Green Lane, and commuted to work in the City: terribly injured, the twenty year old passed away later in the day at the London Hospital. Having received little warning the missiles, mainly 50 kg bombs, caused many casualties among the civilians caught open-mouthed in awe along the streets of the city.

It would be a direct hit by one 50 kg bomb on an infants' school, as the raiders turned for the long flight home, that aroused most anger and demands for reprisals. Five bombs aimed at the London Docks fell on Poplar, one missile going through three floors of the Upper North Street Schools to blast 64 children in a ground floor room. Anxious mothers and families hurried to the scene to find servicemen with tears running down their grime and soot covered faces, as they recovered 18 dead and 30 badly injured infants, all but two under 6 years of age, from the shattered ruins of the school

With bomb racks empty, the Gothas flew towards the Essex coast. In a running dogfight across Ilford, stragglers were engaged by Home Defence machines. A Bristol F2b from No 35 Training Squadron, with Capt C W E Cole-Hamilton at the controls, attacked a Gotha flying over the town. Having fired nearly one hundred rounds in short bursts from his synchronised Vickers gun before it suffered a stoppage, the pilot flew to one side, enabling Captain C H Keevil to bring his ring mounted Lewis gun into action, unfortunately presenting the Bristol as a target to the gunners of the flanking machines. Caught in the cross fire, the unfortunate observer received a fatal wound in the neck.

The two B E.12 biplanes of No 39HD Squadron, testing their guns over the Thames oblivious of the German raiders, had been finally made aware of the air-raid by Ingram ground to air message panels laid out at near-by Suttons Farm aerodrome. Capt S R Stammers caught up

with the Gothas as they crossed Romford, but could not coax his B.E.12 any higher than 10,500 ft. After emptying three drums from his over-wing Lewis gun at extreme range, the enemy aeroplanes were at least 2,000 ft higher, and he returned to North Weald. A second Bristol Fighter from No 35 Training Squadron with a poor running engine also attacked the same Gotha at long range without being able to overtake the enemy machines. Capt T Grant, the other 39HD Squadron pilot who had been on firing practice earlier with Stammers, did not return to North Weald that day. Having pursued a Gotha flying out to sea in his B E 12, he managed to close to within 500 ft, firing before the German pilot opened the throttles and easily outpaced the B.E. biplane. Frustration turned to anger, as anti-aircraft fire from Shoeburyness forced Grant to land at nearby Rochford aerodrome. At least three Sopwith 1½ Strutters from No.37HD Squadron made determined but uncoordinated attacks; between them their observers emptied over twelve drums of ammunition at the homeward bound bombers without success. RNAS machines had been lured away by the decoy coastal attack earlier; however, a single Sopwith Pup 17,000 ft above the Thames estuary, piloted by Flt Lieut F A Fox, dived on a group of Gothas over Southend, firing off a drum from his over wing Lewis. Changing the empty drum with difficulty under fire from three enemy machines, he chased them out to sea, only to be frustrated by a stoppage in the breach of his single Lewis gun, after a dozen rounds from the second. Capt J T B McCudden, No.63

Training Squadron, an experienced front line pilot with 5 enemy machines to his credit, also flying a Sopwith Pup, emptied three drums of ammunition at close range into another Gotha without visible results.

No.39HD Squadron, with their B.E.12 night fighters, were typical example of the Home Defence machines attempting to engage the daylight raiders. The latest versions of the B E biplane still required 33 minutes to reach 10,000 ft, where the maximum speed fell to below 90 mph. Only the two B.E.12 machines from A Flight at North Weald, who were actually airborne as the Gothas struck at London, managed to come to grips with the enemy machines on their homeward flight. Pilots from B and C Flights, airborne from Suttons and Hainault Farm aerodromes, were unable gain sufficient altitude to overtake the unladen Gothas flying at 14,000 ft above the Essex fields.

As London recovered the dead and dying in the sunshine of a June afternoon, shock gave way to anger, and anger to outrage, as the death toll of civilians mounted to 158, with a further 425 injured, plus 4 military personnel killed and 7 injured.

Eluding RNAS patrols across the Channel, all the bombers returned safely to their Belgian bases. That evening, glasses were raised in the officers' casino of Kagohl 3, to the Kaiser, Haupt Brandenburg and to the Meteorological officer, Leutnant Cloesser, who had predicted the weather so accurately for the raid on London. Half an hour after the Gothas were manhandled under cover, a summer storm broke, hail stones the size of pigeon eggs drummed with a deafening roar upon the wooden hanger roofs. German morale soared as an official communique announced, "Today our airmen dropped bombs on the Fortress of London".

Haupt Brandenburg, commander of Kampfgeschwader 3, became the latest idol for German propaganda. The next morning Brandenburg received orders to report to Supreme Headquarters, where the Kaiser and General Staff eagerly awaited his personal report of the London bombing.

The destruction of Naval Zeppelin L48 during the early hours of Sunday, 17th June, did little to appease public anger, following the Gotha raid on the City four days earlier. L48 fell blazing on to the open fields of Holly Tree Farm, Theberton, Suffolk, following the combined attacks of three RFC Home Defence aircraft.

The following afternoon the funeral cortège of Herbert Daniel, killed in the Gotha raid, was met at the gates of St Mary's Church by a large number of railway officials; over forty wreaths were placed on the grave. On Wednesday, 20th June, the funeral of Ilford's second victim of the Gotha daylight raid on London, 20 year old Olive Noakes, took place at St Mary's; her soldier husband, on active service in France, was unable to be present.

On Tuesday, 19th June, 1917, the Albatros C type, ferrying Haupt Brandenburg back to his squadron in occupied Belgium, stalled and crashed on take off. Oblt Freiherr von Trotha, his pilot, an experienced pre-war aviator died instantly; Brandenburg, wearing the `Blue Max' awarded by the Kaiser during the memorable weekend at Kreuznach, survived with very serious leg injuries.

As thousands of east Londoners watched floral laden horse-drawn hearses, bearing the bodies of infants killed in the bombing of the Upper North Street Schools, clip-clop through the cobbled streets of Poplar, the demands for reprisals against German cities grew more strident. With the month drawing to a close, the War Office recommended that the proposed strength of the RFC be increased from 108 to 200 squadrons, whilst the War Cabinet still argued the pro's and cons of public air-raid warnings for the civilian population.

Demands for front line squadrons with experienced pilots be withdrawn from France to combat the Gotha menace, brought No.56 Squadron and their fast S.E.5 fighters to Bekesbourne. Across the Channel No.66 Squadron also pulled away from the front to occupy an aerodrome on the outskirts of Calais to intercept the Gothas on the outward journey with their high flying Pups.

To supplement the B.E nightfighters of No 39HD Squadron, 3 factory fresh S E.5 were supplied to B Flt at Suttons Farm. C Flt at Hainault Farm received the largest machine to see service at the Ilford aerodrome, a 43 ft 6 in span Armstrong Whitworth F.K.8 two seat observation machine, with a top speed of 90 mph. Although not fast it did have an operational ceiling of 13,000 ft.

The 'Big Ack', as it was known in the RFC, manned by Capt W H Haynes, with A M Gellan as observer gunner, was ordered into the air at 07.30 hrs on Wednesday, 4th July, when 18 Gothas returned to England with full bomb racks. Hptmn Rudolf Kleine, taking over command of Kagohl 3 from the injured Brandenburg, bombed military and naval installations at Harwich and Felixstowe, killing 14 and injuring 28 military personnel; 3 civilians were also fatal victims. Just one RFC machine managed to engage the Gothas during the raid. Capt J Palethorpe, accompanied by A J Jessop, flight testing a D H.4 from Martlesham, encountered the Gotha formation. The unfortunate air mechanic managed to empty one drum from his Lewis gun before he was killed outright by enemy crossfire, as Capt Palethorpe tore through the enemy formation. Twenty minutes later the fearless Captain was airborne again, with Lieut Hoffert, but the 'Huns' had flown.

Although Berlin announced, "All our aeroplanes returned undamaged", after the coastal raid on 4th July, at least two Gothas were damaged, when five RNAS Sopwiths from Dunkirk ambushed returning raiders off the Belgian coast.

On Friday, 6th July, No. 56 and 66 Squadrons were ordered to return to Western Front. Above the raging 3rd battle of the Somme (Passchendaele), a dogfight involving 40 aeroplanes evolved. Falling from the sky, an all red Albatros D111 managed a very shaky landing behind the German lines - although wounded, Manfred von Richthofen survived to fight another day.

On Saturday, 7th July, weather conditions prevailed, allowing Kagohl 3 to target London again, following the same flight path used by Brandenburg on the 13th June. Crossing the Essex coast near the River Crouch at 09.45 hrs, Kleine signalled a decoy Gotha to leave the squadron and fly south to make a diversionary air-raid on Margate, along the coast, hoping once again to confuse of the London defences.

At the head of his squadron, Haupt Kleine flew west above Essex, skirting Brentwood, where Capt E Mason, from No 37HD Squadron, attacked single handed, only to have his Sopwith Pup riddled in the crossfire from the bombers. Returning to Stow Maries with a shot through main-spar, a second No.37HD Squadron Pup, piloted by Capt E S Cotterill, also engaged the raiders, but had to land at Hainault Farm aerodrome for 8 minutes to have stoppages in both his Vickers and Lewis guns rectified. Turning north-west, the bomb-laden machines came under fire from AA batteries at Lambourne End, Theydon Bois and Epping. Above Woodford, two RNAS Camels swooped on the formation, disregarding shells bursting dangerously near, and managed to fire 100 rounds apiece before their guns jammed. No 39HD Squadron B.E.12a from A Flight at North Weald engaged the Gothas with both guns above Ongar; plagued with stoppages, Lieut Ernest Gilbert harried the raiders, until he ran out of ammunition for his serviceable Lewis gun. Lieut E S Moulton-Barrett of B Flight, Suttons Farm, had no difficulty overtaking the bombers in his S.E.5. Attacking four machines in turn, he expended all his ammunition without any visible results.

Although the `Big Ack' of C Flight had taken off from Hainault Farm a quarter of an hour before the Gothas had crossed the coast, Capt W Haynes pursued the bombers without getting within effective range to open fire. Lieut Gerald Stoneham, in the rear cockpit of the FK8,

later recorded in his log book, "Followed 22 Gothas to London-Southend and out to sea", where, in frustration, he emptied a drum from his Lewis gun as a parting gesture at the rearmost Gotha.

Furious barking of anti-aircraft guns alerted civilians of the Gotha formation droning towards London on the morning of Saturday, 7th July. Those brave or fool-hardy enough to risk the falling shell fragments to watch the `Hun air show' had 10 persons killed and a further 55 injured by defending gunfire. However, as the streets of the City were not so busy on a Saturday, the total casualties for the air-raid were lower than on 13th June, with 55 civilians and 2 military personnel killed; 190, plus 3 military personnel, injured. Damage amounted to a staggering £205,622

A *Times* reporter, joining the rush for the safety of Blackfriars Underground Station, thinking to himself, "The raiders have London at their mercy, there are no defences against them." A 110 lb bomb damaged the Central Telegraph Office, killing the sentry on duty; this would be the only military target hit in the London area. The majority of the `aerial torpedoes' fell on private dwellings and empty offices; 3 churches and a synagogue were damaged. Once again the enemy airmen appeared to be contemptuous of the anti-aircraft explosions bursting around them and well able to fend off the isolated attacks by Home Defence aeroplanes.

A lone RFC machine flying across London in pursuit of the departing raiders was cheered mockingly by frustrated Londoners, who had watched in vain to see the arrogant `Huns' taught a lesson.

Equally frustrated were pilots of the Home Defence squadrons, who were able to come to grips with the German bombers, only to suffer jam after jam with their synchronised Vickers guns. Pre-war stocks of ammunition had been quickly exhausted and inferior brass used in the manufacture of cartridge cases to meet the ever-growing demand had been partially to blame, the fabric belts feeding the guns designed for ground use where a `number two' fed the belt into the gun by hand was just another of the many causes. The latter would be cured by the introduction of a metal link system introduced later in the year; many front line pilots personally checked each round with a gauge as the armourer loaded the ammunition belts.

Chadwell Heath and Romford anti-aircraft gunners engaged the returning bombers, as 2nd Lieut W Salmon from No.63 Training Squadron, attacking a Gotha single handed in a Sopwith Pup received an eye wound. The unfortunate young officer, attempting to land on his own aerodrome at Joyce Green, lost consciousness and crashed to his death.

Four Sopwith 1½ Strutters from No.37HD Squadron, with the advantage of the altitude gained awaiting the return of the London bombers, dived to attack as the enemy formation approached the Essex coast and flew into a devastating hail of bullets from German machine guns. Capt C B Cooke's biplane, hit by three bursts of machine gun fire, managed to land safely at Rochford. 2nd Lieut J E Young would not be so fortunate; his machine, hit by the withering crossfire, fell into the sea. Young, trapped in the wreckage, drowned, his wounded gunner

AM C C Taylor was rescued by the Royal Navy, but succumbed to his wounds.

A No 50HD Squadron Armstrong Whitworth FK8, piloted by 2nd Lieut F Grace, with observer gunner 2nd Lieut G Murray, did force down an isolated Gotha. Without covering crossfire of the formation, the crippled bomber fell into the sea, to become the only Home Defence success during the raid. Despite their inflatable life jackets and flares fired by the crew of the `Big Ack' trying to attract nearby shipping to the plight of the German airmen clinging to the rapidly sinking bomber, the three man crew perished. Fighting off determined attacks by RNAS Sopwiths from bases along the French coast, the remaining twenty-one Gothas returned to their Belgian aerodromes around 13.00 hrs. Four battle damaged biplanes crashed on landing.

Two hours later an emergency meeting of the War Cabinet took place at 10 Downing Street, the first of many verbal battles that would eventually hammer out an independent air service, as a direct result from the two daylight air raids on London in the summer of 1917.

That same afternoon, a gun carriage, attended by Royal Flying Corps personnel from Hainault Farm aerodrome, carried the mortal remains of 2nd Lieut Eric St Clair Smith along the Ilford High Road, towards the City of London Cemetery. The 25 year old officer had been killed during a wireless training flight from Brooklands aerodrome on Monday, 2nd July, when B.E.2e biplane A8667, piloted by Sgt Watson, carrying St Clair Smith, broke up in mid-air. Faulty material used in the construction of the biplane had been responsible. He was buried with full military honours.

The following morning, Sunday, 8th July, the serious situation brought about by the apparent ease with which the Gothas had been able to bomb London for the second time in daylight, was brought home to No.39HD Squadron, when orders were received for B Flight at Hornchurch to pack all equipment and fly their aeroplanes to join C Flight at Hainault Farm immediately.

One by one, in pouring rain, the aeroplanes of B Flight evacuating Hornchurch landed at Hainault Farm; ground crews, stores and equipment followed by road. Several days of chaos elapsed before the additional influx of officers and men settled in with C Flight personnel at the Ilford aerodrome.

On Tuesday, 10th July, seventeen Sopwith Pups of No 46 Squadron, withdrawn from front line duties in France, took up temporary residence at Suttons Farm aerodrome. The pilot of missing eighteenth Pup had been forced down in the Channel following engine failure. Lieut Charles Courtneidge, brother of Cicely, the musical comedy artiste, was rescued uninjured by a Naval patrol boat.

An important decision by a meeting of the War Cabinet on Wednesday, 11th July, brought about by public demand, set up a committee headed by the Prime Minister and Lieut-General Jan Smuts to review the arrangements for defence against air raids and the organization of aerial operations generally.

On Saturday, 12th July, over the enemy lines along the Ypres front, furious air battles took place; one dogfight involved 60 aircraft. The following day, Major General H M Trenchard received notification from the War Office that 24

Sopwith Camels, urgently required to replace obsolete Sopwith 1½ Strutters of No.43 and No.45 Squadrons at the front, were being re-directed from the Boulton Paul works to No.39 Home Defence Squadron. As there had been no consultation, Trenchard, who had reluctantly relinquished No.46 Squadron for Home Defence duties just three days earlier, was furious and reported the matter to Field Marshal Haig. The Commander-in-Chief of the British Expeditionary Force protested to the War Cabinet that his planned July offensive had reached an advanced stage and that no alteration or modification could be made without grave disadvantage.

Daylight Gotha raids on London were having far-reaching effects: on Tuesday, 17th July, a Royal Proclamation stated that the royal family of Saxe-Coburg-Gotha was henceforth be known as Windsor.

As Ilford families were concerned about the lack of warnings during daylight raids and the plight of 10,000 children in the local schools. Many of the town's men were away in the armed forces and during weekdays a large proportion of the remaining male population commuting to the City on business or their occupations added to the unease.

A meeting of the Ilford Education Committee advised town parents that it would be irresponsible for children to be sent out of the schools during an air raid, in spite of the Poplar school bombing horror still fresh in their minds During the tragic 14th June air raid, as the Gothas returning from London flew over the town, a worried teacher lowered class room window blinds in an act of desperation. One little girl enquired why this was being done and received the reply from the small boy sitting next to her, 'To make them think we are not at home.'

At Hainault Farm aerodrome, the transition from the stable B.E. biplane with in-line engine to rotary engined Sopwith Camels took place, with the aid of the larger, but similar powered, 1½ Strutter, without mishap. The latest Sopwith design would soon acquire a name as a killer among training squadrons. C Flight No 39HD Squadron carried out their first defensive patrol with 10 Sopwith Camels on 22nd July, in response to an expected raid on London. In the event, the Gothas were content with a hit and run attack on Harwich and Felixstowe, leaving 13 dead and 26 injured in an attack lasting 7 minutes

Ten minutes after the raiders had flown out to sea at 08.15 hrs, those citizens of London still in bed were rudely awakened by explosions overhead and assumed that an air raid had begun. In fact the `All Clear' message passed to London's County Hall that Sunday morning had been mistaken for `Take Air Raid Action', despite the colour code accompanying the messages of green for `Warning', red for `Take Air Raid Action' and yellow for `All Clear'. Adding to the confusion, many Londoners had been unaware of the new air raid warning system for the City, consisting of three sound rockets Maroons, fired at five second intervals from 85 buildings around the capital. Eventually `All Clear' placards carried by policemen on cycles appeared on the streets and by 10.00 hrs life in the City returned to what passed for normal in wartime, although more than one Londoner, excited by the explosions, had been disappointed when the Gothas failed to appear. Anti-aircraft batteries along the

Essex coast were also confused and continued to fire at aircraft, damaging two Home Defence machines up to an hour and a half after the raiders had flown home. One Gotha just failed to make the beach at Ostend after coming under attack from Bristol fighters of No.48 Squadron, stationed at Bray Dunes, and fell into the sea.

On Tuesday, 24th July, officers and men at Hainault Farm were officially informed that they were no longer serving with No 39HD Squadron, ending the many rumours that were circulating since the amalgamation of B and C Flights two weeks earlier. The airmen were, in fact, an independent unit, No.44 Squadron, the first of three new Home Defence squadrons being formed to counter the enemy daylight bombing raids. Training began under the experienced eye of Major T O'B Hubbard, who had seen action in France with No.11 Squadron.

As a young 2nd Lieutenant in the small pre-war Royal Flying Corps, he had escaped serious injury when a Short biplane under evaluation crashed with him at the controls. Five years to the day, prior to the formation of No.44 Squadron at Hainault Farm, Tom O'Brien Hubbard officiated as an observer at Fairlop playing fields for the Royal Aeronautical Society. Edward Petre, a test pilot for Handley Page Ltd, (then at Barking) qualified for his RAeC certificate on 24th July, 1912. Three days later, Petre made the first heavier than air flight across London, from Fairlop to Brooklands. Flight training at Fairlop, a sub-station to RNAS Chingford, went on during the summer of 1917, affected more by bad weather than enemy daylight raids.

On Wednesday, 25th July, Field Marshall Haig was forced to postpone the planned third battle of Ypres, until Saturday 28th, when again the big push had to be cancelled due to torrential rain falling in Flanders.

On Monday, 30th July, the second new Home Defence squadron, No.112, an offshoot of No.50 Squadron, was formed at Throwley in Kent, equipped with Sopwith Pups.

The great allied offensive begun at 03.50 hrs on Saturday, 31st July, when the infantry stormed out of waterlogged trenches, capturing most of the first day objectives successfully, with the aid RFC aeroplanes bombing and strafing the enemy lines and aerodromes. A blanket of low clouds cut air fighting above the battle, but the RFC lost 30 machines to ground fire with their close support. Torrential rain returned the next day to ruin what had been a promising start to the third battle of Somme, turning the battlefield into a sea of mud and deep slime-filled craters.

No.44 Squadron, seven days old on the last day of July, 1917, received notification from the War Office, acting upon the urgent review of Britain's air defences carried out by Lieut-General Jan Smuts, that they were now under the overall command of the London Air Defence Area (LADA).

Brigadier-General Edward B Ashmore, a regular artillery officer, had been recalled from France to command the new London Air Defence Area that actually included all south-east England. Upon his arrival at the War Office, Ashmore thought he had probably exchanged the comparative safety of the western front for being hanged in the streets of London.

As a major serving at the War Office in 1912, Ashmore undertook flying lessons at four in the morning, to be at his desk by nine o'clock. As a qualified aviator, he commanded an RFC wing in France in 1915, before transferring back to the Royal Artillery as a brigade commander.

1st August, 1917, brought no respite from the falling rain; soldier and civilian alike blamed the weather on to the massive ten day artillery barrage, the heaviest of the war, preceding the third battle of Ypres.

Major-General Ashmore did not waste the respite afforded by the heavy rain keeping the Gothas grounded in Flanders. At Hainault Farm new machines and pilots were arriving daily to bring No.44 Squadron up to fighting strength.

Lieut Ronald Adam arrived at Ilford from a training squadron, having served in the trenches with the Middlesex Regiment. He transferred to the Royal Flying Corps and was assigned to No 18 Squadron in December, 1915, as an observer, flying in Vickers F.B 5 `Gunbus' machines, until they were replaced by the more reliable Beardmore engined F E.2b. Returning to England for flight training, Ronald Adam received his wings at Rochford on 7th July, 1917, and was immediately ordered aloft in an unarmed B E.2c training machine with a ceiling of 8,000 ft, as a token gesture to the Gotha bombers returning from London daylight raid at 14,000 ft.

His first impression of his latest posting was of a drab and muddy aerodrome that had once been a farm. However, there were compensations - London was less than an hour's drive away. Some pilots spent most of their free time in London, where a box was permanently reserved at the Vaudeville

Theatre for the musical comedy *Cheep*, starring Beatrice Lillie.

The more experienced new pilots soon mastered the Camel, as did Lieut Cecil Lewis, the 19 year old flight commander, who had served two tours of duty at the front, where he had been wounded serving with No 56 Squadron. Credited with eight victories flying S.E 5 scouts over the enemy lines, Cecil Lewis regarded his new highly manoeuvrable Camel superior to the S.E 5; he was, however, less enthusiastic about his new living quarters in the large farm house across the road from the aerodrome.

Flying in from Boulton & Paul via No.3 Aircraft Acceptance Park (Norwich), the new Camels equipping No.44 Squadron were found to be well constructed, with one minor recurring fault of broken tail-skids that would eventually be remedied by replacing plain wooden tail-skids with laminated plywood.

Boulton & Paul were the second largest firm sub-contracting work from the Sopwith Aviation Company during the war and would eventually construct 1,550 of the 5,497 Camels built.

To ensure the whole squadron would be airborne as soon as possible on receiving an air-raid warning, Klaxon hooters, wired to a Morse key in the squadron office, would blare out to bring officers and men running to the flight line. As pilots donned flying kit, ack-emmas primed cylinders and warmed up the 110 hp Le Rhône rotary engines in preparation for the take action order - if received, the whole squadron could be airborne in one minute.

An outline target of a `Hun'

aeroplane, supported by scaffold poles, set in the small lake on the north-east perimeter of the aerodrome, gave pilots with local air to ground firing practice, after the twin Vickers machine guns of each Camel had been synchronised and zeroed at a brick built sand filled bunker adjacent to the armourers workshop. Several large white painted revolving plywood arrows were set around Hainault Farm; visible up to 17,000 ft, they replaced the time consuming laying out of white Ingram panels that had previously been in use to indicate the direction of raiding enemy aeroplanes to pilots.

An increase of activity at Hainault Farm aerodrome during August attracted crowds of spectators at the weekends to watch the new squadron practice formation flying and perform aerobatics in their snub nosed biplanes. Capt T Grant noted that some evenings people flocked to Hainault aerodrome, as it was not ordinary flying being demonstrated, but aerobatics so daring that they trembled with excitement. Posted to No 44 Squadron as Capt Teddy Grant, he was in fact a Norwegian aviator named Jens Herman Tryggve Gran. On Thursday, 30th July, 1914, he made the first aeroplane flight across the North Sea from Scotland to Norway in a Blériot monoplane. As this feat coincided with the full mobilization of the Russian Army following the bombardment of Belgrade by Austrian artillery, his splendid achievement had been over shadowed by the start of the Great War. He would be remembered in Britain however as `Trigger', the young Norwegian ski expert, who accompanied Captain Scott on his last expedition to the South Pole in 1910.

On Sunday, 12th August, a break in the abysmal summer weather encouraged many Ilford families to join day trippers flocking to Southend on Sea.

Almost three weeks had elapsed since the last bombing raid on England and Hauptmn Rudolf Kleine, forced to abandon several planned raids through bad weather, waited impatiently. A number of his airmen had already left their quarters before breakfast to spend the day in Ghent when Kleine received an unexpectedly favourable weather report. By early afternoon enough crews assembled to man 13 Gothas, though intelligence reports of new squadrons swelling the number of fighter aircraft awaiting their return did not bode well for the small force.

Twenty-six Mercedes engines roared into life and slowly throttled back into a tickover, while mechanics made final adjustments. The flyers received confirmation, no doubt to their relief, that Chatham naval base - not inland London - would be the target. Kleine, unable to contact his own pilot and rear gunner, remained grounded. Before climbing wooden steps to board their 'Devil Kites', each airman inflated his rubberised waist-coat by mouth; comrades had drowned, pulled under the waves by waterlogged flying suits.

Two Gothas, suffering engine trouble, fell out of the small formation; the remainder, blown 20 miles off course towards Felixstowe, followed the shoreline south to the river Blackwater, making landfall at 17.30 hrs, Flying alone as a decoy to bomb Margate, another Gotha left the formation.

Telephone lines hummed with warnings, orders and counter-orders. At the L A D A control, the new commander deployed his squadrons to protect London. Eighteen Sopwith Pups of No.46 Squadron patrolling in formation, befitting a front line fighter unit, had been air-borne within one minute of receiving the order at Suttons Farm aerodrome. No less than six of fifteen Sopwith Camels aloft from Hainault Farm were flown by pilots with the rank of captain, resulting from the hurried transfer of experienced pilot officers to the new squadron based at Ilford. With No.39 Squadron B E 12 ex-nightfighters, the two Sopwith squadrons patrolled the approach to London from North Weald to Joyce Green, under orders not to be decoyed away from their designated operational areas. Ironically, the one LADA squadron that did eventually engage the enemy in force had been kept on the ground at Rochford aerodrome in readiness should the 'Huns' have another formation of bombers heading towards England.

Three bombs, aimed at No 61 Squadron lined up in readiness for take off at Rochford, wounded two mechanics and damaged a hanger, prompting Major E R Pretyman to take unauthorised action and order his 'Pups' airborne. The small force of Gothas en route for Chatham, observing the glint of sunshine on wings of defending fighters in the direction of London and aware of the Rochford Pups climbing in pursuit, turned east above Canvey Island, heading towards Southend. Alerted by white arrows uncovered on the aerodromes below pointing towards the

Thames Estuary, pilots from Nos 39, 44 and 46 Squadrons observed anti-aircraft fire directed at raiders some twenty miles away, but could do nothing but wait for the expected raid on London.

Homeward-bound day trippers, many with tired young children, making their way to the railway stations, added to the throng of locals and holidaymakers enjoying the evening sunshine at Southend. Accustomed to the regular sound of gunfire during daylight hours from the nearby artillery ranges at Shoeburyness, they were unaware of the approaching danger. Six 50 kg bombs, apparently aimed at Victoria Station, falling on the streets crowded with women and children in the centre of the town inflicted the worst incident of the evening. The ordeal for Southend had been brief; in five minutes the Gothas dropped 34 bombs in the area where 33 people died, including nine children, some infants in their perambulators; a further 45 civilians were injured.

Twenty minutes earlier, the decoy bomber added an injured woman to the casualty list when 4 bombs fell on Margate. RNAS fighters chased the lone Gotha out to sea. The enemy airmen were harried by no less than 11 fighters and, although one engine had been disabled early in the fighting, the bullet-riddled bomber crash landed on the beach at Zeebrugge. Sub-Lieut Harold Kerby from the naval aerodrome at Walmer chased the crippled Gotha to the coast of occupied Belgium, before encountered the main force, harassed by ten Pups from No.61 Squadron and a mixture of RFC/RNAS pilots, trying to overtake the now empty bombers on the homeward run.

Kerby had the one and only Home Defence success of the raid by attacking a Gotha 4,000 ft below the covering fire of the formation head on, killing or wounding the pilot. The Gotha fell into the sea, where the crew perished in spite of the attempts of Kerby to attract nearby shipping by firing his Very pistol.

With fuel almost exhausted, the equally exhausted pilots attempting to land battle-damaged Gothas in the gathering dusk crashed four of the bombers, bringing the total loss of machines to six, more than half of the actual raiding force.

In the officers' mess at Hainault Farm that evening, the dismay of not being allowed to engage the enemy, who came so temptingly near, did not last for long. Unaware that Chatham had been the original target for the Gothas, the C.O., Major Hubbard, explained that the mere sight of the London defence squadrons had deterred the raiders.

The unfortunate citizens of Southend, protesting at the lack of public air-raid warnings, eventually would have sirens installed in the town.

Fate was kind to Lieut Edward Moulton-Barrett, who exceeded his allotted patrol period during the Gotha raid on Southend by 40 minutes, but crash-landed without injury, having run out of fuel.

Several days later, two Camels, piloted by Capt T Gran and Capt J I Mackay, set out from Hainault Farm to perform aerobatics over London in aid of a War Bond drive. Capt Gran and Mackay looped the loop, flew inverted and spun their machines becoming quite wild and intoxicated in the polluted air above the great city. On returning to Ilford, they repeated their London exhibition above the aerodrome for the benefit of the naval airmen at nearby Fairlop. Pulling out of a loop, Gran fell into a spin and at 1,000 ft found himself desperately fighting to regain control, as the revolving fields rushed to meet him. "I thought I was a gonner," recalled Gran, "when suddenly I remembered Armstrong's advice - as a last way out of it bust the motor."

Under full power the aeroplane once again responded to the controls, but his feeling of relief was short-lived; almost immediately he saw stars and lost consciousness. As he came to, he heard Mackay telling him, "You had the luck of the devil." Around Gran lay the crumpled remains of his Sopwith Camel, a complete write-off. Gran suffered mild concussion and went on a few days leave, owing his life to another colourful character serving at Hainault Farm aerodrome in the summer of 1917.

Lieut D'Urban Victor Armstrong, named after his birthplace, Durban in South Africa, had served with No.60 Squadron in France, flying notoriously inadequate Morane single seaters in combat with Fokker monoplanes prior to returning to Home Establishment early in 1917. His transfer to Hainault Farm from B Flight No.39HD squadron in July coinciding with the arrival of the first Sopwith F 1 Camel at the aerodrome. Completely fearless, Armstrong not only mastered, but became part of, the Camel and a legendary aerobatic pilot during his tour of duty with No.44 Squadron at Hainault Farm aerodrome.

Tall, dark and handsome, Armstrong turned many a female head at the Savoy, although his subsequent engagement to a local girl may have resulted from a party at Reed Pond House in nearby Gidea Park, the home of his aunt, Mrs Edward Royds. Sgt Edward J Mills, a C Flt engine fitter, recalled Armstrong "rolling, looping, and tail slipping over our aerodrome" and came to the conclusion, after clearing away the remains of a Camel that tried duplicating the famous Armstrong flick roll at about thirty feet, that the A Flt commander had become a menace.

To fellow pilots, however, Armstrong would be remembered as charming, unassuming character, whose flying skill prompted Capt Oliver Stewart to remark "the fellow had the hands of a surgeon", after witnessing for the first time Armstrong putting his `Bus' through its paces above the Experimental Establishment at Orfordness.

"He flew across the aerodrome, the wheels of his machine skimming the grass, suddenly, yet without a jerk the machine reared up, turned completely upside down and without raising itself above the level of the shed roofs and flattened out. with the wheels again skimming the grass. Had there been the slightest error of judgment, the machine would have struck the ground".

In complete contrast to the heatwave of August, 1914, the third summer of the Great War proved to be the worst for 50 years. Ignoring his meteorological officer's advice, Haupt Kleine attempted the largest daylight raid of the campaign on the morning of Saturday, 18th August. Kleine's impatience with the weather

No.44 Squadron, Summer, 1917. Lieut George Craig (centre with white silk scarf); behind him Lieut Ronald Adam, in front of a relaxed Captain Tryggve Gran; by his feet in a thoughtful mood is Captain C J Q Brand; 2nd Lieut Charles Banks heads the group on Lieut Craig's right hand (*G A Pidcock/T Henshaw*)

RAF badge

RFC badge

RNAS badge

proved costly in men and machines, for, as predicted, the south-west gale blew the bombers well off course, with Kleine doggedly leading his squadron across the North Sea for three hours, before finally admitting defeat within sight of the Essex coast and firing a washout signal flare.

Releasing their bombs harmlessly into the sea, the anxious pilots checked their fuel gauges, banked for home and watched with relief as their forward airspeed increased by over 30 mph with the resulting tail winds. Nine of the 28 Gothas were wrecked or badly damaged in landing accidents, mainly due the gale sweeping across occupied Belgium. Two crews drowned after Gothas run out of fuel before falling into the choppy sea, two more crews were lost when their machines, blown off course, crashed in Holland. Thanks to the same weather that seriously hampered the BEF in France, it had given Home Defence time to re-organise daytime fighter squadrons to meet the Gotha menace.

The first fatal Camel crash at Hainault Farm aerodrome occurred on Sunday, 19th August, when Lieut George Robert Craig span to his death, although it had been a minor miracle that Capt Tryggve Gran survived a similar crash a few days earlier.

·Lieut George Craig had been awarded his Military Cross for conspicuous gallantry during service with the Lancashire Fusiliers, before transferring to the RFC. On one occasion with a five man patrol in No Man's Land, he fought off a larger German patrol, killing their officer. During another raid on enemy trenches, he found the barbed wire uncut, and sent his party back, remaining with just two men to cut a sufficient passage.

The inquest on Craig's death took place at Ilford Town Hall on Wednesday, 22nd August. B Flt commander, Capt James Ivan Mackay, giving evidence, stated that Craig, on returning from a formation flight, requested permission to indulge in fighting practice with another machine above the aerodrome. Having checked that Sopwith Camel B3-788 was in order, Capt Mackay allowed Craig his second flight that evening. Quickly airborne, Craig dipped the snub nose of his machine in salute to the multitude of evening spectators before engaging in mock combat with another Camel above the aerodrome. Craig completing two spinning nose dives, regained altitude, before attempting or falling into a spin in the opposite direction. Watching below, Capt Mackay became anxious, fearing the pilot had lost control, or, worse, consciousness. The mounting excitement of the crowd turned suddenly to horror, as the spinning machine crunched into a field a quarter of a mile north of the aerodrome at 18.45 hrs. Capt Mackay, among the first to arrive on the scene, found that Craig had been killed instantly by the force of the impact. Sparing the distressed parents of Lieut George Craig further anguish, Captain Mackay had been requested by the coroner to formally identify the remains of their son for the inquest. Giving his eye witness account of the tragedy, Mackay told the coroner that Lieut Craig had been a competent pilot and, from personal experience, knew that giddiness often occurred spinning in an aeroplane. The inquest recorded a verdict of accidental death.

Zeppelins were headline news again on Tuesday, 21st August, as Peter Strasser planned the resumption of Naval airship raids on England that night. The Royal Naval Air Service destroyed another of his vulnerable hydrogen-filled giant flying ships. Zeppelin L23, carrying out a routine patrol along the Danish coast, came under attack from a Sopwith scout, piloted by Sub-Lieut Bernard Arthur Smart. This extremely courageous 26 year old officer had completed his flight training at RNAS Chingford and sub-station Fairlop aerodromes the previous year. His exploits, that entailed the hazardous take off from a makeshift platform above the forward 6in gun turret of the light cruiser HMS *Yarmouth*, the shooting down in flames of L23 with incendiary ammunition fired from a single Lewis gun and the equally hazardous ditching of his Pup near waiting destroyers, had to be kept secret from the enemy, who believed the Zeppelin and her 18 man crew fell victims to the guns of the warships being shadowed by L23.

Bernard Smart was invested with the DSO on 7th November, at Buckingham Palace and later received a bar to his DSO for his part in the carrier strike against the Tondern Zeppelin base on the morning of 19th July, 1918.

Home Defence night fighters rose to the challenge of 8 high flying Naval Zeppelins trying to raid northern England during the night of Tuesday, 21st, and early hours of Wednesday, 22nd August. Cautiously flying in excess of 20,000 ft, out of range of the waiting nightfighters, airship crews were overcome by lack of oxygen and fatigue. The few bombs dropped at random injured one civilian. For Peter Strasser, desperately trying to convince the High Command that the Zeppelin was still a war winning weapon, the raid proved another embarrassment.

22nd August had been a busy day for the commander of B Flight at Hainault Farm. Prior to attending the inquest of the unfortunate Lieut George Craig at Ilford Town Hall during the afternoon, Capt James Mackay had been among the 15 pilots of No.44 Squadron scrambled at 10 15 hrs, as warily the Gothas probed England's air defences. Under pressure from the High Command, Haupt Kleine led all the remaining serviceable bombers of Kagohl 3 in an attempt to bomb London. One after another five of the 15 'Devil Kites' fell out of formation with engine troubles, the last being the red tailed Gotha of Kleine. Attempting to order his deputy commander to take charge, Kleine raised a wide barrel pistol, but the coloured flares failed to ignite, adding to the confusion.

Major T O'B Hubbard flew with his squadron in the defence of London on the morning of Wednesday, 22nd August. Once again the Camels of Hainault Farm, and Pups from Suttons Farm and Throwley were denied the opportunity to attack the raiders. Approaching the Kent coast near Margate, the ten bombers were greeted by a barrage of accurate anti-aircraft fire that sent one Gotha spinning into the sea at Walpole Bay; two crew members perished - the lucky third man was rescued. As deputy commander of the depleted Gotha squadron, Oblt Richard Walter decided that inland London would be to hazardous a target in view of the alerted defences and fired coloured flares for target No 3, Dover. More confusion followed - a Gotha bombed Margate, before being hit by anti-aircraft fire, and fell in several pieces across a golf course, killing the crew. RNAS aeroplanes from Dover, Manston and Walmer made life very uncomfortable for the enemy airmen. The constant anti-aircraft barrage ceased only when Home Defence machines attacked the German aeroplanes at close quarters. Flt Sub-Lieut E B Drake from Manston, flying Sopwith Camel B3844, claimed - along with several A gun crews - the destruction of a third Gotha that fell with one engine on fire into the sea near Dover; again there were no survivors.

Eight civilians and four servicemen were killed, and 12 civilians, plus 14 servicemen, were injured, during what would prove to be the last daylight raid on England by the Gothas of Kagohl 3.

Seven battle-damaged Gothas landed safely after fighting off repeated fighter attacks during the return flight across the North Sea. It was obvious the Germans had lost the initiative gained during the early daylight raids. Aided by atrocious flying weather that curtailed more attacks on London, the L A D wasted no time in re-organising and equipping Home Defence squadrons and anti-aircraft units to combat the Gothas.

On receiving orders to return to France as commanding officer of No 73 Squadron a week after the Gotha raid on Dover, the ubiquitous Major T O'B Hubbard once again told his batman to pack his kit and said his farewells. His successor at Hainault Farm aerodrome,

22 year old Captain Gilbert Ware Murlis Green, had, prior to joining No 44 Squadron, served with No.17 Squadron in Salonica. Murlis Green, a skilled pilot with at least seven enemy machines to his credit, had become well known to his opponents across the Bulgarian/German lines as Captain Green, the English ace.

On Thursday, 30th August, the next of kin at 26 Norfolk Road, Seven Kings, were informed that 2nd Lieut Hugh William Evans had died in Tidworth Hospital. The unfortunate airman had been undergoing flight training at the Central Flying School, Uphaven, when his Sopwith Pup 2171 fell into an air pocket and crashed. 20 year old Evans died from injuries received when his face came into violent contact with the breech of the Vickers gun in front of him - an all too common incident for Great War airmen.

Lieut Albert Earl Godfrey, a Canadian pilot credited with 14 victories with No.40 Squadron, replaced Capt T Gran, the Norwegian, at Hainault Farm, when he flew to join No.101 Squadron in France on Saturday, 1st September. Tryggve Gran officially joined 101 Squadron on the 3rd September, although fully equipped with lumbering two seat FE2b pusher aircraft for night bombing, Gran also had charge of a single seat Sopwith for unspecified duties. The Pup B2188 was housed in an out of bounds hanger, that also contained a modified B.E.2c machine for dropping spies behind German lines. What special duties the multi-lingual Norwegian carried out are not recorded, however. No.101 Squadron records indicate that Gran also flew on 17 night bombing raids, until he was badly wounded by shrapnel, during a

No. 17 Squadron

The Airco DH6 training biplane in which PFO Laurence Pearson made his first solo flight on 3rd September, 1917 (*L H Pearson*)

low level attack near Douai, on the night of 30th November.

Monday, 3rd September, proved a memorable day for PFO Laurence Herbert Pearson, undergoing flight training at Fairlop in an Airco DH6 training biplane. With a total of 78 minutes dual instruction and two landings to his credit, 18 year old Pearson made his first solo flight at 11.30 hrs. It remained an unofficial solo, however, as his instructor, FSL Hughes, mistaking the would-be pilot for a more advanced pupil named Palmer, climbed out of the spacious open cockpit of A9603, after Pearson had made his second landing and said, "You'll be all right, Palmer, take her up!" Without a second thought, Pearson opened the throttle of the idling 90 hp RnF engine and took off. At fifty feet the railway embankment came racing towards him and Pearson yanked the docile trainer into a flat turn towards the hangers, just missing them. At 100 ft Pearson circled Fairlop aerodrome, collecting his wits, before deciding it would be advisable to land. On his sixth attempt he remembered to switch the engine off and made a good landing, to his instructor's immense relief; six days later Laurence Pearson soloed officially at Fairlop and served in France with No.2(N) Squadron. The sight of an RNAS pilot, APFO Pearson, stunting a 'Clutching Hand' (DH6) just across Forest Road at nearby Fairlop aerodrome, provided the airmen of Hainault Farm with an amusing topic of conversation for a while.

It had become a frustrating period for the pilots of No.44 Squadron, especially those that had survived flying obsolete machines in combat over the enemy lines and were ready to meet German airmen on equal terms. These experienced officers made certain the excessive machine gun stoppages that plagued Home Defence airmen during the first daylight raids on London were now a thing of the past. German Army Intelligence were aware No.46 Squadron had returned to France at the end of August; no doubt their presence at Hornchurch had been a deterrent, until new squadrons such as No.44 were fully operational. The few remaining Sopwith 1½ Strutters at the Ilford aerodrome were collected by No.78 Squadron, now at Suttons Farm. At dusk, the routine of pushing the Camels of Hainault Farm back into their sheds for the night had been carried out and pilots not on standby duty wasted little time in heading for the blacked-out bright lights of London.

Apart from the `Hun' (a man undergoing flight training)'s hilarious solo, Monday, 3rd September, had just been another day waiting in vain for the return of the enemy bombers for the airmen at Hainault Farm. The distant hum of aeroplanes approaching Chatham at 23.00 hrs raised no alarm, as, earlier in the day, notice had been given of an air defence exercise planned for that night. An air raid on Dover by two German Army planes apparently in mistake for Calais, 21 miles away, the night before, had prompted Major-General Ashmore to order the night practice.

Five Gothas, manned by volunteer crews from Kagohl 3, were attempting the squadron's first night raid on England; one machine returned to Belgium with engine trouble. At Chatham Naval Barracks lights out had been sounded and hundreds of recruits in hammocks were sleeping, when, without warning at 23.12 hrs, four 110 lb aerial torpedoes struck the Base. Two scored direct hits on a drill hall that had been converted into an over-crowded dormitory, killing 130 Naval ratings and injured a further 88, as the shattered glass roof fell in, adding to the carnage. The death toll at Chatham far exceeded the total of naval and military personnel killed in the previous nine day-light bombing raids by the Gothas of Kagohl 3.

At Hainault Farm, the warning of nocturnal raiders bombing Kent prompted Capt Murlis Green to call for volunteers and telephone the officer commanding the London Air Defence HQ, with a plea for the night flying ban on the squadron Camels be lifted. There is no doubt Ashmore's high regard for this young much-decorated officer, awarded the DSO for shooting down two twin engined Friedrichshafen bombers out of a flight of six on a daylight mission over Salonica on 18th March, prompted him to sanction a trial experiment.

At the Ilford aerodrome, three machines were warmed up in readiness awaiting official clearance and electric torches, in lieu of cockpit lighting, drawn from squadron stores. The wheel chocks were pulled from Camel B3852 at 23.40 hrs, half an hour after the bombing of Chatham. Capt C J Q Brand, the commander of A Flight, was the first away, guided by a makeshift flarepath and the hazy moon. Three minutes later, 2nd Lieut C C Banks, throwing caution to

the wind, followed into the unknown at the controls of B3886. Murlis Green, giving last minute instructions to despondent ground crews, who never expected to have their machines returned in one piece, took off at 23.47 hrs in B3899. To avoid collisions, the C.O. patrolled between Hainault Farm and Joyce Green aerodromes, Capt Brand followed the Thames between Tilbury and the Woolwich Arsenal (a likely target), while 2nd Lieut Banks flew between Hainault Farm and Rochford aerodromes.

No enemy machine was seen, but the safe return to the aerodrome almost an hour and a half later of Murlis Green, the last of the intrepid trio, without mishap, proved to the Top Brass that, unlike the lightweight Sopwith Pup, the Camel could be landed safely at night. Ashmore, unaware that Camels had recently flown after dark in France, remarked that the night flight by No.44 Squadron had perhaps been the most important event in the history of air defence and instructed all the pilots at Hainault Farm to practice night landings.

On Tuesday, 4th September, in expectation of night flying Gothas returning to raid the London area, the aeroplane sheds at Hainault Farm were a hive of activity. Crossley tenders were despatched to depôts early to collect night flying equipment: it did not take the ground crews long to install cockpit lighting equipment and switches to ignite the magnesium landing flares clamped to the under-side of the lower wingtips, thus completing the rapid transition of No.44 Squadron Camels into first class day and night fighters.

Searchlights sweeping the skies a little after 23.00 hrs on Tuesday, 4th September, warned Ilford to be on the alert. Soon the distant bark of anti-aircraft guns could be heard creeping nearer. It was not long before the sinister sound of Gotha bombers passing overhead and the occasional buzz of a single engined night fighter searching for them could be heard. Encouraged by the safe return of his five 'Devil Kites', manned by volunteers, and the lack of fighter opposition the night before, coupled with a spell of fine weather, Haupt Kleine wasted no time in striking at London. Eleven bomb-laden Gothas, camouflaged for night operations, were despatched at five minute intervals, two returned plagued by the usual engine trouble; five visited the capital between 23.20 and 00.50 hrs; whilst the remaining four scattered bombs across Essex, Kent and Suffolk. Following the dull gleam of the river Thames, the German airmen had no difficulty in finding the City. In spite of the enforced blackout, they could discern the streets and buildings of the great metropolis through the clouds below. Capt J I Mackay, an experienced night flier who had served previously with No.39 Squadron, accompanied 2nd Lieut Banks, Capt Brand, and Capt Murlis Green on their second night patrol from Hainault Farm. The 78 ft span Gotha biplanes proved even more difficult to find than the elusive 640 ft long Zeppelins, and one member of No.44 Squadron likened anti-Gotha patrols at night to searching for a fly in a blacked-out room.

Hainault Farm pilots found no raiders in their allotted patrol areas and landed safely despite one Camel being fired upon by enthusiastic anti-aircraft gunners whilst flying over Ilford. Some off-duty pilots had made their way to the Savoy after the theatre. The restaurant was crowded with late night revellers, when the building shook with bombs exploding nearby. Unperturbed, the pilots resumed their supper; they knew the bombers would be long gone before they could return to Hainault through the deserted blacked-out streets of east London. The nearest bomb had fallen a mere 30 ft from the crowded Savoy and Cleopatra's Needle on the Victoria Embankment suffered damage during the raid, when a bomb fell into the road opposite, killing the driver and two passengers of a passing tramcar.

The night raid on London by five Gothas out of nine crossing the coast, left behind 19 fatal casualties and 71 injured; officially it was thought more than 26 enemy aeroplanes had been involved and in the circumstances the casualties plus damage were considered light by the authorities. Two Home Defence machines from Nos.37 and 50 Squadrons countered an isolated Gotha each, but the bombers at once faded away into the surrounding darkness. The Germans later admitted the loss of one machine, probably the Gotha held in searchlight beams for several minutes, enabling Kent anti-aircraft guns to score what appeared to be a direct hit; when last observed the enemy bomber was diving towards the sea.

On Thursday, 6th September, Ilfordians paid their respect as a flag-covered coffin carried on an RFC Crossley tender passed along the High Road. Officers and men of No.44 Squadron escorted the mortal remains

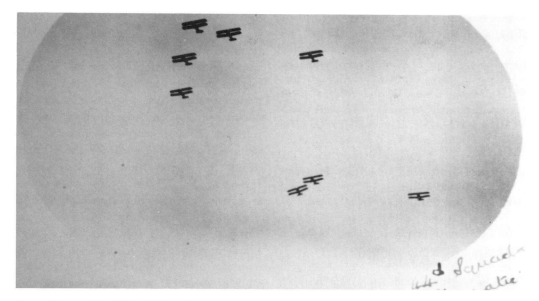

Sopwith Camels of No.44 Squadron in formation over Ilford (*C T Perfect/Redbridge Libraries*)

Major G W Murlis Green at the controls of a Sopwith Camel converted nightfighter making a low pass across Hainault Farm Aerodrome (*C T Perfect/Redbridge Libraries*)

of 2nd Lieut Hugh William Evans, killed in a flying accident at the CFS, Upavon, on 30th August. The funeral procession left the family home at 26 Norfolk Road, Seven Kings, en route for St Mary's Church in the Ilford High Road. Major Evans of the 17th Norfolk Regiment received the news of his son's death shortly after hearing that another of his five sons had volunteered for the Army. Interred with full military honours at St. Mary's, the service was conducted by the Right Reverend Bishop of Barking assisted by Reverend Telford, Vicar of St. John's, Seven Kings.

A picturesque wedding in Ilford on Saturday, 8th September, aroused a lot of interest in the town, where the families of both the bride and bridegroom were well known. The bride, Dorothy Zoë Kapedia, only daughter of a local Councillor and barrister-at-law, A Kapedia, of 13 Endsleigh Gardens, and niece of Sir Frank and Lady Reynolds, married Petty Officer William Stewart, RNAS, of 104 Norfolk Road, Seven Kings, who had seen active service in France. Sixty guests, not including the bridegroom's three brothers serving in the forces overseas, attended the wedding reception held at the Cecil Hall.

In the early hours of Monday, 10th September, RNAS personnel at Fairlop aerodrome turned out to help farm workers fight three haystack fires at Forest Farm, until the Ilford Fire Brigade arrived to deal with the incident at 0130 hrs. On Wednesday, 12th September, the Ilford Fire Brigade broke all records by arriving from the Ley Street depôt within three minutes, when called to the premises of Mr Barnet Bravo, a tobacconist at 58 High Road, where a fierce stockroom fire threatening the Ilford Hippodrome was quickly dealt with.

Saturday, 15th September, began in a relaxed routine manner at Hainault Farm aerodrome, as the 'Huns' had not raided England for a few nights. Just before mid-day Lieut W E Nicholson, the Mess President returned to the aerodrome in triumph, having located a barrel of pre-war ale in Stratford, were his family owned part of the East London paint manufacturing company of Jensen & Nicholson Ltd. The barrel was rolled off the back of the Crossley tender and set up in the officers' mess; at lunch the airmen drank to the health of their Mess President. Two glasses of the brew were enough to get the pilots into high spirits, voting Lieut Armstrong should lead an aerial snake of Camels that Lieut Cecil Lewis proposed to go contour-chasing all over the Essex countryside. The ground staff of No.44 Squadron reckoned the pilots had more than their fair share of luck in getting airborne without mishap and what the German POW's working in nearby fields thought has not been recorded. One of the last pilots to leave the South African and the depleted flying snake skimming the Thames marshes, had been 2nd Lieut. Charles Chaplin Banks. Arriving above Hainault Farm, Banks could not believe his eyes, there were three figures strolling nonchalantly across the middle of the aerodrome. Saturday afternoon or not, he decided to teach them a lesson. What Banks did not know as he dived upon the offending trio, was that Major-General E B Ashmore and his A.D.C had arrived in his absence to discuss the problem of locating the night flying Gothas with the squadron C.O. Captain Murlis Green. Among the pilots watching from in front of the now busy aeroplane sheds, stood Lieut Cecil Lewis, who recaptured the incident for posterity in his autobiography *Sagittarius Rising*, in which he referred to Banks as 'Sandy' on account of his ginger hair. "Down he came like a hawk," recalled Lewis, "the G.O.C. Home Defence was at first amused, screwing his monocle tighter into his eye; but soon he became alarmed and finally sat, panic-stricken, in the mud while the undercarriage of the Camel shrieked by about a foot above his head and the slipstream from the prop blew his beautiful brass hat off. Climbing rapidly to 500 ft, Banks half rolled and dived again forcing the General and his companions to sit on the stubble of the aerodrome making unprintable remarks about the pilot. By the time Ashmore, his A.D.C and the C.O. returned to the aeroplane sheds, the amused spectators had disappeared."

The talk, if not the toast, of No.44 Squadron in the middle of September, had been the Camel pilot who strafed no lesser person than the General Officer Commanding the London Air Defence Area. Fortunately for Charles Banks, 45 year old Major-General Edward Bailey Ashmore learned to fly in 1912 and understood high spirited young airmen. Deprived of his Sam Browne for a mere three days, Banks eventually returned to a leg pulling in the officers' mess. He replied, "Well, I bloody well put the wind up him, anyway!" Capt. G W Murlis Green, who, as Banks' commanding officer, had not only suffered the indignity of being strafed by one of his own pilots, but also waited a further three months for his promotion to Major, the usual rank for a squadron commander.

As the British Expeditionary Force in Flanders prepared for yet another major offensive, the German Army Air Service introduced the Halberstadt CL.11, a purpose built ground strafing two seat battle plane, adding to the miseries of the front line 'Tommies'. The German answer to the Sopwith Camel also began to appear over the front, Manfred von Richthofen's combat report dated 0750 hrs on 1st September, stated, "Flying my triplane for the first time, I attacked, together with four of my gentlemen, a very courageously flying English artillery flyer. I approached and fired twenty shots from 50 meters, whereupon the adversary fell and smashed near Zonnebeke." The German pilot continued, "Most probably the English pilot had taken me for an English triplane, as the observer stood upright in the plane without thinking of making use of his gun." Richthofen's 60th victory had been an R.E.8, the pilot, 2nd Lieut J B C Madge, survived as a wounded PoW, his unfortunate observer, 2nd Lieut W Kember, was killed. The new enemy fighter plane influenced by the climb of the Sopwith Triplane would be a worthy opponent of the Camel, now replacing the Triplane and Pup in front line Squadrons.

France mourned the loss of her much decorated 54 Victory 'Ace' 22 year old Capitaine Georges Guynemer, who fought more than 600 combats in the air, before he was killed in action over Poelcapelle on 11th September.

On Thursday, 20th September, the BEF launched their next major offensive after a night of torrential rain, taking all their objectives and 3,000 prisoners during the first day in the battle for the Menin Road Ridge. German counter-attacks followed for the next five days, in which the RFC, ground strafing and directing artillery fire on the enemy troop

Air Mechanic Frederick A Harvey, RFC, observation balloons, on leave in the garden of the family home, 28 Douglas Road, Goodmayes, 1916 (*Jeffery Harvey*)

concentrations reforming to attack the advanced positions, distinguished themselves.

On Thursday, 20th September, No.7 Balloon Wing officially became a unit of the London Area Defence Scheme, with 10 aprons of three kite balloons in the outer London area. The aprons had 40 weighted steel cables 1,000 ft in length, raised to an altitude of 10,000 ft by three Caquot balloons tethered 500 yards apart. The Wing HQ were in the Royal Forest Hotel, Chingford. No.1 Balloon Squadron Headquarters operated a mile from Barking Great Eastern Railway Station, at Longbridge Farm. No.1 Balloon Apron was at Eastbury House, Ripple Road, Barking; No.2 Balloon Apron at Parsloes Park, Chadwell Heath; No.3 at Gale Street, Barking; No.4 at `Great Gearies', Barkingside, Ilford. `A' and `B' Balloon Detachments were also found in St. James's Park, and Kensington Gardens. No.2 Balloon Squadron Headquarters at `Banavie', Woodford, had Balloon Aprons no's 5, 6, 7, 8 sited between Walthamstow and Manor Park. No.3 Balloon Squadron Headquarters at `Wood Lodge', Shooters Hill, London S.E.15, had a further three Balloon Aprons - 9, 10 and 11 - in the area. The next day, at a demonstration of a London Balloon Apron for Major-General Ashmore, two conscientious Air Mechanics, clinging desperately to the guy ropes, were carried aloft as a violent gust of wind swept the balloons into the air and the airmen fell to their deaths.

Young Arthur Scarborough of Chester Road, Seven Kings, treated the arrival of the balloon barrage as a matter of course: gone were the days when he and his school chums played truant to see an aeroplane at Hainault

Farm. With two aerodromes, anti-aircraft guns and searchlights in the Ilford area, the balloons raised little interest and acquired the nickname of `Pigs' when mentioned in conversation. Although the `Pigs' were plainly visible in daylight, few Ilford civilians knew their true purpose, of forcing night raiders to fly above 10,000 ft, effectively reducing the area of the `blacked out room' for No.44 and other H.D. squadrons around London.

Among the many letters of `thank you' from the armed services received by the industrious volunteers of the Ilford United Women's War Distress Society, now in their third year of war work, arrived a breezy missive from a Canadian soldier at the front, who suspected the bus conductress he had `mashed' when last on leave in Seven Kings, had been responsible for the Society sending him a most welcome parcel from Ilford.

Ilford enjoyed an Indian summer with a continuous spell of fine weather reminiscent of the first glorious autumn of the war; however, after three years of bloodshed, morale in the town, in spite of the propaganda printed daily in the press, was on the decline. The third battle of Ypres raged in France, the heart-breaking daily lists of dead and wounded would exceed 310,000 by the end of the year. Shortages brought about by the U-boat blockade, increased the long patient queues for food and the severe shortage of coal brought about the demands for the fair rationing of fuel during coming winter.

During 1917 horse-racing had been suspended due to the emergency; County Cricket, the Football League and the University Boat Race also disappeared as the situation deteriorated.

At Hainault Farm aerodrome, thanks to the spell of fine weather, more than half the pilots of No.44 Squadron were proficient enough to carry out night patrols. It was a beautiful evening on

Monday, 24th September, with a star-filled sky; it also heralded the first of half a dozen raids that became known as the harvest moon offensive. Warning of enemy aeroplanes off the coast and Zeppelin activity across the North Sea received just before 1900 hrs, was quickly passed to Home Defence aerodromes, AA gun-sites and searchlight crews. The first Gotha crossed the coast a few minutes later, followed at intervals by twelve more, out of a total of sixteen originally intending to bomb London. In response to the telephone message received at the Ilford Fire Station, the red lantern on top of the station had been extinguished, warning those in the vicinity of the approaching danger. Police and Specials on bicycles blowing whistles and shouting warnings, endeavoured once again to warn the remainder of the town's population to take cover. Three of the new Gotha G.V's, eluding searchlights, gunfire and night fighters, dropped bombs on London. One bomb killed 13 and injured 22 people sheltering in the foyer of the Bedford Hotel, Southampton Row; some of the casualties had been out of town guests watching the 'Hun Air Show'. Although his crews welcomed the G.V. as an improvement, the new Gotha had been a disappointment to Hptmm Rudolf Kleine, who intended to resume the more accurate daylight raids. Unfortunately for the Germans the G.V. would not live up to expectation - although slightly faster than its predecessor, it lacked a much needed improvement in its ceiling to face the modern Home Defence fighter aircraft in daylight.

Many of the Ilfordians enjoying the beautiful evening of Monday, 24th September, had been caught out of doors when the Gothas arrived early. The first house at the Ilford Hippodrome, starring Harry Lauder in the revue, *Three Cheers*, still had half an hour to run, when the manager announced an air raid warning from the stage; less than a dozen of the packed audience left. While experienced crews of Kagohl 3 bombed London, six more targeted the unfortunate people of Dover once again; the remainder deposited bombs at random along the Essex and Kent coasts. None of the thirty Home Defence machines sent up to engage the enemy bombers was able to report a sighting, though, not surprisingly, the patrolling pilots encountered other H.D. machines on the prowl beneath the stars. Relying on vision only, the sound of the enemy bombers smothered with the racket of their own noisy rotary engines, Captains C J Q Brand, G W Murlis Green and W H Haynes touched down safely, but frustrated, at Hainault Farm following their patrols. Two hours after the sound of Gotha engines fading out to sea, leaving 21 fatal casualties and 70 injured, the deep drone of Zeppelin motors were heard heading for the softer targets in the Midlands and northeast. At least five out of a force of ten Naval airships led by Kvtkpt Peter Strasser, flying in L46, attempted to raid industrial targets such as the Skinningrove iron works without success; fortunately much of their deadly cargo fell on open land. Casualties were light, with only three people suffering injuries. Across the Channel, airmen from Kagohl 1 inflicted the most serious damage during the night by bombing the

RNAS depôt at St. Pol, sheds containing 140 aeroplane engines were destroyed.

At 11.10 hrs on Tuesday, 25th September, 2nd Lieut Charles Cowley Dennis, of 39 Toronto Road, Ilford, serving as an observer with No.11 Squadron RFC, was killed in action over the enemy lines in France. Bristol Fighter A7124 piloted by Lieut A E Miall-Smith, with Charles Dennis manning the Lewis gun in the rear cockpit, were engaged in a furious dogfight with enemy aircraft above Le-Câtelet. Following a sustained exchange of machine-gun fire with an Albatros scout, the Bristol was observed to break up in mid-air. Parachutes similar to the type demonstrated at the Ilford Whitsun Carnival of 1914 by Mrs Spencer might have saved the lives of the two young officers had they been issued to allied airmen.

At the front, when observation balloons were set ablaze by enemy aircraft, their crews, if lucky, escaped death with the aid of parachutes designed by Capt Spencer. Officially the 'Spencer' was too bulky to be carried by aeroplanes; unofficially, British High Command believed pilots would be tempted to parachute from battle-damaged aeroplanes, rather than try a risky landing.

On Tuesday evening, 25th September, the red lantern on top of the Ilford Fire Station Tower was extinguished, warning people in the Ley Street area that enemy bombers were approaching. Once again, three isolated Gothas attacked London out of a total of 14: the remainder bombed the Kent coast. Due to continued spell of fine weather, patches of mist and fog developed as evening temperatures fell,

hampering friend and foe alike. Hainault Farm pilots were forced by ground fog rapidly spreading across Ilford after take off, to land elsewhere. Capt Brand put his machine down at the Shenfield NLG, Capt Haynes followed 2nd Lieut Banks to the hospitality of No. 39 Squadron at North Weald, and the pilots returned safely the following morning. Several H.D. pilots were forced to return early, due to weather conditions, and two pilots escaped serious injury in landing crashes. During the raid a 1½ Strutter of No.78 Squadron, fired upon by an aircraft flying east, gave chase, returning fire until the exhausts of the phantom machine vanished into the night. Total casualties for the air raid were nine killed, twenty three injured; one Gotha failed to return to Belgium, the crew presumed drowned in the North Sea.

Count Ferdinand Adolf Heinrich von Zeppelin passed away peacefully on 8th March, 1917, aged 79, having lived long enough to witness the demise of the German dream of forcing Britain out of the war with his hugely successful, but so vulnerable, airships. Undaunted and with all the enthusiasm and energy of a person fifty years his junior, von Zeppelin set up a design team at the very busy Zeppelin works to produce giant aeroplanes early in the war and followed their development and construction more keenly after the defeat of his airships by incendiary bullets of the Royal Flying Corps. Multi-engined *Reisenflugzeug* (giant aeroplanes) were tested and flown operationally on the Russian front during 1916; now the second generation of R-planes, Zeppelin Staakens, were ready to bomb England.

Two 138 ft span R-planes, together with 25 Gothas, flew towards England on Friday evening, 28th September; the enemy intended the raid to be the heaviest yet carried out on London. Due to adverse weather, only three of the Gothas managed to reach the coast, both giant Staaken R.IV aeroplanes made their début over England, scattering bombs across Kent and Essex. The six engined giants, each driving propellers up to 14 ft in diameter, had the advantage of generator powered wireless sets carried within their spacious fuselages. The commanders of the seven men crew were able to triangulate wireless beams transmitted from the Belgian coast to navigate among the clouds. A low cloud layer made it impossible for the searchlights to play an active rôle, leaving the gunners to fire blindly at a force estimated by the Home Defences in excess of eighteen machines, no doubt due to the excessive noise of the six engined R-planes.

At Hainault Farm, Capt C J Q Brand, the commander of A Flt, intent as ever on bagging a Gotha, took to the air at 20.15 hrs and climbed above the sea of clouds to be greeted by the brilliance of the full moon, but no enemy machines. Towards the end of his vigil he descended through the murk to find the Hainault landing flares obscured by thick mist. Thankfully he touched down safely at nearby Suttons Farm. Capt W H Haynes and 2nd Lieut C C Banks also followed Brand at intervals, but were recalled as visibility at the Ilford aerodrome quickly deteriorated. The planned heaviest air raid of the war, proved to be a disaster for Kagohl A, three Gothas were reported missing and six crashed on landing, but both giant R-planes returned successfully to base without mishap. There were no civilian casualties and the total bomb damage for the raid amounted to £129. The War Office, warned by allied intelligence reports of giant R-planes at Belgian aerodromes, had deliberately withheld the information from the Home Defences until a few raids later. Only after confused searchlight crews reported single giants as three Gothas in close formation and sound locaters were totally misled, were they eventually informed.

Horace Randall, a local auctioneer and estate agent, offering aircraft Insurance on property or personal injury to readers of the *Ilford Recorder*, received numerous enquiries after the next air raid, when three R-planes carrying the equivalent bomb load of nine twin-engined Gothas returned with the darkness to bomb London.

Saturday, 29th September, continued the spell of fine autumn weather in the London area, and, towards dusk, thousands of Londoners sought the safety of Underground Railway platforms in expectation of the Gothas returning after dark. The mass exodus of families with their bedding created a number of serious problems as the so-called 'Harvest Moon Offensive' went on. Confused Home Defence sightings encouraged daily newspaper reports of 'Hun' bomber squadrons, repelled by the anti-aircraft barrage directed at the few enemy machines that had actually reached London during the latest night raids. Ilford, in the eastern suburbs, received its share of falling shrapnel that ricochetted off cobblestones or shattered roofing slates - only those on duty or the foolhardy remained outside during the ever increasing barrage. For most the novelty of watching the 'Hun Air Show' had worn off.

Screeching Klaxon horns at 20.05 hrs warned No 44 Squadron at Hainault of approaching raiders. Actually Hptmn Kleine had just seven Gothas serviceable for that night's raid; of these, three aborted with engine troubles soon after take off. Mingling with the few Gothas, three giant R-planes again misled the ground defences, each giant being identified as four or five Gothas by sound detectors. Fifty minutes elapsed before the first machine at Hainault Farm was ordered to patrol; once again Capt C J Q Brand was first airborne. Lanterns were be displayed in front of the aeroplane shed in use as a workshop, to indicate the direction and distance of enemy machines when reported by telephone from the LADA control rooms near the Admiralty Arch, Whitehall.

South African Brand, flying Camel B3852, a presentation aircraft named after the Basuto warrior 'Makhabane', was as determined as ever to find and destroy the enemy bombers. Although only 24, Brand behaved and looked older than most of his contemporaries, who, in turn, regarded him as a father figure. A regular army man since 1913, Brand regarded it his duty to set an example to the young pilots and seldom accompanied them to the frequent parties held in London's theatreland, where many found girl friends and brief wartime romance. Unable to draw their Flight commander out of his shell, a mythical girl friend was invented for him - soon his secret passionate affair with 'Flossie Highkick' provided amusing gossip, until the hoax

was revealed to all some weeks later - but the nickname 'Flossie' stayed with Brand long after the war.

Two Gothas and one giant R-plane faced the London barrage; aerial torpedoes damaged rail and rolling stock at Waterloo Station, fortunately with no serious casualties. At nearby London Bridge Station badly wounded servicemen from Flanders were calmly transferred from a hospital train to waiting ambulances non-stop throughout the raid. A single bomb penetrated the thick wooden beer cellar-flaps of the Eaglet public house in the Seven Sisters Road, Islington; the underground explosion erupting through the floor of the saloon bar hurling customers out on to the road; four people were killed outright and another 32 were seriously injured.

Evening mist and fog again affected a number of Home Defence aerodromes, but Sopwith Camels from Hainault Farm were among 33 fighters airborne, again searching in vain for the small scattered force of bombers. Two out of the four Gothas involved failed to return, the massive barrage probably accounted for one lost at sea and a twin-engined Handley Page bomber of the RNAS, returning from a night raid on enemy aerodromes, engaged another off the Belgian coast, forcing it to land damaged in Holland with a wounded crew member. Total casualties for the Saturday night raid, in which the three giant R-planes returned to base without mishap, were 40 killed and 87 injured. Although disappointed with the apparent failure to terrorise English civilians in and around London, the German High Command were aware the air-raids forced the War Office to employ very large numbers of troops to man the defences. London was now ringed with 250 high angle guns, 325 searchlights and eight squadrons of aeroplanes, all badly needed by the B.E.F.

On Sunday, 30th September, a fierce counter attack on the British lines at Polygon Wood by German infantry equipped with specialist flame-thrower units was beaten off.

At home an estimated 300,000 men, women and children packed the London Underground platforms as dusk approached. In Ilford, evening church services had been brought forward to 5 pm to enable their congregations to be in the safety of their own homes before dark. Mist that shrouded parts of the town during the day, cleared suddenly at nightfall - a calm settled over the almost deserted streets, as Ilford waited.

Shortly after sunset the first of ten Gothas, accompanied by a single engined C class machine, began crossing the Essex and Kent coastline at 18.45 hrs. Just one Gotha had fallen victim to the usual engine troubles and turned back.

The pulsating beats of Gotha engines heard above London at 19.40 hrs, were soon drowned by a furious anti-aircraft box barrage, from which steel fragments rained down like hail. Criss-crossing the metropolis at intervals for an hour, six Gothas attacked the capital; the remaining four struck at Dover, Chatham and Margate; a few bombs also fell on Essex The fierce barrage during 3 consecutive night raids depleted ammunition stocks to a dangerous level, some guns; firing as many as five hundred rounds, became red hot and were cooled with buckets of water. Exhausted gun crews; many unfit for front line duty; became temporarily blinded and deafened by the continuous salvos of gunfire. Hands suffering burns from red hot gun barrels were another hazard added to the exhausted and confused gunners.

The *Ilford Recorder* the following week published a report of damage to the town inflicted by the friendly gunfire during the air raid. At 2 Argyle Road, the home of Capt Alexander Christal, an unexploded shell crashed through the roof and two floors, smashing a marble mantelpiece, damaging the drawing room before burying itself beneath the kitchen floor. Another unexploded shell ploughed into the playground of Downsall School. At 41 Grange Road a nosecap from a spent shell damaged the front door of the home of Mr C J Lewis.

Having stayed at her parents house in Seven Kings for the weekend, Mrs Amey and her child returned home to 24 Grange Road on Monday morning to discover that a shell had fallen through the roof front bedroom and into the parlour below, doing much damage. In the next road, Windsor, an unexploded shell also crashed through the roof of no.94, missing the bed by inches and knocking the corner off a table in the lounge below, before passing through a wall to bury itself several feet in the back garden. Luckily Mr Berry and his family were in the front room and escaped injury. 24 and 26 Clarendon Road, Seven Kings, were also damaged by a shell that fell in the road opposite. A house in Auckland Road also suffered damage when a shell fragment ricocheted through a kitchen window. Many 'what goes up must come down' jokes, circulating in Ilford and London, promoted the printing of patriotic and comic postcards featuring air-raid 'fun', adding a little to the morale on the Home Front.

Enough pilots were now experienced at flying the Sopwith Camel as a night fighter to enable Captain Murlis Green to double his patrol to 8 machines during the third successive night raid on 30th September. Although the handling characteristics of the snappy little biplane were giving Camels a increasingly bad reputation as killer of unwary pilots, No.44 Squadron suffered no casualties during the transition to night flying and subsequent nocturnal operations. The first Camel piloted by Lieut D V Armstrong, aided by the flickering lights from two gallon petrol tins filled with burning cotton waste and paraffin, became airborne at 1910 hrs. Two minutes later Lieut Cecil Arthur Lewis, an experienced 19 year old with two tours of duty as a pilot on the Western Front and eight enemy aeroplanes to his credit, started his first night patrol. Twenty year old Lieut Augustus Henry Orlebar, another front line pilot resting with Home Defence, had his first night patrol cut short by engine trouble, returning to Hainault Farm after twenty minutes. Lieut George Henry Hackwill, a seasoned veteran from No.22 Squadron in France before coming home as an instructor and hunting Gothas in the daylight raids, also carried out his first night patrol. Captain Murlis Green, airborne at 1945 hrs, fired a washout flare when persistent engine trouble forced him to land at the aerodrome within the hour. 'Flossie' Brand, determined as ever to come to grips with a Gotha, carried out two patrols between 1945 and 2155 hrs.

What Capt William Harold Haynes was up to when he encountered a London-bound Gotha flying at 6,000 ft above the forest at Lambourne, is open to speculation. As an ex-Intelligence officer, who had been dropped behind enemy lines early in the war, did he suspect German airmen were aware of the 10,000 ft minimum patrol height for night fighters deeming searchlights and anti-aircraft guns less of a risk at a lower altitude than the patrolling high flying Camels? Whatever the reason, it gave a pilot of No.44 Squadron the opportunity to fire his guns in anger, instead of practice on the much patched 'Hun' target at the small pond in Hainault. Haynes closed with the enemy bomber and at 100 yards fired 300 rounds before the startled German pilot took evasive action and disappeared as if by magic. Not content with the outcome Bill Haynes returned to Hainault Farm, re-armed and followed 2nd Lieut Banks into the air for the another search for the elusive Gothas.

Several Gothas were glimpsed briefly by Home Defence pilots, apart from Capt Haynes; a Sopwith 1½ Strutter, crewed by Capt F Billinge and his mechanic E Cooper, fired twenty rounds at one raider that promptly disappeared. The same crew from Suttons Farm encountered another bomber, but lost sight of it before they could get within range. The 30th September air raid would also be noted for the first recorded night sighting of an enemy bomber by a wireless tracking B.E.12 from No.50 Squadron; once again the German airmen managed to elude their pursuer.

The month passed very quickly for 2nd Lieut Herbert Beck of Mayfair Avenue, who reported to No.3 Squadron as a pilot from No.43 Training Squadron at the beginning of September. No.3 Squadron, equipped with French built

Sopwith Camels of C Flight, No.3 Squadron, in France (*G S Leslie*)

No.3 Squadron

Morane Parasol two seat machines, had been engaged in reconnaissance and artillery spotting on the Western Front for three years. The arrival of Bertie Beck at Lechelle aerodrome coincided with No. 3 Squadron commencing re-equipping with Sopwith Camels. His first flying duties entailed ferrying the venerable but obsolete aeroplanes back to No. 2 Aeroplane Depôt. Bertie may have briefly met another local airman serving with No.3 Squadron as an observer, however, with the rapid transition to a scout squadron, surplus observers were quickly posted to other units.

2nd Lieut George Ebbon Randall of Third Avenue, Manor Park, having served with No. 3 Squadron since April, requested and returned to Home Establishment for pilot training.

The fortunes of Stanley Apling of Thorold Road, Ilford, dramatically changed during 1917: his enthusiasm for aviation had not waned since photographing A C Hucks and his Blériot monoplane in pre-war days. Upon leaving Ilford County High School, aged 17, the previous year, he became an employee of the Royal Insurance Company. Stanley volunteered for a commission in the Royal Flying Corps after a former employee, now in the RFC, mentioned the excellent pay - 10/- daily when commissioned, increasing to £1 daily when commencing flying instruction. In March, Stanley returned his application form and heard nothing, until his call-up papers for the Army at a shilling a day, arrived shortly after his 18th birthday in May. Two months of basic infantry training at Cannock Chase ended with notification of

his transfer to the RFC; the following day found him billeted as an officer cadet in an hotel at St Leonards, waited on by girls in the dining hall. October, found Cadet Apling on a three month military aeronautics course at Oxford University.

In the early hours of Monday, 1st October, Colonel John Laurie of 7 Belfort Gardens, Ilford, in charge of a Salvation Army mobile unit, arrived in south west London, where most of the damage had been caused during the latest air-raid. The Salvation Army provided sleeping accommodation for bombed-out families and assistance for those suffering shock. Colonel and Mrs Laurie were still busy at 09.00 hrs when the Prime Minister and Lord French arrived at the scene. During the morale boosting tour of the bombed areas that morning, David Lloyd George and the Field-Marshal were greeted yet again with demands for air-raids on German cities. The Prime Minister placated angry crowds with the promise, 'We shall bomb Germany with compound interest'. Returning to the War Office, Lloyd George urgently summoned the War Cabinet. Adding to the anxiety felt at the meeting, following the fourth successive night on London, Winston Churchill, in charge of munition production, expressed his deep concern about growing absenteeism among the workers on mornings following the increasing night raids. The Cabinet decided that immediate action be taken to commence bombing German targets, with at least one squadron independent of the B.E.F. Field-Marshall Haig received a wire recalling Major-General Trenchard from France.

Eighteen Gothas embarked upon another raid the same evening, but, for various reasons, only 11 bombers crossed the coast; six bombing London. Seven Camel pilots patrolled from Hainault Farm and hawkeyed Capt Haynes saw a

Gotha at 12,000 ft near Epping, but it vanished quickly among the clouds. Of 19 Home Defence pilots aloft during the raid, only Haynes reported a sighting, although the casualties were regarded as light, 11 fatal and 42 injured. Keyed up defences over-reacted to unidentified aeroplanes hidden by ground mist just a few hours later. Shortly after 13.00 hrs, on Tuesday, 2nd October, Ilford Special Constables cycled through the town with air-raid warning placards and gunfire was heard, and schools were hurriedly closed for the rest of the day. Official reports stated the enemy aeroplanes were driven off: had the truth been known, the keyed up population of London would have enjoyed a good laugh along with the airmen at Hainault Farm.

AA defences, uninformed of the urgent summons the evening before, fired upon 3 two-seat R.E.8 biplanes ferrying Trenchard and two staff officers from France. Lack of communication by top brass had been responsible for the 'daylight raid' and the subsequent unexpected half-day holiday for Ilford school children. Greeted by anti-aircraft fire on crossing the Kent coast, Trenchard's pilot prudently landed at Lympne. Continuing his journey to London by road, Trenchard observed at first hand the almost deserted thoroughfares of the City due to the general alert. He reassured the War Cabinet that RFC bombers would soon be operational from an aerodrome near the German border. Two flights of single engine D.H.4 day bombers and nine of twin engined Handley Page night bombers were promised in addition to the squadron already earmarked for

detachment from Headquarters Wing.

On Tuesday, 9th October, in spite of the heavy rain falling for several days, British infantry forded a flooded canal and somehow, under heavy fire, crossed a battlefield knee deep in mud to capture the ruins of Poelcapelle. Among the many casualties was Charles Douglas Young of 110 Grosvenor Road, serving with the Rifle Brigade, who died of wounds on Wednesday, 10th October. Twenty year old Charles had been a founder of the 3rd Ilford Troop of Boy Scouts, Secretary and a playing member of the Grosvenor Athletic, Football & Cricket Club.

On the same day, 2nd Lieut Herbert Beck of Mayfair Avenue, with No.3 Squadron RFC at Warloy Bailon, escaped injury when a Camel he had just collected from No.2 Aeroplane Depôt crashed during take-off in the rain.

The funeral took place at St. Mary's Cemetery on Wednesday, 17th October, for another victim of the 13th June daylight raid on the City that had already claimed 162 lives. The death of 21 year old Miss Nellie Cakebread of 49, Percy Road, Goodmayes, had been due to tragic circumstances. Apparently uninjured by a bomb that fell near to her office, the young woman continued going to business for a few days until she became very ill. Nellie was taken to St Bartholomew's Hospital, where eventually it was discovered that poison gas, presumably emitted from the German bomb, had seriously damaged her lungs. German bombs contained an explosive mixture of 60% TNT and 40% hexanitrodiphenylamine, an extremely toxic substance. Only women workers between the ages of 21 and 40, wearing protective clothing and masks, were allowed to work with TNT and then only for short periods at a time. Such was the wartime sense of humour that, whilst this helped to alleviate nausea and coughing up of thick bitter tasting yellow phlegm and other irritating symptoms, the unfortunate women munition workers were referred to as 'canaries' - due to a yellow discoloration of their skin, another side-effect of working with TNT

On the day poor Nellie Cakebread was laid to rest, two flights of De Haviland 4 day bombers of the new 41st Wing carried out a raid on Germany. No.55 Squadron had, as Trenchard assured the War Cabinet, become operational within days of arriving at Ochey. Newspaper reports of the daylight raid on an iron foundry near Saarbrucken by the Independent Air Force and subsequent raids subdued the clamouring for reprisal bombings of Germany.

On Friday, 19th October, the last Sopwith Triplane constructed by the Ilford Aeroplane Company, N9512, was delivered by road to Hendon; obsolete for front line service, it eventually served at the School of Aerial Fighting, Marske.

A Zeppelin raid on England, planned by Fregattenkapitan Peter Strasser that night, was intended to restore the Naval Airship Service to favour once more with the High Command. Thirteen awesome flying machines, the undersides of their hulls painted matt black to avoid detection by searchlights, giving them a sinister and more warlike appearance, were ready. A change of plan, brought about by the elements, reduced the raiding fleet to eleven, as two Zeppelins were unable to be marched from their sheds because of strong cross winds. Lightened to operate at 20,000 ft, Strasser's flying ships were to target the less well defended north of England. An unpredicted gale at the great height they

were operating, scattered the fleet with disastrous results; five of the massive craft were written off. Had it not been for the unusual atmospheric conditions prevailing, the raid would have caused the defences problems. In fact, at 22.30 hrs all searchlights were covered. The lights would be more helpful to the Zeppelin crews as they struggled in sub-zero temperatures with primitive oxygen breathing tubes to maintain their equipment and engines. L45, blown well off course, careered across blacked-out England unseen and unheard, was taken by surprise as the dimmed-out Metropolis came rushing into view through the clouds below. One 660 lb missile, released in haste, fell on the corner of Piccadilly Circus, demolishing the premises of Swan & Edgar; the second fell on 103 Albany Road, Camberwell; a third hit 13 Glenview Road, Lewisham. By covering the searchlights the LADA had almost concealed the existence of London far below to the troubled Zeppelin commander. Unable to return to base in the face of the gale, L45, attempting to reach Southern Germany, crash-landed in France, where the exhausted crew were taken prisoner.

The disastrous 'Silent Raid', as the 19th October air raid later became known, ended the airship raids on England for 1917.

On the Western Front, American infantry began to take over front-line trenches in the French sector on Saturday, 27th October.

The arrival of American airmen at Ilford the following month went almost unnoticed by the residents of the town, due to the wide variety of khaki army uniforms worn by officers seconded to the

Royal Flying Corps. It came as a surprise, to say the least, for Capt G W Murlis Green to receive a small detachment of cadets from the United States Air Service for flying instruction with his busy Home Defence unit. The tremendous response, following the call for volunteers by the Air Service in the wake of America declaring war on Germany in April, swamped their limited training facilities. Many would-be aviators of the fledgling U.S. air force found themselves training with their British, French and Italian allies.

No.44 Squadron was an eye-opener for six Americans posted to Hainault Farm, via Oxford and Grantham, where the military discipline had been hard. They were delighted to find there was little or no formality in the squadron Mess and soon made friends. Billeted in pairs in the town they were collected every morning by squadron tenders for breakfast at the farmhouse, before flight training. Lieutenants Jack Devery and Clayton Knight were billeted at an off license, run by Mrs Plume and her two teenage daughters. "All in all," recalled Clayton Knight in later years, "it was a wonderful set-up for Devery and me".

The billeting allowance for servicemen in the town paid, 9d (3½ pence) per day, or 2/6d (12½ pence) per day, if meals were required.

On Monday, 29th October, a solitary Gotha, braving the gusting wind and dense cloud, bombed between Burnham and Southend, without causing damage or casualties. Six Camels were sent aloft from Hainault Farm, only to be recalled within half an hour due to rising gale force winds.

On Wednesday, 31st October, ten days after his posting to No.84 Squadron at Liettres in France, Lieut. E W Powell was killed in action over the enemy lines. Powell had been the RFC officer who landed the first B.E.2c biplane at Hainault Farm on 4th October, 1915.

London was again the target for the night of Wednesday, 31st October, when the Gothas launched their first incendiary raid on England. Twenty-two Gothas carrying over six tons of bombs crossed the Kent coast, approached the City from the south to skirt the well defended eastern approaches. Arriving at irregular intervals through the drizzle, at least nine raiders reached the outskirts of the metropolis, to be greeted by a fierce barrage and probing searchlights. Of the twelve pilots patrolling from Hainault Farm during the raid, only Capt W H Haynes had a brief glimpse of a raider at 12,000 ft. Lieut A H Orlebar taking off in Camel B2378, found the Le-Rhône running badly and returned to the aerodrome to resume his patrol in another machine. Wounded by a Turkish sniper at Gallipoli and transferred to the RFC on his return to England, Orlebar had served with No.19 Squadron, where he had forced down two Albatros scouts.

Despite the bad weather, the only mishap at Hainault Farm during the busy night occurred at 02.30 hrs, as a Sopwith 1½ Strutter of No. 78 Squadron from Suttons Farm sheered off its undercarriage attempting to land; the pilot had become lost in the murk. Once again, fortune favoured the defenders; the incendiary bombs did little damage, except in Ramsgate, where a gasometer and private

'Will it still fly, mister?' Ilford schoolboys dying to lend the men of No.44 Squadron a hand with Camel that overshot the aerodrome, landing in Hainault Road (*R Gerrard/G S Leslie*)

No.82 Squadron

property were destroyed. The raiders returned to Belgium, but mist and possible damage accounted for five crashing as they attempted to land. Had anyone in the London area managed to sleep through the anti-aircraft barrages, they were certainly awakened by the 'All Clear', as several hundred Boy Scouts throughout the City blew cheerfully into their bugles. The authorities decided to try bugle calls, then in use as air-raid warnings for the citizens of Paris. A private business company had to step forward with a Lloyds insurance policy, when the Home Office claimed they would not be responsible for Boy Scout buglers killed or injured on air-raid duty.

On Tuesday, 6th November, Canadian 1st and 2nd Divisions captured the ruins of Passchendaele village, after the bitterest and bloodiest battles on the British front. Field Marshal von Hindenburg had ordered that Passchendaele must be held at all costs. From the occupied high ground, exhausted British infantry could now observe, stretching to the far horizon, the plain of Flanders, for the first time since October, 1914.

On Sunday, 11th November, spectators along Hainault Road, watching the aerial fighting practice taking place, witnessed the second fatal crash at Hainault Farm. Three months had elapsed since Lieut George Craig had spun his Camel into the ground half a mile from the aerodrome: the second accident had been no less tragic or spectacular.

Lieut Walter Bertram 'Bert' Wood, MC, had served with No.29 Squadron before his posting to Ilford a few weeks earlier. He had been officially credited with 13 of the 18 enemy machines he shot down in 36 combats over the lines.

Bert had been requested by a less experienced member of the squadron to practice air fighting with him and agreed, after having obtained permission from his Flight Commander. As the two Camels soared aloft in mock combat, 2nd Lieut Robert Mordaunt Foster, another ex-front line pilot, watched through a pair of binoculars and was able to give an eye-witness account of the accident at the inquest, held at the Ilford Town Hall the following Wednesday.

Lieut Foster stated that he 'saw the deceased manoeuvre into a spin away from the other machine, that was a natural thing to do. He had started at about 2,500 ft and at approximately 700 ft stopped spinning and came out on his back; this gave rise in my mind that all was not well, within 200 ft from the ground the machine nose dived, he was then too close to the ground to right himself.'

Captain Henry Hackwill, C Flight commander, had already given evidence at the inquest, saying that, in his opinion, the deceased either lost consciousness or fainted in the air and so lost control of the machine, otherwise so capable a pilot would have been able to get out of any difficulty he might have been in. Dr Frank Collins, in charge of the inquest, asked Lieut Foster, "Do you share the Captain's opinion that he lost control of the machine through unconsciousness?" Lieut Foster replied, "Yes". The inquest found that death was due to accident and sympathy was offered to the parents of Lieut Wood, who had previously lost their older son, Edwin, killed in action on 27th September. At No.44 Squadron it was the opinion, that 19 year old Bert Wood may not have fully recovered from a bout of influenza at the time of his fatal accident. The subsequent transfer of the coffin to Grimsby, for a funeral with full military honours, was carried out by Messrs Gilderson & Son of Seven Kings in Ilford High Road.

After his posting to Hainault Farm Bert Wood had received a letter from Major Chapman, the CO of his old squadron, that went on to say, "It is not for you to thank us, but for us to thank you for all the Huns you shot down for the squadron and for always being so cheery in the Mess, as it helped tremendously to keep up the tails of new pilots in these very strenuous times. I expect you will get a Flight in about a month from now. Have a jolly good rest and take things really easy".

Lieut Charles Stewart Lavers, an experienced 21 year old fighter pilot of No.1 Squadron, replaced the unfortunate Bert Wood at Ilford a few days later.

On Thursday evening, 22nd November, 600 people took part in a Whist Drive held at the Ilford Town Hall, for the benefit of the Emergency Hospital Fund. Organised by members of No.44 Squadron RFC, with the assistance of Mrs Christobel, Miss Flood and Mr Alfred Bott, the whist drive was the largest so far held in the Town Hall. During the interval, Mr Bott auctioned various items donated by the airmen of Hainault Farm, including a piece of alloy framework from the Billericay Zeppelin that fetched 11 shillings; a larger section of the L32 brought in another 21 shillings; a rotary engine cylinder from a British aeroplane shot down in France, bearing a bullet hole, was sold for 3 guineas; it was however a Triplex windscreen from another British machine, complete with a bullet that brought the top price of the sale at £5. A grand total of £20 from the auction was added to the proceeds of the whist drive.

No.44 Squadron stewards, Flt/Sgt's Jennings and Shaw and Cpl Sanders, assisted by Mr Lowe and Mr South of the Mayfield Cricket Club, did all they could to add to the enjoyment of the evening. Most of the prizes were handiwork from local aerodromes; those from Hainault Farm were most conspicuous - they included clock stands, photo frames and walking sticks made from damaged aeroplane components. Three special prizes, presented by the officers of No.44 Squadron, were a plated nut dish and crackers, a salad bowl and a plated tankard. At close of play, Lady Briggs and Mrs Bott presented the prizes, Sir Peter Briggs presented boxes of chocolates to Mrs Christobel and Miss Flood, in recognition of the assistance they had been to the Royal Flying Corps, and thanked the officers and men of Hainault Farm for their generous assistance to the Ilford Emergency Hospital.

Two weeks' leave from France in the middle of November had flown by for 2nd Lieut `Bertie' Beck at home with his family in Mayfair Avenue, fortunately a spell of bad weather prevented enemy air raids from marring the reunion. All good things must come to an end and 2nd Lieut Beck said farewell to his family at Victoria Station to rejoin No.3 Squadron at Walloy Bailion on Sunday, 2nd December.

In the early hours of Thursday, 6th December, sweeping searchlights reflecting for split seconds, the ghost-like balloon apron hanging motionless in the night sky, warned those people of Ilford still up and about of an impending air-raid. A high flying Rumpler biplane off the English coast confirmed by two-way wireless that

19-year-old Lieut Walter B Wood (*Geoffrey Wood*)

Lieut Cecil Lewis, the last surviving
member of No.44 Squadron,
died in January, 1997

conditions were at last favourable to the Gotha Squadron's weather officer. The London area received a warning at 01.30 hrs, as the first of 16 Gothas and two Giants crossed the Kent coast. In Ilford the occasional distant gunfire could be heard, as German aircraft showered incendiary bombs on Whitstable, Herne Bay, Margate and Ramsgate. Three quarters of the bombers' load were incendiary, the remaining half ton of explosive bombs carried by a Giant were dropped on the outskirts of Dover.

It was a cold morning, with roofs and pavements of the town heavily coated with frost; Capt `Flossie' Brand and 2nd Lieut Banks, with the exposed areas of their faces smeared with bear grease as protection against frostbite, patrolled for well over two hours in the intense cold without seeing an enemy machine. The majority of Ilfordians, assuming the danger past after a lull of an hour or so, sought the warmth of their beds, only to be rudely awakened at 05.00 hrs.

The `cock-crow' raid as it became known, began with a barrage of anti-aircraft gunfire, creeping nearer and depositing large amounts of `shrapnel' all over Ilford. One by one, six Gotha bombers struck at the City from different directions, dropping 276 incendiary and 9 explosive bombs. Fortunately, there were only three fatal casualties in the City and one of those died through wounds received from anti-aircraft fire; 15 other people were injured. The London Fire Brigade attended 52 incidents between 04.30 and 06.00 hrs; one of the serious fires destroyed the large furniture store and warehouse of B. Cohen & Co, in Curtain Road, Shoreditch. A cigar-box factory close by; a clothing factory; and the auditorium of the Great Assembly Room in the Mile End Road, were among the badly damaged buildings

The total casualty list for the early morning air-raid of Thursday, 6th December, totalled 8 killed and 28 injured; many of the injuries were inflicted by falling shell fragments. None of the 34 Home Defence pilots, including six from No.44 Squadron airborne during the raid, searching for the enemy machines, made a positive sighting. Thanks to the furious barrage by the anti-aircraft gunners, the `cock-crow' raiders were not allowed to get away unscathed. The crew of Gotha G V/906/16 were forced to jettison their bomb-load after a nearby exploding shell shattered the propeller of their port engine above Canvey Island. The young pilot, Gemeiner [Private] J Rzechtalski, had no choice, as the large biplane, not an easy machine to land under ideal conditions, began to lose height rapidly: the Gotha had to be landed in enemy country in the dark. As Rzechtalski cursed his luck, the aircraft commander, Leut R Wessells, pointed out the flares of Rochford aerodrome in the distance. Approaching the welcoming `L' of landing lights, Wessells, by pure luck, fired the correct colour flare for permission to land. It would have been a good landing, but for the wing striking a tree and slewing the Gotha into a crash landing on the golf course.

Capt Cecil Lewis, who had been transferred from Hainault Farm to No.61 Squadron at Rochford a few weeks earlier, recalled in his memoirs, "Mechanics, thinking it was one of their own, ran to

Captain C J Quinton Brand at Hainault Farm in the cold winter of 1917-18

the crash site. They were much surprised to see three 'Huns' crawling out of the wreck. The Germans were quickly hustled away before they could do any further damage to their aircraft; except for bruises all were quite unhurt. British officers went out to inspect the broken, petrol-soaked bomber: one of them found a flare pistol; as he was showing his prize to another officer, it went off with a glorious flash. A magnesium flare bounced along the ground, and the whole heap exploded in flames; by morning only the charred engines and a twisted framework remained".

The second Gotha downed by AA fire had been hit during the fierce London barrage at 05.00 hrs. Both the pilot, Vizefeldwebel B Senf, and the commander, Leut S Schulte, were on their 13th raid on England. With one engine on fire, the Sergeant pilot successfully landed the Gotha in a small field near Canterbury and the crew surrendered to a Special Constable, after setting the rest of their machine on fire. The crew of a third Gotha perished in the North Sea.

Later Thursday morning, Boy Scout buglers sounded the all clear in Ilford, where the air-raid had come as an unpleasant surprise to many after a five week lull.

At Hainault Farm aerodrome modifications were began on the armament of several Camels. Capt F W Honnett, at Suttons Farm, had converted obsolete Sopwith 1½ Strutters into a single seat machines with upward firing Lewis Guns, to bridge the gap until No. 78 Squadron received replacement Camels. What No.44 Squadron realised on examining the Sopwith 'Comic', as some

wag had named the Hornchurch fighter, was the fact the 'Comic' armed with over-wing Lewis guns could make use of the anti-Zepp ammunition. The mixture of explosive and incendiary bullets were too dangerous for use with synchronised Vickers guns firing through the propellers - if the timing mechanism failed a flat nosed explosive round would shatter the whirling propeller with disastrous results.

Prior to their arrival in Ilford for flying training, the six would-be aviators from America had never seen a Sopwith Camel: the name suggested some sort of hump backed monstrosity. Lieut Clayton Knight soon changed his mind after arriving at Hainault Farm; the Camels, he recalled, were a revelation of trimness and grace in the air. The small group of 'Yanks' were warmly welcomed by the colonials of No.44 Squadron and soon overcame the natural reserve of the English pilots to become close friends. Knight had his first flight at Hainault Farm on the morning of Saturday, 8th December, but not in a single seat Sopwith Camel. Two B.E. 2e biplanes, single bay versions of the machines used so successfully against the Zeppelin the previous year, were used to teach the Americans the rudiments of flying. South African Lieut D V Armstrong could not resist looping B.E. A8646 several times during Clayton Knight's first flight above Hainault Farm. On landing Capt Quinton Brand, Armstrong's Flight Commander told the pilot off in no uncertain terms for stunting a B.E.2e that had a reputation for shedding the top wing if manoeuvred violently. Armstrong just smiled and replied, "Well, I didn't take the extensions off the old B.E." Clayton Knight was not surprised to hear the riggers checked the overhanging wire braced upper wing and to find it had not been strained. Knight maintained it was Quinton Brand who later taught him all he knew about flying, although he did not solo at Ilford.

On 12th December, Hptmn Rudolf Kleine, the CO of the `English Squadron', leading 17 Gothas in a short range daylight raid on British military depôts near Ypres, fell to the guns of Nieuport B6825, piloted by Captain William Wendell Rogers of No.1 Squadron.

The following afternoon the funeral cortège of Air Mechanic Thomas John Crosswell left 133 Ilford Lane, en route for the City of London Cemetery, via the Ilford Broadway. Thomas Crosswell had been attached to the School of Aerial Gunnery at Hythe in Kent, where his wife had stayed at lodgings close by. During the course of his duties on Thursday, 6th December, whilst riding a motorcycle combination without a passenger, he collided with a motor lorry, sustaining head injuries, and died two hours after admission to the local hospital.

A light dusting of snow covered the fields of Hainault Farm on Tuesday, 18th December. It was a perfect morning for flying, but tragedy again struck the Ilford aerodrome. 2nd Lieut Vane Carrington Manuel was a long way from his home town of Vancouver, Canada, and new to No.44 Squadron, when he spun Camel B2A78 into the ground. Once again the verdict of the inquest, held a few days later at the Ilford Town Hall, would be accidental death.

Klaxon hooters, announcing that the `Hun' were crossing the Essex and Kent coasts, blasted the gloom from the Mess at Hainault Farm on the evening of `Larry' Manuel's fatal crash. Lieut J T Collier raced down the flare path at 18.36 hrs, followed a few minutes later by Capt Murlis Green, half an hour into his patrol at 10,000 ft above the goods yard at Goodmayes. Guided by criss-crossing searchlight beams nearby, Murlis Green saw the twin exhausts of an enemy machine. The C.O. of No.44 Squadron, piloting Camel B5192, recently converted with over wing Lewis guns, closed to within 30 yards of the bomber. As the searchlights found and illuminated the Gotha and its tiny pursuer, anti-aircraft gunners below watching fascinated. Attacking from beneath, Murlis Green opened fire to find his right hand gun frozen out of action, the flash from the other Lewis blinded him, but not before he saw bombs falling from the Gotha and banked his Camel swiftly out of their way. Murlis Green closed with the Gotha three more times, in the last attack undisturbed by searchlights, firing 60 rounds at close range, forcing the Gotha to dive; caught in the bomber's slipstream the Camel went into a spin. Quickly regaining control, Murlis Green found to his anger that the enemy had eluded him in those valuable seconds.

The falling bombs, seen by the pilot in his attack, fell on a Canadian military storehouse in Spa Road, Bermondsey, at 19.25 hrs. Having lost his quarry, Capt Murlis Green returned to the waiting flare path at Hainault Farm, refuelled, re-armed and flew off into the night again at 19.54 hrs to continue the hunt.

Murlis Green, remembered as the English `ace' by the enemy flyers in

Macedonia, began to give the Germans bloody noses long before the outbreak of war. As a student at Bad Godesberg in his youth, Murlis Green won a German school boxing championship and, unknown to him that night, he had won another bout with a German. Leut Friedrich Ketelsen's relief at shaking off the aggressive English flier would be short-lived, Murlis Green's sustained burst of machine gun fire had seriously damaged the Gotha's starboard engine. Heading towards the coast, the over-heated engine emitted a sheet of flame and cut out completely. Ketelsen attempted to return to Belgium on one engine, but losing height rapidly and only ten miles out to sea, the pilot realised the crippled machine would not make the crossing and turned back towards the Kent coast. The damaged Gotha belly flopped into the icy water off Folkestone and began to sink at 21.00 hrs. Rescue was at hand, an armed trawler of the Royal Navy arriving in time to save two members of the crew, but the exhausted pilot, clinging to the upper wing, fell into the sea and drowned.

Two other Ilford airmen encountered bombers during the raid. Lieut Jack Collier, in Camel B3859, closed with a bomber and fired 120 rounds before the slipstream from the larger machine flipped the Camel into a spin. Regaining control of his aeroplane, Collier found his cockpit instrument lighting had failed and, unable to locate the Gotha again, Collier wisely returned to Hainault Farm for a safe landing at 19.39 hrs.

Capt George Henry Hackwill, flying Camel B2402, encountered a bomber at 10,300 feet above Woodford. Closing in to attack from the rear, Hackwill also found his machine in an involuntary spin, due to the slipstream of the larger machine. Quickly countering the spin and relocating the bomber, the third Ilford pilot opened fire, only to have his night vision temporarily blinded by the muzzle flash of the two Vickers guns directly in front of his face. Having lost the enemy in those vital seconds, Capt Hackwill safely landed at Hainault Farm twenty minutes later.

Morning papers on Wednesday, 19th December, 1917 carried the news of a pilot's successful attack on a Gotha, forcing it down in the sea near Folkestone. It made cheery reading for Capt Tryggve Gran, recovering from wounds in a London Hospital. The previous night's air-raid had been a very noisy experience, to say the least, for the bedridden patient. On 30th November, whilst carrying out a low level attack on horsedrawn and mechanical transport near Douai, Tryggve Gran received a shell splinter in his leg. With help from his observer, 2nd Lieut G D Shand, he brought the damaged FE2b A5586 back across the lines to an emergency landing ground on the outskirts of Arras.

During the afternoon of 19th December, the Norwegian was pleased to receive a visit from an old friend from No.44 Squadron, Capt George Hackwill, and delighted to learn that another friend, Capt Murlis Green, had been the pilot responsible for downing the Gotha. In the course of their lengthy conversation, George Hackwill described his encounter over Woodford the night before with a huge enemy bomber with five engines - actually the Giant R.12 had six engines coupled in pairs, turning three propellers. The Giant dropped two 660 lb bombs and incendiaries on London; six Gothas also raided the capital, whilst the remainder bombed the long-suffering population of Kent. Well over 5 tons of bombs were dropped during the Tuesday night raid by 13 Gothas and a single Giant; the damaged inflicted on London was the worst since Kptlt Mathy and his crew dropped the first 660 lb bombs on the City during the 8th September, 1915, Naval Zeppelin air raid. Casualties for the latest raid by German Army aeroplanes were 14 killed and 83 injured; during the 1915 Zeppelin raid, 7 RNAS machines were airborne, one BE2c crashed, killing the unfortunate pilot, another returned with engine trouble and a third made a forced landing. Of 47 aeroplanes hunting the enemy during the latest raid, two BE2 biplanes crashed on landing, and another No.78 Squadron 'Comic' sheered off its undercarriage landing.

The safe return of all nine Hainault Farm Camels flying patrols on the night of 18th December, 1917, and the later confirmation of their CO's Hun kept the tails of No.44 Squadron up, following the fatal crash of 2nd Lieut V C Manuel earlier in the day.

The following week the Canadian was buried with full military honours by the officers and men of No.44 Squadron at St Mary's Church in the Ilford High Road. Lieut Clayton Knight, one of the six Americans, acted as pall-bearer; he and 2nd Lieut Thomas Michael O'Neill, a stocky Irishman, being the shortest of the pall-bearers, carried the front of the coffin and more than their fair share of the weight. Clayton Knight recalled, 'In swinging around over the grave,

'Dubs' [O'Neill] nearly fell in; all his Irish superstitions arose as he took this as an omen of his own death.' Five months later O'Neill, flying Camel C 8298 with No.43 Squadron, would be reported Killed In Action, east of Bailleul on 8th May, 1918.

The gloomy outlook for many Ilford people, as the fourth Christmas of the war approached, was not shared by eighteen year old Stanley Apling. Having completed his three month's course at Oxford University, he had been granted a commission and sent home on indefinite leave as a 2nd Lieutenant in the Royal Flying Corps, awaiting flight training. Stanley's leave lasted a whole month, enabling him to share Christmas at home with his family.

Seven Camels patrolled from Hainault Farm on the night of Saturday, 22nd December, in expectation of meeting an enemy bomber. Fortunately for the Home Defences, stormy weather thwarted the German intentions of raiding London; one Gotha that did cross the Kent coast landed south of Margate on one engine and the crew set their machine on fire before police officers arrived by taxi to arrest them. Other Gothas and a Giant were diverted to targets along the French coast; two more Giants dropped their bomb loads in the sea off Ramsgate and Sandwich.

Weather prevented Home Defence pilots south of the Thames from patrolling. All the 18 night fighters airborne, including the Sopwith Camels from Hainault Farm, returned safely. On Christmas Eve, ten single engined D.H.4's of No. 55 Squadron flew 200 miles over enemy territory in daylight to bomb a chlorine gas factory at Mannheim. Several bombs damaged the railway station an hour after the Imperial train carrying the Kaiser and his Staff returning from the Verdun Front to Berlin passed through.

Christmas Day, 1917, had been quiet for 2nd Lieut Bertie Beck and his comrades of No.3 Squadron at Warloy aerodrome; after dark with oil drained from the Camels to prevent it becoming syrupy with the extreme cold in the hangers, the squadron prepared to have Christmas dinner and make merry. Following the toast to the King, presents purchased in Amiens along with the festive fare were brought in to the Mess and placed in front of the CO, Major Raymond Barker, who announced all the presents were in the nature of good luck mascots for his pilots.

One by one, their names were called in alphabetical order, the first being Lieut A G D Alderson, who recalled "the CO with a twinkle in his eye, handed me a small parcel neatly wrapped in brown paper, saying that I had to open it before returning to my seat. Removing the outer coverings according to instructions, a white box was revealed which, when opened, contained something which at first sight I hoped might be a silk scarf, except for the fact it had a lace edging, and, with cheeks I knew betrayed my embarrassment, I held up an example of the most intimate feminine apparel". Amid applause, Alderson thanked the CO for his mascot that he would regard as essential to his future well-being and was pleased to see later that he was not the only pilot in the squadron whose luck now depended upon feminine underwear.

During the evening, Bertie Beck joined in the sing-song around the Mess piano, singing all the popular songs of the day, many being parodied by the young airmen, one song in particular was very popular with the RFC; the verses varied from squadron to squadron, but the sentiment of the following verse was a typical example.

"As the aviator lay dying
These last words he did say,
Take the cylinder out of my stomach,
The connecting-rod out of my brain,
From the small of my back take the crankshaft,
And assemble the engine again."

On Thursday, 27th December, Bertie Beck flew with Lieuts Alderson and Brown on the dawn patrol, led by Capt Eric Hughes. The four Camels attacked German infantry with 20 lb Cooper bombs and machine guns with good results, in spite of the bad weather. Two days later Beck, carrying out another low level bomb and machine gun attack on enemy infantry at 0800 hrs with Capt Michie, Alderson and Christie, witnessed the latter make a safe landing with a leg wound on the advance Landing Ground at Bapaume.

Edward and Ellen Young of Cavenham Gardens, Ilford, received an official War Office telegram; seldom did a W O telegram contain good news. On Sunday, 30th December, HMT *Aragon* had been torpedoed by a German submarine outside Alexandria Harbour; their 19 year old son Air Mechanic Sidney Thomas Young was reported missing, believed drowned. The body of another local RFC man, Air Mechanic William Ernest Ridgewell, also on board the ill-fated troopship, en route for the Egyptian Expeditionary Force, was recovered. His parents William and Sarah Ridgewell, of Brandon Cottages, Marks Gate, Collier Row, were later informed their 36 year old son had been buried in the Hada War Memorial Cemetery, in Egypt.

On the morning of Monday, 31st December, Bertie Beck and C Flight were again carrying out low level strafing behind the enemy lines with machine guns and bombs. The lucky mascots presented by the CO of No 3 Squadron on Christmas day added to the revelry, but Major Raymond Barker knew his pilots needed all the luck they could get. Flying unarmoured fabric covered biplanes on orders from Headquarters for low level support of the Army put his men in extreme danger from massed small arms fire and enemy fighters above.

In spite of heavy losses of machines in action and accidents, the RFC at the end of the year had 8,350 aeroplanes on strength, the RNAS 2,741.

New Year's Eve in Ilford, following the most depressing three months of the war, was not celebrated as in bygone years; the sacrifice of 240,000 British casualties in the third battle of Ypres for so little gain, hung over the town. Russia, the great ally, who many believed, alongside France would win the war in 1914, before the B.E.F could play an active part, had collapsed into anarchy and civil war. On the Italian front, a disastrous retreat at Caporetto in October forced Allied forces to rush 5 British and 6 French divisions to Italy, to prevent another Ally from breaking ranks. Following mutinies among French infantry units during 1917, the total number of men deserting peaked 27,000 by the end of the year. The appointment of Georges Clemenceau as French Prime Minister to form a new government in November, and living up to his reputation as 'The Tiger' at seventy-six years of age, proved he was still the most formidable man in France, who would rapidly revitalize the fighting spirit of the nation.

The first night fighters seen through the eyes of American WWI airman and aviation artist, Clayton Knight. The painting on display at the Pentagon, in Washington, DC, depicts Hainault Farm aerodrome during an air-raid in the winter of 1917/18. (*USAF Art Collection*)

1918

On Thursday, 3rd January, four DFW CV biplanes, on reconnaissance along the British lines, were surprised by four Camels of C Flight No.3 Squadron, anti-aircraft units confirmed that 2nd Lieut H Beck shot one of the German two-seaters down, completely out of control.

The same day saw the formation, at last, of the Air Ministry; Lord Rothermere became the First Secretary of State for Air, and General Hugh Montague Trenchard, Chief of Air Staff.

On Saturday, 5th January, after a cup of 'sergeant majors' and biscuits, Bertie Beck and C Flight left Dignity and Impudence (a St Bernard and a terrier), the squadron mascots, huddled by the fire in the Mess to face another dawn patrol. Resembling Bubelin, the rotund character in the Michelin Tyre Company adverts, the pilots wore heavy leather coats, thigh-length soft leather boots lined with sheep skin, with an extra pair of thin silk gloves inside their leather gauntlets and ladies' stockings worn under their flying helmets. Despite the intense cold, squadron records indicate that the Camels of C Flight did splendidly by dawn's early light, ground strafing supply columns with bombs and bullets.

On the Home Front, the scarcity of timber, in great demand for the war effort, brought more hardship; the people of Ilford now had to apply for a permit to purchase a single plank of wood. Coal rationing did not eliminate the shortage or the queues at the town's coal yards, when it was available. New Year economy campaigns urged civilians 'to eat slowly, you will need less food' and 'by keeping warm, you will need less food'. During the month, agitation among food queues in Brentwood and Chelmsford almost amounted to riots. However, the U-boat menace was now in decline, as the convoy system brought the sinking of allied merchant ships to a new low.

The increasing number of airmen undergoing flight training presented some problems to the expanding RNAS aerodrome at Fairlop. PFO T E W Browne, after being well treated at a hospital in Waltham Cross for mumps, returned to Chingford aerodrome and a posting to the Sub-Station at Fairlop, where his billet was a large canvas tent. In later years, Tom recalled, "sometimes we woke up to find snow lying on the ends of our beds; this did us no harm, but the Mess piano, already weakened by baptisms of beer, gave up completely the day after it had been snowbound."

By comparison with the airmen sleeping and messing under canvas at the RNAS aerodrome along Forest Road during the winter of 1917/18, conditions for the pilots of No.44 Squadron RFC at Hainault Farm were luxurious. The Americans training with the RFC at Ilford were billeted in the town, but they would often stay on after dark to assist and watch their instructors taking off to hunt for enemy bombers. Lt Clayton Knight, would help Capt Quinton Brand on with his heavy leather coat, which was a difficult task, as the airman had been wounded serving with No.1 Squadron and suffered a half-paralysed left arm. One evening, Clayton Knight recalls, the squadron C.O. sat around the open fire in the Mess talking to his pilots, as they made toast on long handled forks. The furniture in the Mess was a mixture of

Anne Adron Brown, fiancée of Stanley Apling (*Stanley Apling*)

Stanley Apling in a much-repaired 50hp
Caudron Box-kite at Stagg Lane Aerodrome, Hendon,
January, 1918 (*Stanley Apling*)

secondhand armchairs and sofas that, according to the American, afforded a certain unforgettable atmosphere. The American also recalled that Major Murlis Green, whose long overdue promotion had arrived in December, and his wife, 'lived in a make-shift house constructed from airplane packing cases on the far side of the flying field'. Enterprising as ever, the Commanding Officer of Hainault Farm had the bitumen felt-covered chalet resembling a railway carriage erected on the aerodrome for good reason; Mrs Murlis Green was expecting her first baby and wanted to be near her husband. Although the Murlis Green dwelling at Hainault Farm looked primitive, the squadron fitters had installed electric light, running water, a bathroom and a telephone; not many homes in Ilford could claim all these items in 1918. When a photograph of the happy couple complete with new born baby and a flock of chickens in front of their unusual home later appeared in the press, Major-General E B Ashmore and the Air Ministry chose to turn a blind eye to the unauthorized building on the Ilford aerodrome.

Over there, on Thursday, 10th January, 2nd Lieut Bertie Beck, with Lieuts Alderson, Hird and Peydon of No.3 Squadron, carried out an afternoon low-level attack in support of the IV & V Army Corps after the weather had improved enough for flying.

Two days later Bertie had a 'Busman's holiday' when C Flight, led by Lieut Alderson, flew in brilliant sunshine to Marquise, near Boulogne, to exchange their 110 hp Le Rhône powered Camels for machines fitted with 130 hp Clerget engines. Above Marquise the young pilots could see the English coast; sadly it was the last time young Bertie saw England.

On Tuesday, 15th January, Lieut Cecil James Marchant was transferred to No.44 Squadron from No.78 Squadron at Suttons Farm; just eighteen days later he would be posted yet again to No.46 Squadron in France, where he had completed a tour of duty flying Sopwith Pups until June, 1917.

2nd Lieut Stanley Apling fondly remembers Friday, 18th January, as the day he met the only girl in the world - Nancy, an attractive, intelligent local lass just five days past her 17th birthday. Christened Anne Adron, she was known as Nancy to her family, who lived at 8 Cambridge Road, Seven Kings. Her father, Chatteron Brown, was the manager of Goodmayes Farm and a familiar figure in the area, going to and fro in his pony trap. Stanley received a telegram ordering him to report to Stag Lane aerodrome, near Hendon, for pilot training with mixed feelings, but he looked forward to flying after three months of intensive study of aeronautics at Oxford. Also the posting to west London was a stroke of luck: by rail he could be home and with Nancy in an hour or so. As there was no accommodation on the small civilian-staffed aerodrome, Stanley found himself billeted with a doctor in nearby Colindale Avenue.

Stag Lane flying school had much repaired 50 hp Gnome rotary powered Caudron biplanes, that, being of pre-1914 vintage, had no flying instruments, just an off-on petrol lever and a domestic light switch for the ignition; the latter would almost be young Stanley's undoing. On Monday, 21st January, 207 TDS at Fairlop suffered the first fatal casualty of 1918, when PFO W E Floyd, flying solo, brought Avro 504j B8602 in to land; on touching down, the machine burst into a fireball, and the unfortunate airman perished in the flames, before he could be dragged clear.

The following day, luck deserted 2nd Lieut H M Beck, who had survived several crashes during his 4 months active service with No.3 Squadron, where the average life span of Camel pilots engaged on hazardous ground strafing missions lasted three weeks. Bertie Beck no doubt saw his attachment to No.6 Squadron, flying R.E.8 observation machines to provide their crews with fighting experience behind the lines, as a welcome respite for a few days. On the morning of Tuesday, 22nd January, flying Camel B9141, the ex-Bancroft School boy engaged in mock combat with a `Harry Tate' of No.6 Squadron, but lost control of his machine at 500 ft and spun to his death. He was buried with full military honours in the Military Cemetery of St Pierre, Amiens.

As Commanding Officer of No.3 Squadron, 24 year old Major Richmond Raymond-Barker had the unenviable task of writing a letter of condolence to Amy and Herbert Beck, at 45 Mayfair Avenue, Ilford, after they had received a War Office telegram informing them their son had been killed. Bertie's C.O. explained the circumstances of the fatal flying accident and continued, "He was one of the finest and stout-hearted fellows I have met during this campaign and I never want a better in the Squadron; his absolute devotion to his work was an example to everyone and his ceaseless cheerfulness was a byword in the Squadron, both among his brother officers

and the men. I was going to recommend him for Flight Commander".

It was not the first such letter that Raymond-Barker had sent to grieving families and would not be the last - until Saturday afternoon, 20th April, 1918, when No.3 Squadron lost two Camels on an offensive patrol. In a battle with Fokker triplanes over the enemy lines, Raymond-Barker fell to his death in a burning Camel - the 79th victory of von Richthofen. A second Camel was shot down by von Richthofen a few minutes later; luckily the pilot, 2nd Lieut D G Lewis, although wounded, survived the crash as a prisoner of war.

After two and a half hours flight training, spread over several weeks, 2nd Lieut Stanley Apling was allowed to fly a Caudron biplane solo on the afternoon of Saturday, 26th January. Circling Stag Lane aerodrome prior to landing the fragile aeroplane, he saw that a fellow student, 2nd Lieut Charles Hesketh, also on his first solo flight, had reduced his Caudron to a pile of wreckage on the airfield below. Undismayed, Stanley flicked the ignition switch off to descend: nothing happened, the 50 hp Gnome rotary continued buzzing unchecked. With all the assurance of youth, the young man clenched his gloved fist and struck the offending electric light switch a hefty blow, cutting the ignition, enabling him to complete his first solo to the satisfaction of his instructor.

When the winter weather permitted, Stanley Aplin flew the primitive little Caudron box-kite, until he had completed one and a half hours solo, and received a posting to Northolt aerodrome for training on the more advanced Avro 504 machines with 100 hp rotary engines.

At the end of January, 1918, the small detachment of Americans were posted away from Ilford to UK training squadrons; one died in action, another killed in a flying accident, two were shot down wounded and made prisoners of war, two survived physically unscathed.

The evening of Monday, 28th January, became misty in and around the London area, as East End families, including many refugees, made their way to the warmth and safety of designated air raid shelters, opened nightly for the public. A large crowd from the nearby tenements gathered outside Bishopsgate Goods Station waiting for the Railway Police to unlock the gates to the shelter area. A queue of people was also waiting at the Olympia Music Hall, Shoreditch High Street, opposite the Railway Station, for the second house, when loud explosions were heard nearby. The more nervous mistook the air-raid warning rockets' loud detonations for falling bombs and surged towards the shelter gates, before the Railway Policemen had time to unbolt them. In blind panic, some forced their way through a smaller side gate used as a staff entrance. In the confusion someone dropped a camp-stool and attempted to stoop and pick it up, only to be overwhelmed by the surge of bodies from behind that quickly piled one on top of the other in a mass of thrashing limbs and cries of pain and warning. Fourteen civilians, including children and an infant that fell from its mother's arms, died and many more were severely injured, before the first bomber droned across the capital; a similar tragic stampede also occurred at a nearby Mile End air raid shelter.

The familiar beat of Gotha engines was heard and bombs fell on east London at 20.30 hrs, inflicting casualties and damage, despite the furious anti-aircraft fire. Fortunately for the defences, fog across aerodromes in Belgium prevented many of the Gothas from taking part in the raid; three out of the seven that crossed the coast between Harwich and the North Foreland struck at London, to be followed by one six-engined Giant with two 660 lb bombs in its racks.

A short lull followed the initial attack on the capital until 21.45 hrs, when a third Gotha, greeted by the London barrage, unloaded its bombs in the Hampstead area and banked north-east for the return journey over Essex and through the patrol lines of No.44 Squadron. Sweeping searchlights caught the raider in their beams, but each time Untoff Karl Ziegler skilfully piloted the bomber out of their glare. Those seconds of exposure, however, had attracted the attention of two Home Defence pilots on separate patrols from Hainault Farm. At 10,000 ft above Romford, the tell-tale glow of twin exhausts revealed the exact location of the dark sinister Gotha to the two converging Camel pilots.

With no means of communicating in the dark, the two Ilford pilots carried out a combined attack on the Gotha, no doubt practised above Hainault Farm aerodrome during the weeks of waiting for the German bombers to return to London.

2nd Lieut C C `Charlie' Banks, in Camel B3827, opened fire after closing in underneath from the left at 30 yards, whilst Capt George H Hackwill, flying Camel B2402, attacked from below right, also at close range. These tactics made it difficult, if not impossible, for Untoff Walther Heiden, the rear gunner, to get

Hainault Farm Camel pilots, Captain George Hackwill and 2nd Lieutenant Charles Banks inspect remains of the Gotha they brought down at Wickford, 28/29th January, 1918 (*Illustrated War News*)

either night fighter in the sights of his Parabellum machine-gun. It was general knowledge in Home Defence that the Gotha carried a sting in the tail, the designers having covered the bomber's vulnerable area by providing a tunnel through the slim fuselage, enabling the rear gunner to protect the underside of the tailplane, but the narrow fuselage restricted the gunners' field of fire either side. For ten minutes ground defences from Noak Hill to Billericay watched bursts of tracer bullets pointing out the twisting and turning raider trying to escape the pugnacious Camels. To Charlie Banks' dismay, his nine cylinder Le-Rhône engine developed faults, as he reluctantly turned for Hainault Farm. George Hackwill, unaware of his comrade's plight, still fired short bursts into the Gotha. Glancing back over his shoulder, Banks saw the Gotha falling like a comet, trailing a flame, and watched it crash below, erupting into a blazing funeral pyre at Frund's Farm, Wickford, at 22.10 hrs.

A lone Giant crossed the coast fifteen minutes later as the last of four Gothas, having bombed Kent, droned out to sea. The crew of a No.39 Squadron Bristol Fighter, on patrol from North Weald, encountered a 'four engined Gotha' over Harlow. Attempting to attack from the rear with his forward firing machine-gun, Lieut J G Goodyear flew straight into the slipstream of the Giant's 14 ft diameter airscrews and the Bristol was tossed to the right, almost out of control. The turbulence created by the six-engined monster also foiled his second attempt and, as the pilot again wrestled with controls, the Giant's gunners opened fire.

Undaunted, Goodyear dived beneath the monster to allow his observer AM W T Marchant to fire his ring mounted Lewis gun up into the belly of the massive enemy machine. A stream of accurate fire from the Giant's gunners wounded his Air Mechanic and punctured the main petrol tank, forcing the gallant Goodyear to break off the combat. Fortunately the landing flares of North Weald were visible to the southeast; minutes later the engine cut out, but Goodyear glided down to a safe landing.

Having disposed of an aggressive night fighter and clipping the outer edge of the Chingford balloon barrage, removing three heavy steel streamers in the process, the Giant flew on undamaged and undaunted by Polygon, the new anti-aircraft barrage aimed to encircle the raider with exploding shells, and it roared on to London. The Savoy Hotel, sheltering nearly a thousand visitors, had a fortunate escape shortly after midnight, when a 660 lb bomb fell on nearby Savoy Hill, close to and - seriously damaging - Savoy Mansions, recently commandeered as offices for the new Air Board. At Covent Garden a smaller missile fell on the Floral Hall, but the most serious incident of the night and of all the London air raids throughout the Great War, occurred after a second 660 lb bomb fell alongside Messrs. Odhams Press in Wilson Street, Long Acre. The basement doubled for a public air-raid shelter for 600 people of whom thirty-eight were killed and nearly one hundred injured, as a wall collapsed and heavy printing presses crashed down on victim and rescue worker alike. 2nd Lieut R N 'Bob' Hall, on patrol in Camel

B9177, plagued with gun stoppages, pursued the Giant from Woolwich to Foulness, where it flew out to sea just after 01.00 hrs. It had been a night of mixed blessings for the airmen of Hainault Farm aerodrome. Lieut Gerald W Gathergood, returning from patrol in Camel B2517 after the raid, overturned and suffered a broken nose; he had been slightly injured a month earlier when the same machine lost a wheel on a formation flight over the town, but on that occasion, Gathergood managed to land his one wheeled machine with little damage. Gotha G V/938/16, destroyed by Hackwill and Banks, gave No.44 Squadron the distinction of claiming the first enemy bomber brought down by Home Defence aircraft on British soil.

After breakfast on Tuesday, 29th January, the two airmen drove through frost covered Essex countryside to inspect their handiwork. On arriving at Frund's Farm they found the remains of the burnt-out wreckage, cooled sufficiently to attract a coating of hoar frost. At 6th Brigade headquarters, they studied the two pilots' combat reports, noting that Banks' Camel carried, in addition to the standard twin forward Vickers, an upward firing Lewis, loaded with the new RTS incendiary/explosive bullets. An inquiry began at once to determine if the new ammunition had been responsible for the destruction of the Gotha, although the body of the unfortunate pilot revealed he had been shot through the neck by a standard bullet.

The morning of Tuesday, 29th January, showed that the previous night's air-raid had claimed 67 fatal casualties and a further 166 injured, all but two of the dead and seven of the injured, being in the London area. During the morning, Major Murlis Green, telephoned Lt Col C Buckle, in charge of local anti-aircraft units, to pass on the thanks of his pilots to the searchlight crews for holding the bomber in their beams and the gunners, who ceased fire when they flew in to attack at close quarters. Four of the seven Gothas that had taken part in the night raid crashed on landing; during the previous London raid a night fighter (Murlis Green) destroyed one and seven were damaged or written off in landing accidents.

The morale of Bogohl 3, having lost their second Commanding Officer Hptmn Rudolf Kleine the previous month, was very low, but the return of Ernst Brandenburg, supplementing his artificial leg with a stout walking cane a few days later, restored the confidence of the depleted bomber crews. Brandenburg, realising the plight of his surviving airmen, requested a break in the London bombing campaign for at least six weeks to re-equip and train replacement air-crews. It remained up to the men of Rfa 501 and their half dozen four- to six-engined Giant bombers to maintain the bombing of England, until the Gothas returned.

As Hackwill and Banks inspected their downed Gotha, German ground crew, forty to a machine, were preparing four Giants to bomb London again, for the second night running. Engine trouble developed crossing the Channel, forcing R12, responsible for the previous night's carnage in Long Acre, to unload its lethal load on the French coast. Sound detectors reported fifteen enemy aircraft crossing the coast, as the remaining three bomb laden Giants, flying at 60 mph, droned in at intervals; the first R39 arrived over the river Blackwater just after 2200 hrs. Camels from Hainault Farm were already airborne. Keen as ever to bag his Gotha, Capt `Flossie' Brand roared down the flare path at 2159 hrs, followed minutes later by Capt George Hackwill and five others, with Major Murlis Green bringing up the rear at 2215 hrs. Capt Arthur Dennis of No.37 Squadron encountered R39 at 2215 hrs southwest of his aerodrome at Goldhanger in brilliant moonlight and emptied a drum of ammunition at close range; reloading, he closed from behind and flew into the turbulence of the tandem four propellers; on recovering control of his machine, the Giant had disappeared. Skirting the patrol lines of No.44 Squadron, the Giant circled around the outskirts and approached London from the north-west, bombing Acton and Richmond Park in error for Charing Cross and the West India Docks.

An anti-aircraft battery at Acton reported `a small machine chasing another with a heart shaped tail, quite double its size' at 23.41 hrs. What the AA gunners actually observed silhouetted against the moon at about 11,000 ft was the Giant R39 with a span of 138 ft, pursued by a 28 ft span Camel from Hainault Farm. The Giant was not twice as large, but five times the size of the Sopwith Camel; the tailplane of the enormous craft exceeded the wing span of Bob Hall's night fighter. Plagued with gun stoppages the Ilford pilot pursued the

German past Roehampton, until it vanished from sight in mist. Alerted by searchlights, a Camel pilot of No.78 Squadron, patrolling the Thames, picked up the Giant flying at 10,500 ft. It had fired a hundred rounds in two swoops, when a tracer bullet striking the Camel's propeller temporarily blinded Capt F Luxmoore, who returned safely to Suttons Farm aerodrome. George Hackwill, from No.44 Squadron, flying Camel B2402 that vanquished a Gotha the previous night, took up the pursuit of R39, now down to 9,500 ft, and travelling with throttles wide open. Fuel shortage prevented the flight commander from more than firing 600 rounds at long range, before the Giant flew out to sea near Hythe. A quarter of an hour before 2nd Lieut Bob Hall, flying Camel B9177, gave chase to R39; the Ilford pilot had attacked another Giant near Benfleet. R25 made landfall near Foulness at 22.50 hrs, to be greeted by a B.E.2e from No.37 Squadron; the pilot emptied a drum of ammunition from below, but lost the raider whilst reloading. Bob Hall's luck was no better, his Camel guns jammed repeatedly whilst pursuing R25 towards London. In his frantic efforts to clear the recurring gun stoppages, he lost the R25 and shortly after gave chase to the R39 as previously described, believing it to be the same machine.

Another Camel from Hainault Farm joined in the fray; 2nd Lieut H A Edwardes, in Camel B3827, managed to get three long bursts from both his guns at the R25, before a synchronizing gear malfunction disarmed his machine. Edwardes boldly switched on his navigation lights and flew above A25;

The War Office turned a blind eye to the unofficial married quarters built by No.44 Squadron for their CO, Major G W Murlis Green and his wife, who were expecting the arrival of their baby daughter, January, 1918 (*Redbridge Libraries*)

during his formation flight with the `Hun' for more than twenty minutes, he attracted more Camels. Irishman, 2nd Lieut `Dubs' O'Neill, had taken off from Hainault Farm at 22.17 hrs, flying Camel B5412, and rattled off over 300 rounds from above and below, before both his Vickers guns jammed. Major Murlis Green, flying `Comic' B3815 armed with two Lewis guns, gave the Giant R25 the best part of two double drums of RTS incendiaries, until stoppages forced him to return to Hainault Farm to have them rectified at 23.44 hrs.

The airmen of Hainault Farm had experienced another bout of serious stoppages with their machine guns and, misjudging the size of their enormous opponent, opened fire before they were in effective range; however, nearly 90 rounds had found their marks during the determined attacks. Instruments were damaged and a radiator was holed by bullets, and this put one of the port engines out of action, as R25 cleared the Brentwood area, slowly losing height: the Germans, undaunted, flew a bee-line towards London. Major Murlis Green followed the bomber to the outskirts of Ilford, where he landed at Hainault Farm, re-armed and re-fuelled, to became airborne again in eleven minutes. Just after midnight the damaged bomber dropped its entire bomb-load on open fields around Wanstead. Luck still flew with the crew of R25. Unseen by twenty or more night fighters hunting for them, R25 crossed the coast near Shoeburyness at 00.30 hrs. R26, the third Giant, came inland at 22.45 hrs above the Naze, also en route for London, but turned for home

when two engines developed faults and were switched off. R26 disposed of its bombs in empty fields near Rayleigh, before flying out to sea at about 51,000 ft; anti-aircraft batteries at Billericay were given credit for driving the raider off. With two thirds of the Giants' bombs falling on open countryside, the casualties were mercifully light - ten killed and ten wounded. The RNAS and RFC flew eighty patrols during the alert; sixteen of them were carried out by Camel pilots of No.44 Squadron; all returned to Hainault Farm safely, although the Giants' gunners had put bullet holes in several machines.

Two blessed events took place in Ilford during the air-raid; Harold Suckling came into the world at his parents' cottage near Barkingside Railway Station. At the unofficial married quarters on edge of Hainault Farm, during the height of the air-raid Mrs Murlis Green, wife of the Commanding Officer aloft fighting, gave birth to a daughter' attended by the Squadron Medical Officer.

At Bogohl 3 the `English Squadron' replaced its losses in men and machines and the handful of Giants of Rfa No.501 were undergoing extensive overhauls, London had a respite. On the night of Wednesday, 30th January, the people of Paris suffered their first air-raid since July the previous year. In a combined effort by Gotha and Friedrichshafen bombers from Bogohls 1, 2, 5 and and 7, fourteen tons of bombs fell upon the French capital, killing 61 and injuring 198 civilians.

The newspapers made comforting reading as Ilford entered the second month of 1918; the last two air-raids had been failures thanks to anti-aircraft gunners and airmen who drove off `waves' of German bombers. It became local knowledge that Hainault Farm airmen were responsible for the burnt out Gotha pictured in the press somewhere in Essex.

On Friday, 8th February, following his promotion to Captain, Cecil James Marchant just 24 days with No.44 Squadron, flew off to rejoin No.46 Squadron in France, where he would be credited with 9 enemy aeroplanes during the following six months, until being wounded in combat on Tuesday, 2nd July.

The men of No 44 Squadron said farewell to Christopher Joseph 'Flossie' Quinton-Brand on Friday, 15th February; promoted to Major, he flew to Throwley to take command of No 112 Squadron, who were in the process of replacing their Sopwith Pups with night-flying Camels.

The Ilford squadron lost another formidable pilot on the day of Brand's departure; Lieut Walbanke Ashby Pritt became hospitalized when Camel B7332 suffered engine failure after take-off, stalled at 500 ft, and span into the ground. In a photograph of Pritt taken the previous summer, as a pilot serving with No.66 Squadron in France, he looks like a 14 year old schoolboy with a lump of toffee in his mouth and holding his pet dog, 'Dickebusch'. The youthful-looking airman, credited with 5 enemy aeroplanes and awarded the MC for his single handed low level attack on an enemy aerodrome, insisted he was twenty. Dickebusch frequently shared the small cockpit of his master's Sopwith Pup for a flip this side of the lines and unofficially accompanied Pritt home to dear old Blighty for a well earned leave. During his service at Hainault Farm, Pritt had a galloping 'Dickebusch' towing the fuselage roundel painted on the sides of his machine.

On Saturday, 16th February, another gallant airman lost his life at Hainault Farm. 2nd Lieut H A Edwardes, who during the last air-raid flew in formation above a German bomber with his aircraft's lights on to attract other night-fighters, plunged to his death in B5192, when the converted 'Comic' suddenly broke up in mid-air.

Twelve pilots from No 44 Squadron were airborne after dark when four Giants were reported crossing the coast, taking advantage of clouds and minimal moon-light. Virtually unseen by ground defences and sixty nightfighters, two six-engined bombers struck at London, fortunately the casualties were light - 12 fatal and 6 injured. Just before midnight, 2nd Lieut W. Algie of No 78 Squadron from fog-bound Suttons Farm, landed at Hainault Farm, at least three Home Defence machines had crash landed.

On Sunday, 17th February, local airman, 2nd Lieut S J Clinch from Seven Kings, flying BE2c biplane 1172 from No.35 Reserve School, Oxford, received injuries after trying to bank close to the ground, losing flying speed: the machine side slipped and crashed. Major V R Rees, the other occupant, was also injured. Clinch had volunteered for the RFC in 1914, served in France for two years, received the Distinguished Conduct Medal for gallantry in the air as a Flt Sergeant, and had been granted a commission in November, 1917.

On Sunday night a lone Giant, R25, roaring across the coast near Allhallows, stirred up a hornets' nest of nearly 70 nightfighters, including twelve Camels from Hainault Farm. Several pilots reported firing at an enemy bomber, although the crew of the R25 were unaware of being attacked. A B.E.12, piloted by 2nd Lieut Sydney Armstrong of No.37 Squadron, caught fire after crashing, killing the unfortunate pilot, was at first thought to have been in combat with one of the raiders. Anti-aircraft gunners made the night memorable for a number of the defending fighter pilots, who were fired upon; whilst other pilots were fired at by `friendly' unidentified aircraft. The R25 had been the only Giant aeroplane serviceable to raid England that night: alone, the lumbering monster had dropped 26 110 lb bombs, plus incendiaries, the majority of the 21 killed and 32 injured in the air raid were victims of the last stick of bombs that fell on St Pancras railway station and hotel.

On Monday, 18th February, Clark B Nichol, one of the six American aviators who had been stationed at Hainault Farm prior to a posting to Stamford aerodrome at the end of January, died of injuries sustained in a crash on his first solo flight.

Nearly three weeks elapsed before the return of the German airmen; during that time, Ilford Councillors were discussing a letter from the Police Commissioner, New Scotland Yard, recommending, "When an air raid notice is given, red lights should be substituted for green on public buildings," when Councillor Davis pointed out that "lights on public buildings made good targets, German airmen would be delighted at our kindness in marking them". He then wished "those in charge

had a little more gumption and common sense". Busy Fairlop aerodrome, a Sub Station to RNAS Chingford, became No.207 Training Depôt Station in the ever expanding air services.

Wednesday, 7th March, had a moonless night and cloud cover, which enabled five Giants to bomb England by their ability to carry wireless as a navigation aid. A sixth machine, suffering from engine troubles, returned shortly after taking off from Rfa 501 new aerodrome at Scheldewindeke. Frustrated by thick ground mist only 42 Home Defence machines became airborne during the raid and a number of those were recalled early due to the weather.

The first Giant flew in above Deal at 22.56 hrs, followed by three more during the next twenty minutes via Maplin; the fifth raider made landfall over Broadstairs at 23.35 hrs. Compared with the single handed raid by R.25 on 17th February, the resulting casualties and damage were light - two further killed, five more injured, and an additional £3,733 of damage inflicted. Once again the most serious bombing incident occurred in London where a 1,000 kg missile fell upon Paddington, totally destroying four and damaging a further 140 houses. St Paul's Cathedral suffered slight damage during the raid, when an unexploded anti-aircraft shell struck the roof of the south transept.

Although only four Camels went aloft from Hainault Farm hunting the raiders, the aerodrome had a hectic period between 01.45-02.00 hrs, when three Bristol Fighters from No 39 Squadron were forced to make emergency landings at North Weald, due to the weather conditions. One of the Ilford Camels, C1561, flown by Lieut G. Shiner, who, for reasons not recorded, escaped serious injury in a crash-landing at Chingford aerodrome at 01.18 hrs.

No. 49 Home Defence Wing suffered the loss of two experienced night flyers when an SE5a, flown by Capt H M Stroud from No. 61 Squadron at Rochford, collided with a No 37 Squadron BE12 from Stow Maries, piloted by Capt R B Kynoch, in the darkness above the open Essex countryside. It came as some consolation for the Home Defence to learn that two of the returning Giants crash-landed in Belgium.

The potato shortage still caused concern in Ilford, posters appealing to the people to grow more potatoes and be self supporting appeared, warning that Essex had consumed 133,900 tons of potatoes the previous year and grown 89,600 tons.

In France, the Royal Flying Corps, responding to a rapid build-up in the back areas of the 2nd, 17th and 18th German Armies, begin to transfer squadrons to reinforce those already in the British sector opposing them. The plan, to thwart the German build-up behind the lines with extensive bombing and ground strafing, would be hampered by extremely bad flying conditions.

At Hainault Farm aerodrome, although no longer a novelty, No.44 Squadron pilots stunting their Camels in fighting practice, still drew spectators at weekends, if the weather was suitable for flying.

A football match arranged between Ilford Police and airmen from the local RFC aerodrome, in aid of the Ilford Emergency Hospital was eagerly awaited.

On Tuesday, 12th March, No.78 Squadron still in the process of re-equipping with Sopwith Camels at Hornchurch, under the influence of Capt D V Armstrong, recently transferred from Hainault Farm as a Flight Commander, suffered the loss of 2nd Lieut William Hays Pickup, when his machine C1625 spun into the ground from 100 feet.

That same evening three Giants, endeavouring to make use minimum moonlight and cloud cover, were to keep the pressure on London, whilst five Naval Zeppelins carried out their first air-raid on England since October the previous year. Engine failure forced one Giant, the R.33, to return shortly after take off; approaching the Kent coast engine problems beset the R13, and Boulogne, the alternative target, received the bomb loads of the R13 and the R39.

Crossing the Yorkshire coast, three Naval Zeppelins, flying at heights between 16 to 18,000 ft, dropped bombs on Hull and the surrounding area, killing one civilian and causing minimal damage.

Confused by thick cloud below and faulty navigation, the remaining two airship commanders dropped their entire bomb-loads harmlessly into the sea.

Nine pilots from No.33, 36 and 76 HD. Squadrons attempted to penetrate the blanket of cloud in search of the raiders; two machines from No.33 Squadron returned early due to the adverse weather, the remaining seven completed patrols without sighting the enemy and returned safely to their own flickering flarepaths.

On Wednesday, 13th March, over the enemy lines, ferocious dogfights took place as Camels and Bristol Fighters defended two Squadrons of DH4 bombers against the 'Flying Circus'. A No.73 Squadron Camel B5590, piloted by Lieut E E Heath, became von Richthofen's 65th victory during the dogfight. Lother, the Red Baron's younger brother, credited with 28 allied aeroplanes, was seriously injured, attempting to land his triplane, after shedding the upper wing in combat with another No.73 Squadron Camel B7282, flown by Capt A H Orlebar, recently transferred from No.44 Squadron at Ilford. Ten days later Harry Orlebar was wounded flying the same machine; returning to the front in August, he flew with No.43 Squadron to increase his total of enemy machines to seven. Surviving the war, Orlebar became well-known as a pilot in the Schneider Trophy Team of 1929/31, and served in WW2.

At 19.15 hours on Wednesday, 13th March, 3 Naval Zeppelins, approaching the Midlands, were recalled by Fregatten-kapitan Peter Strasser, who had personally led the previous night's unspectacular raid. The Leader of the German Naval Airship Service was concerned about a similar forecast of rising north-easterly winds that had resulted in the loss of five airships during the ill-fated October 19/20th raid six months earlier. Strasser's caution was also tempered by the more recent 'Ahlhorn Disaster' of Saturday, 5th January, when explosions and fires destroyed another five vulnerable hydrogen-filled airships in their sheds. Kptlt Martin Dietrich, commanding L42, chose to ignore the order and flew over the Durham coast, bombing Hartlepool. Although the docks and town were ablaze with lights until the first whistling bombs detonated without warning, only 8 people were killed and 29 injured. L42 was pursued 40 miles out to sea by an FE2d of No.36 Squadron, with the pilot, 2nd Lieut E C Morris, desperately trying to coax the 'Fee' above its ceiling of 17,000 ft. Before the L42 disappeared into clouds 20,000 ft over the North Sea, Morris and his observer, 2nd Lieut R D Linford, had fired 330 rounds from their Lewis guns at extreme range.

Some significance can be read in the fact that the Leader of Airships was not at Nordholz to greet the return of L42. Fortified by lunch, Dietrich reported to Strasser and received a cool reception, as expected, for disobeying orders. Eventually the relief of the safe return of a precious Zeppelin and crew and a full account of the mission, brought a smile to the face of his superior officer, who joked, "In honour of your successful attack, I name you Count of Hartlepool."

Four days of continuous heavy rain prevented the RFC from confirming intelligence reports of the increasing arrival of reinforcements of enemy troops opposite the British Third and Fifth Armies in France. At 04.40 hrs on Thursday, 21st March, the expected German 'Push' began with five and a half hours bombardment of the British lines by no less than six thousand medium to heavy guns, plus three thousand mortars. At 09.40 hrs thirty-two divisions of German infantry stormed and captured much of the shell shattered 54 mile wide front lines held by nineteen divisions of British troops. Mist and fog covered the extent of German gains until the afternoon, when the RFC were able to report a massive enemy break through. The BEF had nineteen divisions in reserve at this critical stage, the advancing German Army twenty-eight.

Wounded servicemen in hospital blue were among the variety of uniforms mingling with two thousand spectators gathering at Gordon Fields in the afternoon sunshine of Saturday, 23rd March, 1918. Two teams preparing for a well advertised charity football match in aid of the Ilford Emergency Hospital Fund were the attraction. Ilford Constabulary and Specials versus a team from No.44 Squadron RFC formed at Hainault Farm the previous summer. Major Gilbert W Murlis Green, the squadron commander, was expected to arrive by air and, despite many rumours about a serious set back on the Western Front, the prevailing atmosphere reminded many of happier pre-war days. On his arrival, following the brief flight across the town, Major Murlis Green circled the playing fields with its sea of upturned faces and commenced blipping his rotary engine, confirming his intention to land. Amid enthusiastic cheering from spectators thronging the boundary of the improvised landing ground the Camel touched down and rolled to a standstill.

Gunfire from the battle raging 180 miles away across the Channel had been heard in the town the previous day. The Germans had three objectives; first smashing the right wing of the BEF where the British and French front lines merged; second, forcing the two British army groups back to the Channel coast, to clear the way for the third objective - the capture of Paris, before the build up of the American forces on the Western Front enabled the allies to launch their own offensive. Paris came under bombardment from a fearsome 131 ft long barrelled gun with a range of 80 miles. The 'Paris Guns' would inflict more fatal casualties during the next forty-four days of bombardment than all the air raids during the previous three and a half years of war.

On Sunday, 24th March, as the people of Ilford read the first official War Office bulletin published in the town since early December the previous year, the Fifth Army desperately fought for time, as a hastily prepared defence line was dug on the Somme. No less than 17 RFC Squadrons were forced to abandon aerodromes threatened by the Germans rapid advance. Due to fog, a number of machines had to be burnt to prevent them falling into the hands of the advancing enemy. An improvement in the weather enabled the RFC to support the hard pressed 'Tommies'. Capt John Trollope, No.43 Squadron, shot down six enemy aircraft during two patrols flying Camel C8270, but the RFC losses by nightfall were 11 missing during low level strafing, 46 wrecked, burnt or abandoned. German losses for the day - 12 aeroplanes.

Loss of RFC personnel and aeroplanes ground-strafing during those four days, in an all out effort to halt the German onslaught, reached crisis proportions, and requests for urgently needed replacements arrived at Hainault Farm.

On Thursday 28th March, five pilots of No.44 Squadron waved farewell as their Crossley tender pulled away on the first stage of their journey en route for the Pilots Pool at St Omer in France. Among the five were Lieut C C Banks, destined for No.43 Squadron, where he would add eleven German machines, including another twin engined bomber, to the Gotha brought down at Wickford, before the war ended. Also transferred to No.43 Squadron was 2nd Lieut T M 'Tubs' O'Neill, who was to be killed in action over the enemy east of Bailleul on Wednesday, 8th May, 1918.

Lieut R M Foster, who already had one enemy aircraft to his credit whilst serving previously with No.54 Squadron in France, would be credited with a further fifteen EM, following his posting to No.209 Squadron from Ilford.

On Good Friday, 29th March, as another batch of experienced Hainault Farm pilots made preparations to leave for the front by air, a shell from the 'Paris Gun' fell on the roof of Saint Gervais, a church filled with worshippers. Tons of masonry collapsed upon the congregation below; 88 persons were killed and 68 injured - many of the unfortunate casualties were women.

The following morning at Hainault Farm, Lieut Ronald Adam posed for a photograph with Sgt Edward Mills and his ground crew, having secured Adam's kit bag over the centre section of Camel B9M07, he was flying as a replacement to No.73 Squadron at Beauvois. Minutes later, circling above the Ilford aerodrome, he was joined by three more Camels, piloted by Lieut J C Collier, 2nd Lieut J Paine and 2nd Lieut J L Wingate, who fell into a tight diamond formation, before crossing the Thames for the Kent coast. Leading the formation, Ronald Adam confidently climbed above the clouds to cross the Channel and made landfall over Calais at 8,000 ft. In an effort to recognise landmarks from his days as an observer with No.18 Squadron in 1916, Adam gradually lost height, until at 200 ft, buffeted by a stiff gale and keeping an eye upon Jack Collier who had tucked his machine in too close for comfort, he saw the massive spire of Aire Cathedral and, although having flown between Aire and St. Omer many times in the past, he chose the wrong road and only realised he was lost when he glanced at his compass bearing.

Fortunately for Ronald Adam, now frantically searching for a familiar landmark, a large aerodrome soon came into view and, before he could signal his intention to land, Paine's Camel had already touched down. Adam followed and taxied towards the hangers and, as Jack Collier followed, a fierce gust of wind caught his machine, flicking it over on to its back, like a toy. Wingate's Camel was missing and Adam realised that two of the four Camels flown from Hainault Farm an hour or so before were already out of action. Apart from an officer and a few ground crew the aerodrome was empty. German prisoners working nearby were called and, with the aid of ropes, set Collier's Camel upright. Whilst this was going on, Adam, with the help of two ground crew, attempted to push his machine into a hanger; on lifting the tailplane, another sudden gust of wind threw his Camel on to its nose, leaving them with one serviceable aeroplane. Lieut Adam eventually managed to get through to St Omer by telephone and, after much delay, received orders to send Paine and the only available machine immediately to an aerodrome at Hesdingneul, whilst he and Collier waited to be collected by a tender from the Pilots' Pool.

On arrival at St Omer, they were relieved to find Wingate safe and sound. His engine had cut out near Aire, forcing him to alight in a ploughed field, with the result that his Camel overturned violently. He escaped injury and thumbed a lift in a staff car to St Omer. At the Pilots' Pool, Wingate was greeted by Charlie Banks and some of the gang who had left

Lieutenant Ronald Adam, 44 Squadron, about to fly from Ilford to France in March, 1918. Note the kitbag strapped to the centre section of his Sopwith Camel (*G S Leslie*)

No.73 Squadron

Hainault Farm two days earlier.

During breakfast on Sunday, 31st March, the two ex-Ilford contingents were reunited, with the exception of 2nd Lieut J Paine and Lieutenants Foster and Lomas, who were already with No.9 Squadron RNAS at Clairmarais. The Naval squadron was about to be re-designated No 209 Squadron, with the merging of the RNAS and RFC to form the Royal Air Force the following day. After breakfast Lieuts Adam and Collier reported to the aerodrome office and signed for two replacement Camels to fly to No 73 Squadron. After another round of farewells and exchanges of good luck with the dwindling ex-Ilford group, they were about to take off for the front line squadron, when an orderly arrived with a weather report warning of heavy rain and orders to wait at St Omer overnight - and yet another round of fond farewells the following morning.

On Monday, 1st April, the Royal Flying Corps and Royal Naval Air Service became the Royal Air Force; the female branches of the respective services were also amalgamated to form the Women's Royal Air Force. The changes brought about by the transition to a completely new service was not popular with many of the Naval airman, steeped in the proud traditions of the Senior Service. Gone overnight at Fairlop and Chingford were the Naval ranks, a Squadron Commander RN became a Major RAF, Flight Commanders were now Captains, and Petty Officers, Sergeants. To the airmen at Hainault Farm, who considered the customs of the Naval types along Forest Road, far from the sea with their 'Liberty Boats', 'Master at Arms' and 'Ship's Bell', etc, a constant source of amusement, but were reluctant to relinquish their own

individual regimental uniforms and distinctive RFC 'Maternity Jackets'.

It had been inevitable, because of the date, the RAF would become 'Royal April Fools' until the novelty wore off. Orders placed with British textile mills for uniform material before the collapse of the Russian Empire were made available to the new air service. Pale grey-blue in colour, the bolts of ex-Russian Army cloth contrasted with the drab khaki and dark blue of Britain's wartime services and was not popular with some airmen, especially as, when attired in the new uniforms, they became known as 'Gertie Millar's Own' - Gertie Millar, a beautiful Edwardian musical comedy star, was remembered for her flamboyant dresses.

With many aerodromes over-run by the advancing Germans, the infant RAF in France had problems: Lieuts Adam and Collier, en route for No. 73 Squadron, eventually found their way to Hesdingneul in the late afernoon, only to discover some 200 British aeroplanes of all types picketed on the field and have difficulty finding space to land.

As the British front line finally held fast, after conceding up to twenty miles in some areas, the RAF had to relocate forty-five squadrons to alternative airfields. To support their offensive the German High Command had 822 aeroplanes, at the cost of leaving just 367 machines facing 2,000 aircraft along the French front.

Outnumbered, the RAF, with 645 aircraft, was forced to send out patrols in two or more squadron strength. In one major air battle on Wednesday, 3rd April, Nos.65 and 84 Squadrons, with 27 machines, fought for the sky above the front lines with 30 enemy fighters for more than an hour, claiming 5 EA destroyed.

On the afternoon of Saturday, 6th April, Lieut Ronald Adam found himself in the thick of it with No. 73 Squadron, ground strafing massed German troop concentrations.

Flight Commander Capt Geoffrey Pidcock was an old friend from No. 44 Squadron and the Commanding Officer, Major T O'B Hubbard, had been C. O. at Ilford prior to Adam's arrival there in August, 1917.

Later the same evening Adam, with Collier, flew again to Hesdinguel to collect two new Camels, returning to No. 73 Squadron at Beauvois in the fast-failing light. Adam's service with No. 73 Squadron would be brief, but exciting.

At 10.00 hrs the following morning Major T O'B Hubbard led the entire squadron with the intention 'of giving the 'Circus' a dusting over the lines'. Due to the lack of lighting in the hastily-erected hangers, armourers and mechanics were unable to test the two new machines thoroughly, and untried Camel D6554 proved to be the downfall of Ronald Adam. Over the enemy lines in 'V' formation, with B Flight looking for trouble, Adam found more than his fair share: amid the coughing 'Archie' bursts, his engine began to splutter, the tiny propeller wind-driven pressure pump seized, forcing him to pump manually every two or three minutes - exhausting work at 16,000 ft. Despite a fur-lined face mask, he felt his face becoming frost-bitten, due to perspiration from frantically working the hand pump and constantly turning from side to side searching the sky for 'Huns'.

Suddenly B Flt Commander began to dive; Adams followed the yellow streamer fluttering from his leader's tail, when, without warning, the air filled with Fokker triplanes, many still sporting black Maltese crosses on their wings. Orders had been issued the previous month to replace the Maltese with a straight-sided Latin cross on German aircraft by 15th April.

Strung to the highest pitch of excitement, Adam pressed the gun triggers as a triplane flashed into view and nothing happened! The enemy machine half-rolled and went under the Camel; Adam responded with an 'Armstrong' turn, but the Fokker had vanished. Diving again into the dogfight raging beneath, Adam attempted to fire at another 'Tripe-hound', but both Vickers guns refused to operate: there was no sign of a jam and Adam realised the Constantinesco gun gear had not been correctly set on his new 'Bus'. To add insult to injury, the Camel's rotary engine, starved of fuel, petered out; in the heat of battle he had forgotten to use the hand pump to maintain that all-important pressure.

Adam's plight had not gone unnoticed; as he furiously pumped to restart the free-wheeling rotary engine, a Fokker came in from behind firing, followed by two more at angles on either side beneath his tailplane. The hard-pressed pilot pushed the nose of his powerless biplane down in a slow corkscrew dive, down, down. At 8,000 ft, feeling dizzy, he straightened out and recommenced pumping vigorously to restart the engine. Almost immediately, smoking tracer bullets forced Adam back into a spiral dive; another attempt to restart the fuel starved engine brought yet more bullets ripping through the fabric-covered aeroplane. A rather tattered-looking D655A levelled out once again; a glance at the altimeter confirmed just 6,000 ft left: it had to be now or never for the exhausted pilot, who began pumping to the accompaniment of sputtering machine gun fire and the crack-crack of bullets passing his head. Suddenly the engine fired and burst into life; with full throttle and raised spirits Ronald Adam flicked the now frisky Camel in the direction of the British lines. The new-found energy expired as bullets holed the tank with a loud bang and the pleasure totally disappeared. Demoralised, with the persistent `Hun' again on his tail firing away, the dismayed Camel pilot in a fit of insanity thought, "Better dead than captured", and dived nose first into the ground. Ronald Adam recalled hitting the sleepers of a railway track with a tremendous crash followed by the dis-integrating Camel completing several somersaults.

An old sack was thrown over the `body' of the English airman in the remains of his wrecked machine until a salvage party arrived. On recovering semi-consciousness, Ronald Adam startled a German who had lifted a corner of the sack. "Not dead? Not wounded?" enquired the soldier, who proceeded to free Adam from the wreckage and, after several tries, help him to stand upright unaided.

As a prisoner of war, Ronald Adam witnessed at first hand the mental cruelty inflicted upon Capt W Leefe Robinson VC by the Germans at the notorious Holzminden Camp. Adam returned home in December, 1918, as he put it, `just short of my 22nd birthday, young in years and old in spirit'.

During WW2 he served at RAF Hornchurch as Controller of Fighter Operations, attaining the rank of Wing Commander and being awarded the OBE in 1946. He wrote three novels based on his WW2 experiences - *Readiness at Dawn*, *We Rendezvous at Ten* and *To you the Torch*. As an actor he appeared in over 150 films and numerous rôles on stage and television.

As the people of England read in their daily newspapers of the enemy spring offensive being fought to a standstill, the second phase of the push began with a horrific four hour bombardment on Tuesday, 9th April, 1918. Aided by fog, fresh German troops advanced; the British 40th and Portuguese 2nd Divisions were completely overwhelmed by superior numbers, forcing an 8½ mile wide breach in the front line.

Major Christopher Draper, in command of No. 208 Squadron (ex-No. 8 Naval Squadron), on being informed that retreating Portuguese soldiers were swarming across his aerodrome at La Gorgue, sought permission to evacuate his men and took responsibility for setting fire to 19 Camels on the fog-shrouded field to prevent them falling into enemy hands. Surviving airmen of `Bloody April', 1917, now in the Royal Air Force - an independent service not yet two weeks old - were facing an even more disastrous April twelve months on.

During the next two days, the hard fought battles of the BEF the previous year had been in vain - Ploegsteert and Messines were once again under German occupation. The fall of Armentières, where the Germans claimed 6,000 prisoners and 100 guns, prompted Field-Marshall Sir Douglas Haig to make the following appeal to the BEF on Friday, 12th April. 'There is no other course open to us but to fight it out! Every position must be held to the last man: there must be no retirement.

With our backs to the wall, and believing in the justice of our cause, each one of us must fight on to the end. The safety of our homes and the freedom of mankind alike depend on the conduct of each one of us at this critical moment.'

By this date the weather had improved and visibility, reported as exceptionally good, enabled the RAF to fly a record number of hours over the enemy lines dropping 45 tons of bombs and claiming 49 EA forced down. Thirteen of the enemy were claimed by No.43 Squadron's Capt H W Woollett, who downed six during the day. Lieut C C 'Sandy' Banks crashed an Albatros DV. This made his second EA with No.43 Squadron; on the 6th April, whilst looking for ground targets, he spotted an Albatros DV diving with engine off and followed it down to 50 ft firing until it crashed into the ground. Although the ex-Hainault Farm pilot, again flying Camel D1815, came under heavy small arms fire from the ground, he cleared the front lines by 100 ft, landing at Senlis with a holed tank and elevator cables shot away; enemy airmen had not seen the last of this Camel merchant.

Shortly after 21.00 hrs on Friday evening, 12th April, five Zeppelin airships of the German Navy, carrying fifteen tons of bombs, droned across the Midlands. Their reliable new Maybach motors, carrying them to altitudes of 20-22,000 ft, presented the same wearisome problem to the pilots of No.48 Wing, attempting to intercept the 'Zepps' with obsolete F E and B.E night fighters. Forced to fly four miles high whilst over England no doubt accounted for the fact much of their deadly load fell on open countryside, instead of Leeds, Sheffield or Coventry.

During the early hours of Saturday, 13th April, Camels of No.44 Squadron were ready to take air-raid action, when LADA headquarters reported a Giant nearing the Kent coast, but the expected air-raid on London never materialised.

The phantom raider made little difference to the routine at Hainault Farm, where replacements for experienced pilots rushed out to front line squadrons were practising night fighting in readiness for resumption of the expected bombing offensive on London.

On Thursday, 18th April, it came as little surprise to the people of Ilford, after hearing all the bad news filtering back with the wounded from over there, to read that conscription for military service had been raised to 51 years. Younger, fit men on essential war work in the area suddenly had their deferments cancelled and were called up for the Army.

During the next day, in spite of snow and hail storms or because of them, the BEF fought the German advance on the River Lys to a standstill and the RAF, with little opposition from enemy aircraft, dropped more than 13 tons of small bombs, slaughtering horses pulling badly-needed supply wagons to the front.

Fine weather on Sunday, 21st April, brought with it a resumption of fierce air battles along the Western Front. Anti-aircraft machine gunners gave covering fire to a low flying Camel pursued by an enemy triplane, in turn fired upon by another Camel flying low across the Australian lines. The enemy pilot, intent on adding the Camel to his total of eighty victories, had made a mistake that cost him his life. Manfred von Richthofen crossed the lines in error; Capt A R Brown of No.209 Squadron gave chase to a red triplane chasing a newcomer to his flight, under orders to recross the lines if enemy machines were encountered. Canadian Roy Brown, flying Camel B7270, and several Australian infantrymen claimed to have shot down the `Red Baron', who died of a single bullet wound as the all-red triplane crash-landed in a field alongside the Bray-Corbie road, inflicting further injuries to the body.

Lieut R M Foster flew numerous night patrols in defence of London from Hainault Farm prior to serving with No.209 Squadron in France. He shot down an Albatros two-seater on the morning that Capt Roy Brown pursued von Richthofen's triplane. On the evening of Monday, 22nd April, Bob Foster, with other members of No 209 Squadron, dropped messages over the enemy lines confirming that Rittmeister von Richthofen had been fatally wounded in aerial combat and buried with full military honours that morning. Such deeds had become commonplace, but the death of this much publicised 24 year old aviator, already a legend in his own lifetime, was a setback for the German propaganda machine.

On Saturday, 27th April, the airmen of Hainault Farm were called upon once again to do their bit for the Ilford Emergency Hospital Fund. Following the success of the charity football match organised by the Loxford Ward the previous month, between No.44 Squadron and Ilford Police and Specials, a team from the Crystal Palace Royal Naval Depôt were invited to play the local RA Squadron on Gordon Fields. A detachment of Ilford Specials had little trouble keeping the enthusiastic spectators in order, assisted by the spirited rendering of popular music and patriotic songs by the Canadian Railway Troops band.

At precisely 15.00 hrs, in brilliant sunshine, Major Murlis Green D.S.O. A.C. kicked the ball into play; soon after, the ball passed in front of the airmen's goal, where, with a mighty kick from Ordinary Seaman Lancaster, the flyers went one goal down, to the cheers of the Navy supporters. By half time the airmen were three goals to nil down, in spite of some very skilful football from the team that had beat the Ilford Police and Specials seven goals to nil the month before. During a very exciting second half, it appeared as though the tables would be turned completely on the airmen, when, just before the final whistle, Cpl Graham scored for the airmen, making it seven to one in favour of the Royal Navy. Both teams were entertained to tea at the Drill Hall, after Councillor Smith put up the ball with which the game had been played for mock auction no less than three times in aid of the Hospital Fund. The last purchaser, on behalf of Ilford's Special Constables, presented it to the winning team amid cheers from everyone present.

As the month of April came to a close, the German Army, following the capture of Mount Kemmel, were unable to continue their advance due to the solid British defence along the Lys.

Gordon Fields was the venue of another charity football match in aid of the Ilford Emergency Hospital played on Saturday, 4th May. The event highlighted the many changes that had taken place in the town due to the Great War - a ladies' team from the London General Omnibus Company were to meet the undefeated ladies of the Sterling Telephone & Electric Company from Dagenham.

On Wednesday, 8th May, B Flight,

Lieutenant John D Baird had been performing low level aerobatics when his Camel flew into the machine gun butts at Hainault Farm on 8th May, 1918 (*G S Leslie*)

The funeral cortège of Lieutenant J D Baird, DSO, MC, with fellow officers of No.44 Squadron entering the City of London Cemetery, Manor Park, 20th May, 1918. The band is that of the Cadets of the 13th Battalion, Artists' Rifles (*R Gerrard/G S Leslie*)

under the command of Lieut C R Wentworth Knight, were airborne from Hainault Farm, to practise formation flying for the expected return of German bombers during daylight. All had gone well during the practice, the final manoeuvre - a spin from 6,000 ft before landing - was indicated by a hand signal from Wentworth Knight before allowing his own machine to enter a spinning nose dive. Taxi-ing up to the aeroplane sheds and switching off, he was informed one of his flight had spun below the level of the trees in the distance and must have crashed. Eye-witness, Air Mechanic John Worral, watched the spinning Camel, as the engine burst into life at no more than 50 ft from the ground. It crashed headlong into a solid brick-built machine gun butts on the aerodrome, some yards away from where he stood. 2nd Lieut John Donald Baird DSO MC died instantly in the impact. Twenty years of age from Prestwick, Scotland, he had served with distinction with the Army and shown great promise as a pilot. Sgt Major Edward Hutton testified later at the inquest, that, when he had flown Camel D6649 prior to the deceased officer, 'the machine had been in good order'. A verdict of accidental death was brought in and another unexplained fatal crash added to the Sopwith Camels growing reputation as a killer of friend and foe.

A premonition of impending doom during the funeral of 2nd Lieut V C Manuel, killed in a Camel crash at Hainault Farm the previous December, unfortunately came true five months later. 2nd Lieut Thomas Michael O'Neill, who had confided his fear to fellow pall-bearers after almost falling into the open grave at St Mary's, was killed in action over the enemy lines, east of Baillelll, flying Sopwith Camel C8298 with No.43 Squadron on 8th May, 1918.

On Thursday evening, 9th May, officers and men of No.44 Squadron were entertained by local residents at the Seven Kings Library Hall, where they sat at five tables covered with excellent wartime fare, drinks galore and an abundant supply of cigars and cigarettes, etc. The hall, covered with national flags of Britain's allies and bunting, presented a jolly scene as the festivities got under way. After the health of the King had been proposed and the National Anthem sung in the flag bedecked Library Hall, Councillor G R Davey presiding, on behalf of the local business men and residents, told the mixed audience at the beginning of a well-received speech, 'This evening is in honour of the men of the Royal Air Force, who arrived in the district for the protection of people and property during air-raids. It is no light task,' he observed, 'to plant large numbers of men in a residential area, but they have conducted themselves admirably and like gentlemen". He then extended to the officers and men of No.44 Squadron the gratitude of everyone in the district.

Lieut Roberts, apologising for the absence of his commanding officer, returned the thanks of No.44 Squadron and spoke of the gracious way they had been welcomed by the people of Ilford. The evening continued with musical entertainment provided by local artists. Miss Wilson, Bartlett, Hurley, Roberts, Roberts, (sisters), Miss Sidney and Mrs Wells, aided and abetted by Frank Conner, Phillip Fuller, Bert Nicholls and Layard Nuttell. Mr and Mrs Walter Hammond, caretakers of Seven Kings Library Hall, were commended on their successful catering and general arrangements that ensured the evening had been enjoyed by all.

Although 41 year old Archibald Pilkington of 21 Grange Road had been rejected three times for military service, his sudden death, following a heart attack, came as a shock to his family and fellow employees at the Ilford Aeroplane Works. The funeral of the Ilford carpenter, who had suffered from Brights disease, took place on Thursday afternoon, 9th May, at the Ilford Council Cemetery, attended by his young widow, family and workmates.

On Tuesday, 14th May, the body of 2nd Lieut John Donald Baird, killed in the accident at Hainault Farm aerodrome the previous Wednesday, was carried in a Union Jack covered coffin upon a No.44 Squadron tender along the Ilford High Road. A cortège of officers and men from the Squadron, including a detachment of the Women's Legion attached to the aerodrome, were escorted by the band of the Essex Regiment from the Warley Depôt, the Romford Drum and Fife Band and a contingent of the Artists' Rifles from Gidea Park. The unfortunate airman was laid to rest with full military honours in St Mary's churchyard.

On Thursday, May 16th, a surprise bombing raid on Cologne by six DH4's of No.55 Squadron carried the horror of bombing home to German civilians. Forty townsfolk were killed and over 100 injured; 38 buildings, including water and electricity works, were damaged and important rail movements delayed for eight hours.

On Sunday, 19th May, Captain Tryggve Gran, having returned from convalescence leave in Norway, found himself again at Suttons Farm aerodrome, now occupied by No.78 Squadron. Although it had been less than a year

since his departure from Hornchurch to Hainault Farm for the formation of No.44 Squadron, he was surprised at the large number of brick buildings now surrounding the original wooden huts of the expanding aerodrome.

German bombers, attempting to put the vital Étaples bridge, carrying the only north-south rail link across the British sector of the Western Front, out of action, hit the nearby British military hospital, resulting in an horrific death toll of 182, with a further 643 wounded, including nursing staff.

Whit-Sunday had been fine and warm in and around London, with a slight mist forming during the evening; this, combined with the Bank Holiday exodus from the City, no doubt helped to reduce the death toll of the biggest aeroplane raid on the capital. London's defences were alerted at 22.42 hrs, LADA headquarters were deluged in reports, as 28, out of a force of 38 Gothas despatched, began to cross the Kent and Essex coasts at short intervals. Eleven minutes later, aerodromes of No.6 Brigade began to receive patrol orders; at Hainault Farm the first Camel became airborne at 22.55 hrs, Lieut J H Summers being followed at one minute intervals by Lieut W E Nicholson, Capt R N Hall and Capt W H Haynes.

Accompanying the Gothas attempting the biggest raid on London were the surviving three Giants of Rfa 501; earlier, two single engined Rumpler machines had reported favourable weather conditions over England before bombing Dover.

Ilford airman, Lieut William Goodleff Scotcher of 80 Balfour Road, led the Camels of No.112 Squadron on patrol at 23.00hrs; his Commanding Officer, Major

C J Q Brand, in the sixth machine from Throwley aerodrome, took off at 23.15 hrs. Within minutes of being airborne, Brand could not believe his luck, 200ft above his Camel D6423, flying across Faversham, at 8,500ft were the twin exhaust glow of a Gotha. 'Flossie' Brand, who had been frustrated in his efforts to bag a Gotha as a Flt Commander at Hainault Farm, climbed under the tail of the now visible bomber and fired two 20 round bursts into the starboard engine at close range. As the tunnel gunner opened fire, the South African pilot aimed three 25 round bursts in return. Suddenly the enemy bomber dipped its nose and banked steeply in an attempt to shake the Camel off. In a tight turn, the experienced Camel pilot closed to point blank range and fired again; the Gotha exploded into flames and singed the Major's moustache and eyebrows. Watching the burning remains fall to earth, he checked his watch and realised he had been airborne for just eleven minutes - and continued his patrol. The remains of the Gotha crew shot down by Major Brand were later buried with full military honours in St Clement's Churchyard, Leysdown.

Above Loughton, Camel B4614, piloted by Lieut W E Nicholson, developed a fault due to a broken pressure valve, forcing the experienced night flyer to break away from a Gotha after two attacks and wisely putting the 'Comic' down safely on the flare path at Chingford aerodrome.

Capt W H Haynes had been on patrol from Hainault Farm for just over half an hour, when he encountered a bomber above Romford, heading for east London.

At 23.00 hrs. Capt Haynes' machine, B3816, also a converted Comic, carried two over the wing firing Lewis guns, the right hand gun angled upward at 45 degrees to eliminate the trajectory curve when aiming. An exponent of the Camel and night flyer second to none, Bill Haynes manoeuvred the little biplane 500 ft beneath the bomber to avoid its slipstream, emptying a drum of armour piercing rounds from the right hand gun, forced the large machine to slowly zig-zag. Haynes pursued the lumbering machine across London, where bombs fell on Bethnal Green, and back across Essex. Attacking all the time, until his ammunition ran out over North Benfleet, Haynes reluctantly abandoned the chase and returned to Hainault Farm with bullet holes in his wings and propeller.

Five minutes into Bank Holiday Monday, 20th May, the crew of No.39 Squadron Bristol Fighter from North Weald, on patrol at 11,000 ft, saw the tell-tale glow of a twin engined bomber to the north of Hainault forest. Lieut A J Arkell pushed the stick forward and opened the throttle of the Rolls-Royce Falcon engine, swiftly overtaking the Gotha from beneath, allowing his observer 1st AM A T C Stagg, to open fire with his Lewis gun, before delivering a long burst at close range from his forward firing Vickers. The bedeviled Gotha dived and turned repeatedly, its two gunners trying to return fire, as the two man crew of the Bristol Fighter fired bursts in turn to avoid over-heating their weapons. At 1,500 ft, the starboard engine of the Gotha caught fire, after receiving the attention of Stagg's Lewis at close range.

Slowly the machine spun towards the ground, two of the crew jumped or were thrown to their deaths. The third German airman perished in the remains of the bomber that fell in flames on an allotment near Roman Road, East Ham. Lieut Arkell and AM Stagg in C4636, aptly named 'Devil in the Dusk', returned safely to North Weald at 00.45 hrs: their victory was the first for No.39 Squadron since the invincible Zeppelin myth had been shattered by them in autumn, 1916.

During the three hour air-raid on the 19/20th May, numerous attacks on enemy aeroplanes were reported by pilots; this was due to the largest force of bombers over south-east England so far, good visibility and the ever improving London defences. There were a few disappointed night flyers, however. On his return to Hainault Farm out of ammunition, it had been suggested to Bill Haynes that the Gotha he attacked time and time again may have been a much larger Giant, whose twin nacelles housed two engines apiece in tandem. Giants, with a span 60 ft greater than a Gotha, had misled Ilford airmen on previous raids into opening fire at extreme range; this theory does not explain the battle damage sustained by Haynes' Camel, inflicted by the return fire of the Germans.

Capt D'Urban Victor Armstrong, who had established his reputation as the premier aerobatic pilot of the Sopwith Camel at Hainault Farm the previous summer, also had his share of bad luck during that night. On patrol in Camel C6713 (Doris) from No.78 Squadron Suttons Farm aerodrome, Armstrong encountered a Gotha clearly visible in the moonlight near Orsett at 23.55 hrs. He too carried out repeated attacks, closing to within 50 yards before firing, clearing a stoppage in one Vickers gun without losing sight of the enemy aeroplane, and emptied the remainder of his ammunition belts point blank at the Gotha, now flying at 9,000 ft between Hainault and Suttons Farm aerodromes towards London, before returning to Hornchurch empty handed.

Pilots of No.6 Brigade were credited with destroying a third Gotha during the air-raid, Major Frederick Sowrey, awarded the DSO whilst serving with No.39HD Squadron for the destruction of Naval Zeppelin L32 above Billericay during the night of 23rd September, 1916, engaged the ill-fated Gotha first. After a tour of duty with No.19 Squadron in France during 1917, Frederick Sowrey returned to England with a further 12 enemy machines to his credit, before taking command of No.143 Squadron, a new Home Defence unit, on 14th February.

During his patrol Sowrey, flying S.E.5a C1804, actually encountered two Gothas, the first just fifteen minutes after take off from Detling, flying north-east of Maidstone. Emptying a drum of ammunition into the belly of the enemy machine, Sowrey accidentally dropped the empty drum and lost his prey retrieving it from the cockpit floor before tossing it over the side. Forty minutes later he emptied two drums into the underside of an outward-bound Gotha that took violent evasive action. Pulling back on the stick to bring his forward firing Vickers in to action and stalling in the process, the S.E.5a span a few times, losing contact with the Gotha, before Sowrey regained control. The following morning an expended Lewis drum, used by Major Sowrey, was handed to Maidstone Police by Mr Roland White, who reported it had fallen through the roof of his house, as he stood in the street watching the chase.

Unseen by Sowrey, the damaged Gotha crashed near Frinsted around 00.45 hrs Whit Monday morning. The CO of No.143 Squadron did not claim the enemy bomber in his combat report, but No.6 Brigade at first credited him its destruction. One member of the crew survived the crash with a broken arm, confirming that Sowrey had wounded the pilot, before they came under fire from another night fighter. The wounded German pilot had intended to set his damaged machine and crew down on the Frinsted NLG flarepath, when they came under fire from Bristol Fighter C851 of No.141 Squadron. Lieut Edward Turner had carefully positioned his machine, before allowing his gunner, Lieut Henry Barwise, to open fire, putting the port engine out of action with his first burst; a stoppage after the third burst did not matter. The Gotha rapidly lost height and Turner experienced some frustration, as his engine throttled back for the attack, but took its time to open up again. Again as in the case of the S.E.5a pilot from Detling, the crew of the Bristol never saw the enemy machine crash, but eventually the credit went to Turner and Barwise of No.141 squadron for their text-book attack, making the bomber the first German aeroplane destroyed by airmen from Biggin Hill aerodrome.

Ground defences accounted for no less than three Gothas shot down in flames during the Whitsun, 1918, air-raid and another Gotha, possibly battle damaged, crashed returning to base. All three Giants over England, in spite of encountering terrific barrages of anti-aircraft fire and night fighter attacks, also returned to their Belgian aerodromes. Casualties totalled 49 dead, plus 177 injured, and the bomb damage reviewed in the aftermath was regarded as light by the authorities, taking into account the large enemy force involved. All the fatal casualties were from London. However, two days later the newspapers carried a message from the Lord Mayor to Brigadier-General Ashmore in recognition of the air defences.

"The citizens of London are filled with admiration and gratitude for the splendid defensive measures taken by the Air Services against the enemy's attack, and will be glad if their appreciation and thanks may be conveyed to those who gallantly and successfully protected the capital on that occasion."

It had been the last air-raid of the Great War on London. The German High Command had not ended the aerial bombardment of London for humanitarian reasons; alarmed Rhineland mayors, expressing concern about the bombing of their towns and cities by the RAF, had been brushed aside by Field-Marshal von Hindenburg the previous month. The changing fortune of war, however, dictated that the Gothas of Boghohl 3 targeted the rear areas of the BEF.

The next night, German bombers destroyed 6,000 tons of ammunition during a raid on BEF dumps in France. Again, after dark on Tuesday, 21st May, German bombers struck at BEF dumps, causing fires that destroyed a further 5,600 tons of ammunition, including 69 million rounds of small arms ammunition; clearly, experienced night fighters were required urgently over there.

Hptmm Ernst Brandenburg, making use of a lull at the front, organised a night raid against London for Monday, 1st July, only to have it cancelled at short notice by High Command, as were all further attempts by the redoubtable Brandenburg to raid London.

Expectation of heavier air-raids continuing by day and night did not allow Home Defence squadrons to rest on their laurels, but five days later at Hainault Farm another near-fatal accident with the unforgiving Sopwith Camel occurred. On Saturday, 25th May, Lieut H J L Taylor, trying to stall turn in `Comic' B9287 at 200 ft, suffered serious injuries, when he lost control of the machine and crashed.

Fatal accidents on busy wartime aerodromes were not always due to air-frame or engine failure; the unfortunate Lieut Francis Beacroft Smith MC, serving with 207 TDS at Fairlop aerodrome, died on the morning of Tuesday, 28th May. During the inquest, held the following Friday morning at Ilford Town Hall, it emerged that a momentary lapse of concentration cost the 24 year old airman from Glasgow his life. The accident happened shortly after 06.30 hrs, when 2nd Lieut Charles Homewood, practising landing in Avro 504k D7657, touched down and switched off; Lieut Frank Smith swung the propeller of Homewood's biplane and the warm rotary barked into life to enable the pilot to continue his circuits and bumps. Eye witnesses

watched in horror as the unfortunate airman stooped as if to pick something up and was struck by the invisible whirling propeller of the 110 Le Rhône engine and thrown over the aeroplane. Still alive, but suffering terrible injuries, the casualty was rushed to the Ilford Emergency Hospital, where he died at 15.30 hrs that afternoon. Lieut Francis Beacroft Smith RAF, who had been awarded the Military Cross whilst serving with the Royal Naval Division, was buried with full military honours in the City of London Cemetery, Manor Park.

Just before midnight on Friday, 31st May, Lieut C C Banks, flying Camel D1894 of No.43 Squadron, shot down a Friedrichshafen bomber caught in search-lights behind the British lines. Since his posting to France, Charles `Sandy' Banks had added four enemy fighters to the Gotha he shared with Capt G H Hackwill over Essex in January.

Lieut Banks' victory over the Friedrichshafen bomber was the first for an RAF night fighter on the Western Front and had come following an appeal from No.58 Squadron, whose aerodrome at Fauquembergues was the target of nocturnal `Huns'. The unparalleled number of German bombs now falling on British ammunition dumps and aero-dromes under cover of darkness, resulted in an urgent demand for an experienced nightfighter squadron be flown to France to assist. In less than two weeks a new squadron would be formed and ready at Hainault Farm aerodrome destined for over there. Charles Banks returned to daylight patrols with No.43 Squadron, involving much low level strafing and survived the war with twelve enemy aircraft to his credit.

The sight of an RAF vehicle on the streets of Ilford was not unusual, but passers-by in the High Road on the morning of Friday, 31st May, saw the spectacular crash of an RAF Crossley Tender. Travelling at speed along the High Road, the WRAF driver turned right into Havelock Street, mounted the pavement and crashed head on into the glass shop-front of Messrs. Grey and Co, local tailors. Three large plate glass windows were shattered, showering the driver and her companions, another member of the WRAF and an RAF Corporal, with fragments. Dr Murphy attended to their wounds; fortunately, all were minor cuts and bruises. The vehicle sustained slight damage, but the shop front and much of the stock that had been on display had been ruined. The shocked staff of Grey and Co quickly recovered and made tea for their unexpected guests, after pushing the vehicle back out on the road, enabling the trio to return to the Hainault depôt.

By the early summer of 1918, Stanley Apling - now 2nd Lieut Apling RAF - under canvas at Northolt aerodrome, had progressed to flying Avro 504K machines solo. Unlike his days at the Stag Lane flying school, his first flights at Northolt were with an instructor who had the reputation of being a dare-devil to live up to. On one memorable occasion they landed with a length of telephone cable trailing from the machine, but had no idea how this came about. Stanley enjoyed flying the Avro solo and soon became confident enough to hedge-hop and fly alongside trains travelling the Northolt line embankment, before overtaking them with ease. Showing off by teenage pilots in their training machines was usually overlooked by their commanding officers, most of who were still young enough to remember the thrill and excitement of their own first solo flight.

It was a fine sunny morning at Northolt aerodrome and 2nd Lieut Stanley Apling did not bother to don his heavy flying coat or gauntlets before climbing into the waiting Avro biplane. After fastening his seat belt, he checked the aneroid set by the previous pupil; a few pumps brought the pressure back to the required three and a half pounds needed to supply fuel to the 100 hp Monosoupape rotary engine. Adjusting his goggles, he nodded to the Ack Emma standing by the propeller, who shouted, 'Switch off, petrol on.' Stanley complied and opened the petrol lever wide. A mechanic revolved the propeller, before shouting, 'Petrol off.' Stanley closed the petrol lever, and the Ack Emma took a firm grip of the propeller, before shouting, 'Contact.' Stanley flicked the ignition switch, and one hefty swing brought the engine back to life, as Stanley opened the petrol lever. Pulling the joystick back and 'buzzing' the rotary engine slowly, until the oil began to pulsate in the glass dome of the pulsometer on the instrument panel, Stanley then increased the petrol flow a fraction at a time, until the engine ran smoothly. Giving a hand signal for the wheel chocks to be pulled clear, Stanley, with joystick still held well back, taxied clear of the hangers before turning head on into the wind for take off. Ensuring that there were no other aircraft in the vicinity, Stanley opened the petrol lever, pushed the stick forward to raise the tailplane, and quickly became airborne, steadily climbing above the aerodrome.

He had been planning to show off to his parents in Ilford and his girl friend in Seven Kings for some time; the fine morning, combined with the heady aroma of burnt castor oil, doped fabric, varnished woodwork and a steady 1,200 rpm on the instrument panel, decided him. Stanley carried no map, but the River Thames to starboard made a useful guide. Crossing east London, Stanley arrived over Ilford, where he made several round trips above the family homes in Thorold and Cambridge Roads, flying low over the blue grey slate roofs. Returning for another buzz on Thorold Road, the slipstream snatched the goggles from his forehead, distracting him long enough for the port wings to slice 66 feet off a poplar tree in the garden next door but one to his parents' house. Being a local man, Stanley, anxiously watching the fluttering fabric on the damaged wings, flew to nearby Fairlop, some two miles away, where he had frequently watched Avros of the RNAS on training flights the year before. RAF personnel at Fairlop were still wearing RNAS overalls when they inspected the damaged Avro 504k. To his dismay, he was told that his aeroplane would be grounded for a day or two.

The arrival of 2nd Lieut Stanley Apling in his foliage-adorned Avro at the Ilford training aerodrome aroused little interest among the busy ground crew, long since resigned to the antics of the teenage airmen. Having signed the visiting pilots' book, a motorcycle combination, complete with rider, was made available to transport him to the railway station, just off the Ilford Broadway. He would return to Northolt by train with the ignominy of being improperly dressed - a cap and Sam Browne needed to complete his uniform were hanging in a locker at Northolt. He made a detour first to Cambridge Road, Seven Kings, where Nancy and her family, not knowing of his mishap, were surprised to see him; then on to Thorold Road, where his family, who had witnessed the incident, were relieved to see him uninjured. Reporting to his Commanding Officer on his return to Northolt, Stanley explained the pruning of the tree by saying

that the Avro's engine had choked and he had dived to clear it. Col Henderson looked at the young pilot and said, 'You must be careful you have too much confidence.' Of course, had he known Stanley lived in Ilford his comment would have been different; it was a standing order to remain within gliding distance of the aerodrome, but Stanley had already explained he thought it would be good practice to make a longer flight that morning.

On his next visit to his home in Thorold Road, Stanley retrieved his goggles, which had been found in a neighbour's back garden and was greeted by a lad he did not know, with the question, 'When are you coming over again?'

Stanley graduated to flying single seat Sopwith Pups at Northolt. Much to his surprise on one occasion, the little 'Scout' nosed over on landing, leaving him suspended upside down in the open cockpit by his seat belt. With difficulty he managed to release the belt and tumble out, as an ambulance came speeding across the grass-covered aerodrome to his aid, though he was again uninjured. His confidence returned in full when he found out the reason for the crash - a wheel had come off in flight.

Before Stanley graduated from Pups to Camels at Northolt, the latter were replaced with the S.E.5a - this was good news to the young man, who had been warned that if a Camel got in to an accidental spin turning the wrong way, it was impossible to regain control and a crash was inevitable. There would be no practical tuition on the new single seater, fitted with an in-line 200 hp Hispano Suiza. On one occasion Stanley's 'Hisso' powered S.E. stuck in the mud as he taxied back to the hangers after a flight;

annoyed, he pushed the lever throttle forward too hard, with the result the machine stood on its nose, shattering the wooden propeller.

A night fighter squadron, required urgently to defend the BEF rear areas, presented no problem, causing just a few days of chaos at Hainault Farm aerodrome, where No.151 Squadron was officially formed on Wednesday, 12th June, 1918. One flight of Sopwith F.l. Camels, equipped for night fighting and flown by experienced pilots from No.44 Squadron, were brought up to full squadron strength with a further flight each from No. 78 and 112 Squadrons.

The day previous, Major Arthur Travers Harris arrived at Hainault Farm from No.45 Squadron in France. Credited with five enemy aeroplanes destroyed, Arthur Harris had served with Home Defence in 1916, hunting Zeppelins with B Flight No.39 Squadron from nearby Suttons Farm aerodrome, Hornchurch.

No.151 Squadron went to France, under the command of Major G W Murlis Green, on Sunday, 16th June, leaving Major Harris commanding No.44 Squadron at Hainault Farm aerodrome.

On Sunday, 16th June, there was another serious training accident at Fairlop, when 2nd Lieut J Herries, flying solo in Avro 504k D162, stalled on a turn and spun into the ground.

On Sunday, 23rd June, No.151 Squadron established an aerodrome at Fontaine-sur-Maye; the new Squadron suffered the loss of Lieut W S Bannister, who died of injuries sustained in a landing accident in Camel C6159 en route to join the squadron on Tuesday, 25th June.

Hardly had the pilots of No.151 Squadron familiarised themselves with their area when on Thursday, 27th June, A Flight received orders to fly to Famechon and escort the FE2b bombers of No.101 Squadron on night raids. B and C Flights of No.151 Squadron began regular night patrols of allocated back areas, as flown with Home Defence squadrons in England.

Capt D V Armstrong, flying Camel C6713 (Doris), attacked the first enemy bomber for No. 151 Squadron on Saturday, 29th June, when he fired at an LVG caught in searchlight beams near Estree at 20.35 hrs, sending it down out of control into the darkness.

Unlike the experienced South African, Lieut W Aitken, transferred from No.112 to No.151 Squadron, flying Camel D9445, also fired upon a bomber the same night before it escaped into the clouds; the crew of the next enemy machine he fired at would not be so fortunate.

A number of `Comics' had been flown to France with No. 151 Squadron; those from Ilford sported a knight's helmet with the flight colours of No.44 Squadron on either side of the fuselage. The limited range of the small tank fitted to the converted Camel made it unsuitable for patrols beyond the enemy lines.

At the end of June, as the rapid build-up of American troops in Europe exceeded one million men, the German High Command planned to launch their fifth major offensive of the year.

On Monday, 1st July, Major Murlis Green returned to England, taking command of No.112 Squadron at

Sergeant Pilot William Rowland Felton (*Ilford War Memorial Gazette*)

No.112 Squadron

Throwley, leaving No.151 Squadron in the capable hands of Major Quintin 'Flossie' Brand. Lieut W G Nicol of No.151 Squadron, on patrol the following night, had a narrow escape when Camel B3852, damaged by anti-aircraft fire, crashed and caught fire on landing at Le Touquet. B3852 had been flown by 'Flossie' Brand at Hainault Farm on many anti-Gotha patrols the previous winter and, as a presentation aircraft, carried the name of 'Makhabane', after the Paramount Chief of the Basuto Nation.

Lieut W F H Harris of M Flight No. 151 Squadron, attached to No.101 Squadron, also had a narrow squeak when he crashed, landing after night operations in Camel D.9509.

Closer to home, local pilot Sgt William Rowland Felton of 375 High Road, Ilford, died from injuries received, following a crash at 11.50 hrs in BE2e 9989 of 203 T.D.S during a solo flight on Tuesday, 2nd July, and was buried with honours the following week in St Mary's in his home town.

No.44 Squadron at Hainault Farm suffered another casualty when Camel D6686, piloted by 2nd Lieut H F M Wise, flying low, stalled on turn and crashed, injuring the pilot on Friday, 5th July.

The Le Rhône engine of Camel D9441 of No.151 Squadron cut out on take off, wrecking the converted nightfighter, fortunately the pilot, Lieut L Cook, escaped serious injury.

The large number of German bombers active after dark over the British back areas in France, encountered pilots of No.151 Squadron frequently, but it proved difficult for the night fighters to confirm fallen enemy machines unless they fell in flames or behind allied lines. Capt Reginald Hearne RMC driving along Forest Road past busy Fairlop aerodrome on the afternoon of Monday, 8th July, observed an Avro biplane flying at about 400 ft turn to the left without banking, stall and spin slowly into an open field fifty yards away from the road. Capt Hearne drove across to the wreck of Avro C5843 and with the aid of airmen who ran across to help, released the pilot trapped in the wreckage and drove him to the aerodrome sick ward. On examination 2nd Lieut Charles Homewood, the injured pilot, had suffered two broken legs, a fractured right arm and serious abdominal injuries. He was rushed to the Ilford Emergency Hospital by ambulance, where he died a few hours later without regaining consciousness. 2nd Lieut Homewood from Stapenhurst in Kent had witnessed the propeller accident involving the unfortunate Lieut Frank Smith at Fairlop six weeks before.

A simple flying accident robbed the Royal Air Force of Major James T B McCudden VC, officially credited with 57 German aeroplanes. The experienced airman who had come through the ranks from an air mechanic in the pre-war Royal Flying Corps, died of injuries following a crash when the engine of his SE5a choked after take-off in France on Tuesday 9th July.

On Saturday night, 13th July, Lieut Alfred Victor Blenkiron of No.151 Squadron, a former SE5a pilot with No.56 Squadron, fired at a Gotha beyond the enemy lines just before midnight, but lost it in the darkness.

During the night of Monday, 22nd July, Blenkiron put one engine of a Friedrichshafen bomber out of action and followed it down to almost ground level, but could not confirm the enemy had crashed. The same night, Maj C J Q Brand, CO of 151 Squadron, flying Camel D6423, was forced to land with engine trouble without serious damage; it was another presentation machine from Basutoland named 'Makhabane 11', the same machine he brought down the Gotha in Kent the previous May.

Local airman, Lieut George Ebben Randall, from 3rd Avenue, Manor Park, flew as an observer with No. 3 Squadron in France, before returning to England for pilot training. By July, 1918, he was again in France, flying Bristol Fighters with No. 20 Squadron in action over the enemy lines. On Wednesday evening, 24th July, George Randall, flying D8086, with Lieut G V Learmond as his observer, shot down a Fokker DV11. During the next four months, George Randall would be credited with another nine of the formidable Fokker biplanes, plus a Pfalz D111. Lieut G V Learmond, flying frequently as Randall's observer, would be credited with nine enemy aeroplanes. On the evening of Thursday, 25th July, the airmen at Fairlop aerodrome, redesignated No. 54 TDS four days earlier, saw the new unit's first fatal flying accident. 2nd Lieut William Meff had been airborne from Fairlop for twenty minutes in Camel E1420, before he got into difficulties and span into the ground from 500 ft. The unfortunate 22 year old airman from Aberdeen, with just 27 hours flying time in his log book, died of a fractured skull,

another victim of the deadly but dangerous Sopwith Camel.

No. 54 TDS, with Headquarters still at the ex-RNAS Station in Chingford, was formed at Fairlop to train two fighter squadrons up to front line service standards. Sopwith Camels were issued to the Depôt for advanced pupils. What the rapid expansion programme of the RAF and demand for more and more pilots in the summer of 1918 had on the Ilford aerodrome can be judged by the increase in fatal flying accidents. July, in particular, proved to be a black month for Fairlop aerodrome.

Another successful encounter for a patrolling night fighter of No. 151 Squadron took place in the early hours of Thursday, 25th July. Capt A B Yuille sighted a twin engined bomber at 00.45 hrs above Étaples. Closing to within 30 yards range in 'Comic' D5673, Capt Yuille fired 50 rounds, wounding the gunner. His second burst put one engine out of action; his third, the other engine. Unseen by Capt Yuille, the Friedrichshafen GlVa fell within British lines, later the surviving crew members confirmed the No.151 Squadron pilot's combat report.

Low cloud and heavy rain marred the visit of King George V and Queen Mary to No.44 Squadron at Hainault Farm on Friday 26th July, accompanied by Prince Albert (later King George VI) and General Sir William Robertson, Commander in Chief Great Britain, Major-General E R Ashmore, commanding LADA and Captain B Godfrey-Faussett RN. An eye-witness account also included the Rt Hon Winston Churchill, Minister of Munitions, among the entourage.

When the Brown family of 252 Kingston Road were informed their eighteen year old son, serving with the RAF had been posted to the nearby aerodrome at Hornchurch for flight training they were delighted. Sadly, Flying Cadet Charles David Brown, flying Avro 504K 1482 of No.189 Training Squadron, collided with another machine piloted by Lieut G E Taylor, whilst practising aerial fighting near Dartford. The collision occurred at 17.30 hrs on Saturday, 27th July, at 2,000 ft and young Charles fell to his death, when his Avro disintegrated with the force of the impact. Lieut G F Taylor's damaged Avro overturned on landing; the pilot suffered a broken leg, badly cut head and bruises all over.

No.54 Training Depôt Station, Fairlop, in the summer of 1918 was gearing up to train two single seat fighter squadrons to front line standard. At the same time nine large canvas hangers housed 24 Avro trainers and 24 Camels; officers and N.C.Os under instruction numbered 120. The establishment of 573 personnel at Fairlop included 110 WRAF, plus another 42 women on household duties. Transport at the ex-RNAS aerodrome included a touring car, 8 light Tenders, 8 heavy Tenders, 6 motor cycles, 4 sidecars and 3 trailers for the movement of aeroplanes by road. When fully trained, the Fairlop airmen were expecting to proceed overseas at squadron strength, flying Sopwith Snipes ordered in large numbers to replace the Camels.

Hainault Farm Home Defence aerodrome officially sited one mile east of Fairlop, the boundaries of the two aerodromes were much closer. No doubt when airborne, the more experienced airmen at Hainault Farm gave the trainees at Fairlop a wide berth.

The worst mid-air collision at Fairlop aerodrome during the Great War took place on Monday evening, 29th July. Flt Sgt Arnold Bean from Staffordshire, a pupil under instruction by 2nd Lieut Harold Blake Hatcher from Bristol, flying Avro D7660, collided at 20.30 hrs with Camel F2104, piloted by 2nd Lieut Laurie Bell. A report in the *Ilford Recorder* of the inquest on the accident that took place at the Ilford Town Hall the following week entitled TRIPLE AIR FATALITY, quoted eye-witness, Capt. Edgar Winter RAF, describe how the Camel, piloted by Bell, dived upon the Avro flying 500 ft below cutting it in two. 2nd Lieut Hatcher fell out of the wrecked two seater as the wings of Bell's Camel slowly folded into a V and fluttered free following the fuselage to the ground. All three airmen lost their lives.

Flt Sgt Bean was found in the sitting position, still strapped in the front half of the Avro fuselage, his instructor's body was found unmarked thirty yards away in the grass where it had fallen. The wingless Camel crashed close by, 2nd Lieut Bell from Bournemouth was found to have almost every bone in his body broken.

The same day, Lieut L C Sheffield, No.151 Squadron, having lost his bearings, crashed, attempting to land near Totes, escaping injury.

July almost claimed another 54 IDS pilot as a fatal casualty, when 2nd Lieut Harry Croyle Curtiss, at the controls of Camel B5659, flew to Chingford reservoir on the evening of Tuesday, 30th, to practice diving on a target. During his third attempt he misjudged the height, allowing the Camel wheels to hit the water, flipping the machine over on to its back and sink. The fortunate pilot escaped drowning and serious injury.

Unlike the purely defensive role of No.44 Squadron, No.151, the other Camel squadron formed at Ilford, became the first night fighter squadron in the RAF to adopt an offensive role by flying intruder patrols over enemy aerodromes.

During the night of Thursday, 1st August, Capt S Cockerell, on offensive patrol in Camel C6717 of 151 Squadron, arrived over the bombers lair at Estrees, just as a machine was landing. He released a bomb that exploded 50 yards from the bomber. Capt Cockerell fired 200 rounds at another bomber preparing to land, when all the ground lighting was extinguished; losing sight of the bomber, he dropped two more bombs on the blacked out aerodrome below before ending his patrol.

During the next two months, No.151, the second squadron formed at Ilford during the war with the most experienced Home Defence flyers, became the undisputed Nightfighters of 1918.

A lighter moment in the history of Hainault Farm aerodrome during the summer was provided by the workmen of Messrs A Roberts, contracted to build permanent living quarters for the officers and men of No. 44 Squadron. With the consent of the CO, Major Arthur Harris, the Ilford contractors arranged an horticultural show in the new brick built officers' mess on Friday afternoon, 2nd August, in aid of the Red Cross Fund. Three long tables displayed vegetables from local allotments and gardens and smaller tables were arranged with fruit and flowers. Judges awarded prizes totalling five pounds ten shillings for the best exhibits.

Many Ilford gardens grew vegetables during the war, following numerous appeals by press and posters to overcome the serious food shortage brought about by the U-boat blockade. Following prize-giving in the officers' mess, the produce was auctioned off by Lieut Shakell, with very spirited bidding from Lieut Maxwell, representing the officers and F/Sgt Courtney for the Sergeants' mess. A grand total of £16, the proceeds of the auction, went to the Ilford Emergency Hospital Fund.

August witnessed the tonnage of British merchant ships sunk by U-boats halved from 300,000 during August, 1917, to 150,000 tons, thanks to the convoy system introduced by the Royal Navy.

New ration books issued in Ilford the following month ensured a fairer distibution of essential foods.

Two machines of No. 151 Squadron again carried out offensive patrols over German aerodromes on the night of 2nd August, despite low cloud and rain. Major C J Q Brand, flying Camel D6423, dropped two 20 lb Cooper bombs on hangers at Guizancourt aerodrome, before attacking a two seater attempting to land. He fired a further 100 rounds at the machine on the ground, before the lights being placed around it to warn other retulning bombers of the danger were put out. Dropping another two bombs in front of another bomber attempting to land, he was fired upon by an enemy night fighter. Empty of bombs and bullets, `Flossie' called it a night after 40 eventful minutes over the enemy airfield. Capt S Cockerell, flying Camel C6717, also dropped bombs on hangers at Guizancourt, visible in the glare of landing searchlights, before firing on each light until they were extinguished. At 00.45 Capt Cockerell shot up another bomber preparing to land; immediately all the landing lights were extinguished and the Gotha crash landed two miles from the aerodrome.

An early Bank Holiday attraction for some Ilfordians took place when the Essex County Cricket Ground, Leyton, was the venue for a baseball match between American and Canadian military personnel on Saturday afternoon, 3rd August, 1918, and attracted a crowd of curious good humoured spectators.

Sunday, 4th August, saw the fourth anniversary of the Nation's declaration of war, observed in Ilford by special services at all the churches and a united demonstration around the bandstand in Valentines Park, from the roof of which fluttered flags of the Empire and the Allies in the summer breeze. The band of the Salvation Army were flanked on either side by choristers from St Clement's, St Mary's and other Ilford churches. The stillness of the vast congregation during the prayers was profound experience for those present; few had been left untouched by four years of war. Small contingents of airmen from nearby aerodromes were in attendance at the various parades across Ilford, but the ever present threat of the Gotha's return, ensured No.44 Squadron maintained a state of readiness around the clock.

The spell of fine weather saw dawn to dusk flying at Fairlop aerodrome, as 54 TDS made use of the long summer days to ensure the extensive flight training programme did not fall behind schedule. A lightship sighting of five Zeppelins heading towards England in the twilight of Monday evening, 5th August, set in operation a chain of events that resulted in the destruction of the Zeppelin L70

and the end of the Imperial Navy's bombing campaign against England.

Commissioned the previous month, 694 ft in length, the new airship, powered by 7 engines developing 1,715 hp had exceeded 80 mph on trail runs and had the capability to operate at above 20,000 ft. Why the Germans did not wait for darkness, instead of disclosing their intentions of raiding the Midlands by arriving off-shore at dusk where they were seen, and why L70 was caught by RAF fighters flying as low as 17,000 ft will never be known. 35 RAF machines from No.4 Group, the ex-RNAS Stations along the Norfolk coast, and No.6 Brigade aerodromes inland, answered the challenge.

Major Egbert Cadbury and Capt Robert Leckie, flying D.H.4 A8032 from Yarmouth, found L70 above the clouds. Cadbury opened the throttle of the 375 hp Rolls-Royce Eagle, as Leckie cleared the Lewis ready for action. Both airmen were experienced Zeppelin fighters; in November 1916, Cadbury played a major rôle in the destruction of L21 and Leckie L22 in May, 1917. Explosive bullets blew large holes along the side, igniting the hydrogen that tore the monster in two, blazing wreckage fell through the clouds carrying the entire crew, including Kvkpt Peter Strasser, a last minute passenger, to watery graves.

Two million cubic feet of blazing hydrogen turned dusk into day above the clouds warning the commanders of L53, L56, L63 and L65 that the same fate awaited them if they continued. Bomb loads were jettisoned into the sea and, despondent, Zeppelin crews returned to base without their brave, but fanatical,

Lieutenant Herbert T Flintoft (3rd from left, back row) with fellow pilots of No.56 Squadron

No.56 Squadron

Leader, Peter Strasser. The Imperial German Naval Airship bombardment of Britain had come to an end.

Marshal of France, Ferdinand Foch, appointed Generalissimo of all the Allied forces in France during the desperate days of March, 1918, unleashed a massive counter attack on the Western Front. Preceded by artillery bombardment. at 04.20 hrs Thursday, 8th August, 1918, six hundred tanks led the attack by the combined British 4th and French 1st Armies at Amiens. As the German Army was fought back towards the River Somme, RAF pilots began low level bombing of the bridges, vital to rush urgently needed reinforcements into the battle. Losses were high on both sides. By dusk, the Germans had been pushed back nine miles and were in such disorder that General Erich von Ludendorff described it as `the black day for the German Army'.

Lieut Grady Touchstone, the American aviator who had received basic flight training at Hainault Farm before his transfer to Stamford in January, was wounded and taken prisoner after being shot down flying an S.E.5a with No.1 Squadron RAF at Fienvillers in France.

Major C J Q Brand and Capt D V Armstrong, No.151 Squadron, were over the enemy lines again after dark. Returning to Estrees aerodrome, they shot down a machine attempting to land in flames, both pilots then bombed and shot up landing lights and hangers.

On Saturday, 10th August, Lieut Herbert Flintoft of 100 Lansdowne Road, Seven Kings, became a PoW. Flying with No.56 Squadron, his S.E.5a D6094 was forced down during combat with enemy fighters well over the lines. Patrolling night fighters of No.151 Squadron attacked a bomber lit up by searchlights over Doullens, but Captain A B Yuille, flying Camel D6573, did not open fire until he closed to within 25 yards. Three short bursts disabled an engine, two more set a fire raging in the fuselage. The Germans had risked a Staaken Giant to attack a target just 16 miles behind the front line in a well defended sector and paid the price; the burning mass of the Giant five engined R.43 crashed near Talmas at 23.50 hrs. Five of the seven man crew attempted to escape by parachute, but perished with their comrades. The same night, two ex-Hainault Farm Comics, piloted by Lieut C E Knight and Lieut J H Summers now serving with No. 151 Squadron, were responsible for a `Gotha-type' last seen out of control beyond the enemy lines.

On Sunday morning, 11th August, Zeppelin L53, commanded by Kvtkpt Eduard Prolss, shadowing the Harwich Light Cruiser Force off the island of Terschelling, became the last Imperial Naval Zeppelin to fall to the guns of a British airman. While six Coastal Motor Torpedo Boats carried in pairs by the cruisers, set off to attack enemy shipping in the River Ems, attempts were made to get three Curtis Hl2 flying boats aloft, but a choppy sea prevented the large twin engined machines from getting airborne, and returned to be floated back on to their lighters towed by destroyers. A fourth destroyer towed a lighter fitted with a platform and a Sopwith Camel with a wheeled undercarriage, enabling the well trained deck crew to get the fearless pilot aloft. 22 year old Lieut Stuart Culley had the skill and nerve to take off from the tiny 53 ft long platform towed by *Redoubt* at full speed into the wind. Stuart Culley wasted little time on his subsequent report of the destruction of the 644 ft long airship and her nineteen man crew.

"08.58 hours, flew from lighter to attack Zeppelin from 300 feet below. Fired seven rounds from No 1 gun that jammed and a double charge (47 round Lewis drum) from No 2. Zeppelin burst into flames and was destroyed."

A large patch of bubbling oily scum and flotsam briefly marked the watery grave of the last German airshipmen killed in action. Technology had so advanced the aeroplane during four years of war that the Zeppelin had lost its propaganda value. Running low on fuel, Culley eventually located the *Redoubt* and set his Camel down with little damage on the sea nearby, Camel N6812 was swiftly hoisted aboard. Stuart Douglas Culley was awarded the DSO on 2nd November, for a most difficult undertaking.

On the Home Front, parishioners of St Mary's were told that their vicar, Rev H V Eardley Wilmot, acting as Chaplain to an artillery division in France, had suffered shrapnel wounds to his back and legs, and thefts of vegetables from local park allotments were a serious problem.

The Allied push in France was halted to enable heavy artillery and tanks to catch up with the infantry; overhead the RAF were fighting large formations of enemy fighters with combined squadrons, Nos 20 and 29 Squadrons escorted by 74 and 85 Squadrons carried out low level bombing on busy Courtrai railway station and sidings, leaving four fires burning. after dark. German bombers struck at Calais, destroying a BEF motor transport depôt containing ½ million pounds worth of badly needed tyres and inner tubes. Night fighters of No.151 Squadron were active, Lieut A C McVie, flying Camel D9572, escaped injury after crashing at Le Crotoy.

As the middle of August approached, the Ilford Hippodrome, as usual, played to packed houses with the popular revue *The Bing Boys Are Here*, starring George Robey and Violet Loraine; there was little regard given to the expected return of German bombers. Such was the mood of the town, the strident American marching song 'Over There', likened by many to 'Tipperary', was being played, sung and whistled with the same optimism as in the early days of the war.

Tuesday, 13th August, proved to be lucky for 2nd Lieut S A Grimwade, an advanced pupil undergoing flight training with 54 TDS at Fairlop. He escaped serious injury in a landing mishap that wrote Camel E1419 off charge at the Ilford aerodrome.

Five RAF and one American squadron, attached to the British, carried out a low level raid on Varssenacre aerodrome, near Bruges; petrol and ammunition stores were set on fire, six Fokker biplanes on the ground were left in flames, two more were destroyed by direct bomb hits.

Fokker DVIIs replaced Albatros and Pfalz fighters as fast as they could be built in 1918, friend and foe alike agreed they were the best fighters in service when the more powerful 185hp BMW engine began replacing their 160hp Mercedes power units during the late summer.

Hangers, including a large Gotha type, were badly damaged, all the Allied machines taking part returned, despite heavy anti-aircraft fire damage inflicted upon them.

On Wednesday, 14th August, local airman 2nd Lieut Donald Stephens, serving with No.57 Squadron as an observer to Lieut G Anderson, piloting a D.H.4 returning from a bombing raid, shot the wings off one of the many enemy fighters trying to break up the tight formation of the British squadron. Two German pilots were seen to jump from burning aeroplanes and descended by parachute, during the long battle to regain the safety of the Allied lines. After dark, Lieut A V Blenkiron, on patrol in Camel D9577, added another bomber to No.151 Squadron's tally. He watched a twin engined machine held in searchlights near Bapaume and closed in for the kill. Several short bursts of fire from the Camel sent the AEG down on fire, falling inside the British sector; the crew members of Bogohl 3 were captured.

The parents of 2nd Lieut Donald Stephens at 21 Clarendon Gardens got a telegram stating that their son serving with No.57 Squadron in France had been reported missing in action on Friday, 16th August. His D.H.4 D9267, piloted by 2nd Lieut W H Kilbourne, was last seen by members of the squadron fighting their way back across enemy held territory, gliding down apparently under control.

Saturday, 17th August, saw a return match between the Ilford Aeroplane Works Athletic and the local Police Cricket Club, in aid of the Emergency Hospital, played at Gordon Fields. The first match had been won by the 'Works' by 50 to 33 runs; at the close of the return match, only nine runs divided the two teams - Ilford Police C.C. had 51; Aeroplane Athletic 42.

On Wednesday, 21st August, the Third Army, attacking in fog to the north of Amiens, caught the Germans off guard, forcing them back 3,000 to 4,000 yards on a wide front.

A stall, following a flat gliding turn, ended the young life of Lieut Frederick Charles Barlow of Highland Gardens, Ilford, who was at the controls of D.H.9 C1319, flying from No. 49 WTS Catterick, when he crashed.

Ordered in large numbers, 3,204 D. H. 9's were completed by the end of 1918; they had been intended to replace the D.H.4 now bearing the brunt of RAF daylight bombing raids. The D.H.9 not only suffered numerous problems with their 230 hp Siddeley Puma engines, but also proved inferior in performance to the machines they were replacing.

Searchlight crews were earning praise from No. 151 Squadron in ensuring the 'Hun' bombers, unable to fly over the British lines by day, were not only caught by their beams, but were held long enough for the patrolling Camels to attack: nights of hunting a fly in a dark room were just memories.

On Friday, 23rd August, Lieut W Aitken on patrol in Camel D9445, saw an enemy machine caught by searchlights. As Aitken closed in, the searchlights lost their quarry, but the gunners of the elusive Gotha opened fire on him at 40 yards range. Aitken returned eighty rounds, before the intruder dived away. Lieut Aitken followed, firing two short bursts, before he lost sight of the enemy and returned to his aerodrome. Gotha GVb 9/22/18 had crashed, bursting into flames

No. 44 Squadron took part in football matches, whist drives and other events in aid of the Ilford Emergency Hospital Fund. A three-legged race is about to be run by service personnel and civilians of Hainault Farm Aerodrome. (*Joe Mitchie via Barry Gray*)

near Beauquesne at 00.30 hrs; none of the three crew members survived.

Also on patrol for No. 151 Squadron in the early hours of that night, Captain A B Yuille and Lieut C R W Knight engaged a sinister Friedrichshafen G111 bomber, trapped in the glare of the ever vigilant searchlights. Capt Yuille fired two short bursts and overshot the lumbering machine. Lieut Knight, in Camel D6660, closed under the enemy's tailplane before opening fire; 100 rounds sent the large twin engine machine crashing in flames north of Arras at 01.15 hrs.

Capt Robert Mordaunt Foster, posted to No. 209 Squadron as a Flight Commander from Hainault Farm in April, had escaped injury throughout the fierce fighting over the enemy lines and adding 11 EA to his credit, but his luck almost deserted him this Friday morning, when his airborne Camel C61 collided with a Camel piloted by 2nd Lieut J E Gibbons. Both pilots survived to fight another day, but accident-prone Gibbons was to be killed on 9th October when his Camel F3223 collided with an observation balloon cable.

On Saturday afternoon, 24th August, unsettled weather may have been responsible for the smaller than usual turn-out for another charity football match at Gordon Fields in aid of the Ilford Emergency Hospital. The teams were No.44 Squadron RAF v Ilford XI, none of the pre-war Ilford team was available and several members of the homogenous team had been co-opted from No.7 Balloon Wing, serving in the area. Capt Robert Hall, acting on behalf of Major Arthur Travers Harris, the C.O. of Hainault Farm aerodrome, who was unable to attend, kicked off. The state of the pitch left much to be desired - during the match an injured player lay hidden in the long grass for several minutes as No.44 Squadron Camels buzzed low over the fields. Described as well balanced, the RAF team won the match 6 goals to 3, the latter all scored by Capt Kaye of the barrage Balloon section for the Ilford XI.

A dance held in the Gordon Fields Drill Hall in the evening was a great success enjoyed by all.

German bombers were busy again after dark behind the British lines. 12 aircraft of No.48 Squadron were destroyed in their hangers during a raid on Bertangles aerodrome. No.151 Squadron were in their element. Captain D V Armstrong, leading his Flight on patrol west of Arras, dived on Gothas netted by sweeping searchlights, Lieut F C Broome, Camel D6102, opened fire, but flying into the slipstream of the raider's powerful engines momentarily span out of control. Capt Armstrong, Camel C6713, fired at the same machine, but turned away to avoid a collision. Broome returned to the attack with a long burst that sent the Gotha spinning slowly into the ground near Haute-Avesnes at 22.0 hrs; two of the 3 man crew survived as prisoners of war. Lieut C R W Knight, the third member of Capt Armstrong's flight, again flying ex-Hainault Farm Camel D6660, sent another Friedrichshafen G111 down in flames, bombs exploding on impact with the ground, shortly after midnight on Sunday, 25th August.

Another 'Big Push' early the next morning, 26th, saw khaki infantry men going over the top into another bloodbath at Arras. Pouring rain and low clouds hampered much of the close support needed from the RAF.

On Monday afternoon, one notable

action involving the American 17th Pursuit Squadron attached to 111 Brigade BEF, flying Camels in RAF colours and markings, did take place. Experienced BMW powered Fokker DV11 pilots of Jasta's 2 and 7 accounted for six 17th Aero Camels shot down behind the German lines, three American aviators died, three remained as PoWs. Only in the hands of pilots as skilful as ex-Hainault Farm `Camel Merchant' Capt C C (Sandy) Banks of No.43 Squadron were able to hold their own in combat with the Fokker biplanes. Banks, flying Camel F9514, shot down a DV11 on Sunday, 29th August.

On Sunday, lst September, 2nd Lieuts S H Apling and J A Massey arrived as replacements for a front line SE5a squadron at Izel-le-Hameau. No.64 Squadron had sustained heavy casualties ground attacking in support of the Canadians during the battle of Arras and the new pilots went into action at once.

At Fairlop aerodrome Captain Charles Bailey, watching fellow instructor, Captain Lorwith Gwilym Davies, performing aerobatics in Avro 504k D2l10 during the afternoon of Monday, 2nd September, saw the biplane nosedive into the ground a mile away. Bailey accompanied the station ambulance to the scene of the crash, helping to release his friend from the wreckage, but the unfortunate 25 year old officer died shortly afterwards.

2nd Lieut Stanley Apling had not been destined to remain in action for long. On Wednesday, 4th September, two fellow officers collided and another went missing in action, bringing to light a serious lack of training among some of the arrivals. 2nd Lieut H T McKinnie, the missing officer, had served with the squadron just nine days, whilst 2nd Lieut Sifton Monmouth, injured in the collision, had only three weeks service. Lieut A M Stahl, having survived more than three months in action with No.64 Squadron, was killed in the accident.

Two weeks of bad weather severely hampered the Germans desperate bombing of the British back areas, giving the nightflyers of No.l51 Squadron some well earned respite.

On Thursday, 12th September, there was another body blow by the Allies, when 660,000 American and French troops, supported by 250 French tanks and 1,481 aeroplanes, went into action along the St. Mihiel salient. Among the heavy casualties suffered by the AEF flyers were Lieut David Putnam 139th Aero, with twelve confirmed EA, and Lieut Wilbur C Suiter, one of the `Yanks' of Hainault Farm aerodrome, who were billeted in Ilford the previous winter. Young Suiter was killed in action flying a D.H. 4 with 135th Aero.

On Friday night, 13th September, nocturnal `Huns' were again trying to avoid the searchlights over the British lines when an unlucky Gotha was illuminated long enough for Capt Harold Haynes of No.151 Squadron, patrolling in Camel E5142 to fire two-thirty round bursts at close range. The Gotha fell in flames near Bapaume at 21.25 hrs, making up for the one that got away over Lambourne End the previous year.

Minutes later Haynes engaged a twin engined Friedrichshafen, again at close range. Two fifty round bursts sent the ungainly bomber slowly spinning with

Lieutenant William G Scotcher in RFC uniform
(*Ilford War Memorial Gazette*)

No.50 Squadron

W G Scotcher, as a Flight Commander
with No.50 Squadron, in a Sopwith Camel
(*Douglas Whetton*)

spluttering exhaust flames down behind enemy lines at 21.40 hrs.

A minor mishap at the controls of his SE5a brought Stanley Apling to the attention of his commanding officer Major B E Smythies, who, on learning the young Ilford airman had no experience at all in formation flying, transferred Stanley back to Northolt on 18th September for further training. More experienced pilots were arriving daily at the front now thanks to the vast expansion of RAF training programme.

No. 151 Squadron brought down a third enemy machine on the night of Friday, 13th September, ten minutes after Capt Haynes' last action. Lieut E P Mackay fired 50 rounds at close range into the fuselage of a Friedrichshafen G111 held in searchlights near Peronne. Signal flares began to explode in the rear cockpit of the bomber; the pilot immediately dived to lose height quickly and crashed, attempting to land behind Allied lines.

On Sunday, 15th September, local airman, Capt William Goodleff Scotcher, No.50 Squadron Bekesbourne, flying Camel C6754, spun in from a steep turn near the ground at 21.50 hrs and died instantly. Capt Scotcher, the eldest of three boys who lived at 80 Balfour Road, Ilford, returned from South America, where he held an appointment with the Central Argentinian Railway Company, to fight in October, 1914. Commissioned in the East Yorks Regiment, he served at Galipolli with distinction, before being awarded the Military Cross for conspicuous bravery on the Somme. Transferring to the RFC as an observer,

he eventually trained as a pilot and was on patrol with his C. O., Major C J Q Brand, the night in May when 'Flossie' bagged his Gotha over Kent.

German aeroplanes bombed Paris during the night and 7 civilians were killed, 30 injured. The last long range German shell had fallen the previous month and this air-raid would also be the last.

Yet another Staaken Giant was squandered on a short range mission over the British lines, where the Camels of No.151 Squadron patrolled the night skies. Unable to hide coned in searchlight beams, the four engined Giant was unable, in spite of six machine guns, to fight off the determined attack of Capt F C Broome, flying Camel F6102; riddled with 500 bullets, the Giant crashed in flames near Bapaume at 22.20 hrs. One member of the crew survived as a Prisoner of War.

Major Brand had to abandon his attack upon a Friedrichshafen the same night; his bullets punctured the bomber's oil tanks, smothering him and his machine with engine lubricant.

On Tuesday, 17th September, French and Serbian forces advanced 20 miles into Bulgarian-occupied Serbia, as resistance of that German ally weakened.

Clouds were of no help to German bombers again over the British lines after dark. Major 'Flossie' Brand in his now oil-free Camel D6423 set fire to a Friedrichshafen that disintegrated as its bombs exploded east of Havincourt Wood at 22.41 hrs.

At about the same time, Captain D V Armstrong, flying Camel C6713 (Doris), sent another Friedrichshafen spinning

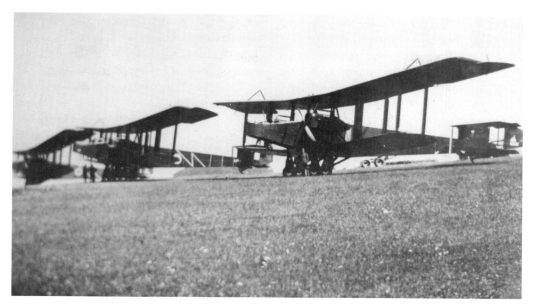

Handley Page 0/400 heavy bombers of No.215 Squadron, RAF (*Colin Ross*)

No.215 Squadron

down to burst into flames on crashing east of Bapaume, killing the crew.

Lieut E P Mackay, on patrol in Camel F1979, shot down the third raider for No.151 Squadron during Tuesday night, 17th September. 250 rounds sent the AEG GV down to crash and catch fire at 20.55 hrs south-east of Estrées-en-Chausée. No.215 Squadron RAF also lost a Handley Page O/400 bomber and crew that night. C9658 was brought down during a raid on Frescaty and Lieut Eric C Jeffkins, one of the two surviving crew members, became another Ilford PoW. Eric Jeffkins' address was The Lodge, Village Homes, Barkingside, and he was an ex-member of Ilford Town Hall staff.

In Palestine the battle of Megiddo opened with an artillery bombardment along a 65 mile front at 04.30 hrs on Thursday, 19th September; three hours later the demoralised Turkish front line troops had been over run.

Ilford had another military funeral when the cortège of Captain William Goodleff Scotcher MC, killed in a flying accident the week before, left the family home at 80 Balfour Road at 13.30 hrs. Venetian blinds along the route were lowered as a mark of respect. An RAF tender carried the Union Jack-covered oak coffin upon which laid the deceased's RAF cap. Airmen from local aerodromes provided a one hundred strong guard of honour and eight pallbearers; a service was held at St Clement's Church, attended by family, fiancée Miss Ethel Lupton, and many friends, including officers and men of No.50 Squadron. Following the service the procession reformed and continued its sad journey to the Ilford Council Cemetery, near St Mary's Church, where

the gallant Ilfordian was buried with full military honours.

Lieut L C Sheffield, No.151 Squadron, escaped serious injury after the engine of his 'Comic' E5165 spluttered and stopped whilst on night patrol; making a forced landing, his 'bus' ran into a shell crater at Bapaume.

On Friday, 20th September, bright moonlight betrayed a tubby twin engined AEG GV, flying at 7,000 ft, to the patrolling Camels of No.151 Squadron. The experienced Lieut F C Broome again in the cockpit of Camel F6102, sent the enemy machine down in flames, its bombs exploding on impact at Tincourt.

At the same time - 21.35 hrs - the following night Lieut A A Mitchell, in Camel C8227, drove down another AEG that crashed on landing near Cambrai. Maj C J Q Brand, in Camel D6423, and Lieut J H Summers, D6568, accounted for yet another twin engined AEG bomber that crashed, killing the crew, at Gouzeaucourt.

The same night - Saturday, 21st September - 2nd Lieut George Norman Troth of 210 Cranbrook Road, Ilford, who had flown as an observer gunner on 40 night bombing raids with No.101 Squadron in France, was killed in action; his pilot, 2nd Lieut F A Browning was wounded and died later.

Living up to his reputation acquired in No.44 Squadron at Hainault Farm aerodrome, Capt D V Armstrong, now serving with No.151 Squadron in France, could not resist invitations from Allied squadrons to show-off the performance of 'Doris', his legendary Camel. It was after a demonstration of the South African's

Captain Arthur Newman (left in back row of this 1912/13 Ilford Hockey team photograph) of 4th Essex Regiment and, later, No.57 Squadron (*Redbridge & Ilford Hockey Club*)

No.57 Squadron

aerobatic skills at the USAS flying school at Issoudun that Lieut Temple N Joyce, a flying instructor encouraged by Armstrong, became the first aviator in the AEF to execute the half roll out of the top of a loop. On another occasion Armstrong, on a courtesy visit to Escadrille SPA 103, had a mock combat above the French aerodrome with a SPAD XIII piloted by Capitaine René Paul Fonck, destined to become the French and Allied ace of aces, with 75 confirmed victories. René Fonck's SPAD was outflown by Armstrong's Camel, but in combat the handsome young Frenchman's deadly marksmanship was as legendary as Armstrong's aerobatics.

On Wednesday, 25th September, Lieut T R Bloomfield, on patrol for No.151 Squadron east of Bapaume, engaged an AEG bomber at approximately 21.00 hrs, firing 150 rounds at 100 yards range. He saw sparks fly from the bomber's right hand engine nacelle, before the slipstream tossed Camel F6084 into a spin. Forty minutes elapsed before he found another enemy machine in his sights; fifty rounds were fired, some hitting the oil sump of the Gotha engine. Oil spraying back over the Camel and pilot forced Bloomfield to disengage and return to Vignacourt.

An unusual accident robbed No.151 Squadron of an original 'Camel merchant' from Hainault Farm on the night of Thursday, 26th September. Returning from a night patrol, Captain W H Haynes taxied into a ditch and overturned; crawling from the upturned Camel in his bulky flying gear, he was inspecting the machine for damage when a mechanic entered the upside down cockpit to clear the live rounds from the machine guns breech blocks. Bill Haynes, on one knee examining the engine by torchlight, was hit in the chest by a bullet and died instantly when the mechanic accidentally triggered one of his guns.

On Sunday, 29th September, A Flt Commander, Lieut Arthur Newman, and his observer, 2nd Lieut C Wilkinson, in DH4 A7723 of No. 57 Squadron, were forced to put down at Treizennes aerodrome, after fighting their way home from a daylight bombing raid far behind enemy lines and accounting for two of their attackers. Arthur Newman had been awarded the Military Cross for rescuing a wounded comrade lying out in 'No Man's Land', whilst serving with the 4th Battalion of the Essex Regiment at Gallipoli. Returning to his squadron at Vert Galand the same day, Newman who had flown on one hundred bombing raids, now looked forward to returning home to Cranbrook Road, Ilford, on leave.

On the last day of September, 1918, Bulgaria surrendered to the Allies, unrest in the Central Powers, after four years of total war and near famine, were bringing demands for peace from the multi-racial Austro-Hungarian empire. While rioting was taking place in Germany, there was also unrest in England - a strike in Ilford by omnibus and tramcar crews was settled by a pay rise of an extra five shillings a week.

Damascus, the capital of Syria, was entered by British cavalry on Tuesday, 1st October.

On the Western Front the Allies retook St Quentin; the following day Ypres Ridge was recaptured and aeroplanes of the RAF dropped 13 tons of rations to British troops advancing beyond their supply lines.

A wrecked Felixstowe F2A flying boat (*Ted Wiles*)

No.151 Squadron

On Friday, 4th October, Capt Trevor William Stewart Harris, a local airman, stationed with the RAF at Felixstowe, lost his life in a flying boat accident. Four crew members survived the crash that occurred when N4537, a twin engined Felixstowe F.2A, powered by two 375 hp Rolls-Royce engines, crashed into the harbour, with Harris at the controls during take off.

After leaving Hainault Farm for further flight training, Clayton Knight, now a Lieutenant in the US Army Air Service, had been posted to No. 206 Squadron RAF in France. On Saturday, 5th October, Knight, piloting DH9 D560 with 2nd Lieut J H Perring, took off from Alquines aerodrome and joined the formation circling overhead for a daylight bombing raid on Courtri. Knight and his regular observer were flying a new untried machine and were ordered to fly at the rear of the formation in case they fell out with engine trouble. Over the enemy lines the ten strong formation of bombers suddenly lost the accompanying bursts of anti-aircraft fire, as several yellow tailed Fokker biplanes dived out of the sun. Knight's observer fired a red flare, warning their comrades, as Oblt Harald Auffarth, intending to make the rearmost De Havilland his 23rd victory, swooped under the tailplane of the English machine, putting a burst of machine gun fire through the ply flooring of Perring and Knight's cockpits setting it on fire. Stamping and beating out the flames as the DH9 spun slowly out of control, Knight eased the smoking bomber off at 1,500 ft, to be met head on by the German ace intent on the kill. Pulling back on the stick and correcting his aim with the rudder bar, the American forced his opponent to bank away with a with a burst of fire from the forward firing Vickers gun. Wounded in the leg by an incendiary bullet, Knight brought the machine down in a wheat field and was captured with Perring attempting to set the upturned bomber on fire again. Many years later Clayton Knight found out that his bullets had damaged the Fokker's engine, forcing Auffarth to make a forced landing, wiping off the undercarriage in the process.

On Thursday, 10th October, the funeral cortège of Flight Commander Trevor William Stewart Harris set out from the family home at 3 Grosvenor Road, Ilford. Officers and men from 54 TDS Fairlop acted as pall bearers and escort, accompanied by the band of the 13th Cadet Artist Rifles, and laid the unfortunate airman to rest in the grounds of St Mary's Church with full military honours.

Lieut Claud Handley Trotter, a 23 year old Canadian serving with No.44 Squadron at Hainault Farm aerodrome, was blinded by a searchlight beam on the night of Sunday, 13th October, whilst on patrol in Camel E5147 and lost his life in the resulting crash.

By Tuesday, 15th October, 'Spanish Flu' was causing concern in Ilford and all schools were forced to close for short periods. Among measures taken by the Ilford Public Health Committee were to telegram the War Office requesting that Dr Oates, on leave from military duties, be allowed to remain in the town to assist with the outbreak of the epidemic that would claim millions of lives worldwide before it finally subsided in 1919.

On Wednesday, 16th October, 2nd Lieut F W Halliwell, flying Sopwith Pup

Pilot Lieutenant Claude H Trotter
(*Walter Hearne*)

A propeller hangs in memory of
C H Trotter in All Saints' Church, Chigwell
(*Revd V C Brown*)

C1515 with 54 TDS Fairlop, span into the ground, to survive the crash with serious injuries.

A guard of honour from No.44 Squadron lined up outside the gates to present arms, as a trailer bearing the flag-covered coffin of Lieut C H Trotter entered All Saints Church grounds at Chigwell on the afternoon of Thursday, 17th October. As this gallant officer, twice wounded flying as an RFC Observer in France, was laid to rest, a firing party from the 13th Artists Rifles fired a salute and Camels of No.44 Squadron from nearby Hainault Farm circled overhead.

On Friday, 18th October, Capt F B Sedgewick, stationed at Fairlop, died in a spectacular Camel crash when F1417 was observed to stall, cartwheel and sideslip into the ground.

The following day 54 TDS Fairlop received its first two-seat dual control Camel for training purposes.

2nd Lieut C A Firmin, former Assistant Scout Master of the 1st Seven Kings Troop of Boy Scouts, returned to France from leave on Monday, 21st October. Due to the rapid advance along the Front he did not rejoin his Squadron until Friday, 25th. By Monday, 28th October, 2nd Lieut Firmin was back in action with No.59 Squadron, flying as an Observer in RE8 E1105, piloted by Lieut F Whitburn. Three miles over the enemy lines Firmin's machine came under attack from a Fokker concealed in the clouds overhead. Although wounded in the thigh, Firmin caught the German machine with a burst of fire as it emerged from the clouds for the kill; the Fokker fell away into a spin trailing a spiral of smoke. The RE8 pilot, also wounded, had almost reached their aerodrome before crashing.

Charles Firmin jumped clear and rolled on the ground to smother his burning leather coat, before returning to the blazing 'Harry Tate' to drag his unconscious pilot clear.

As the Allies continued their advance on the Western Front, No.151 Squadron moved to a forward aerodrome at Bancourt in close support. Lieut C E Hocking lost his life when Camel F1979 crashed at Burlon, near Cambrai, on Tuesday, 28th October. After dark, Lieut L L Carter on patrol in Camel F1887 chased a Gotha, but, closing in, he was caught in the turbulence of the bomber's large propellers, span out of control and lost sight of the enemy machine in the darkness.

It was the Commanding Officer, Major C J Q Brand, who destroyed the last enemy bomber credited to No.151 Squadron during the war. The action took place on the evening of Wednesday, 30th October, when 'Flossie' Brand, on patrol in Camel D6423 - his venerable 'Makhabane II' - fired on a Friedrichshafen GIIIA, coned by searchlights. The bomber burst into flames, but continued flying level until, absorbing 230 rounds in short bursts, the fuselage broke in two and fell 9,000 ft on open land at Fôret d'Andigny, inside Allied lines.

No.151 Squadron accounted for 21 confirmed and 5 probable night bombing machines in its four months active service in France from July, 1918. Obviously the formation at Hainault Farm the previous June, with a flight each of experienced night flyers from the Essex Home Defence aerodromes of North Weald, Hornchurch and Hainault Farm, were the reason for the spectacular success of No.151 Squadron.

At noon on Thursday, 31st October, Turkey officially surrendered to the Allies; the following day the Serbian Army re-entered Belgrade, that had been lost after fierce fighting with the Austrian Army in October, 1915.

In France, the BEF continued their advance. Between the 1st and 4th of November 19,000 German prisoners were escorted to the rear and 450 guns captured; German rearguard units being in a state of chaos.

Captain Bentfield Charles Hucks, the Essex pioneer aviator, who Stanley Apling photographed in Loxford Park during the peaceful summer of 1913, survived four years of war as a test pilot to die on Wednesday, 6th November, 1918 - another victim of the influenza epidemic.

The last fatal wartime casualty of 54 TDS at Fairlop aerodrome also occurred on 6th November, when 2nd Lieut Harry Walter Jassby, a Canadian officer, crashed to his death after his Camel E1422 had been struck by another machine. Because the official records of 54 TDS were later destroyed and no inquest recorded in the local press, details of the occupants and type of machine remain a mystery.

On, 8th November, Major Charles Edward Murrey Pickthorne, the Ilford airman from Endsleigh Gardens, who survived flying obsolete DH2 pusher scouts in action during the spring of 1917, took command of No.84 Squadron at Bertry in France.

On Saturday, 9th November - barely eight months after Field-Marshal Haig made his desperate `Backs to the wall' speech to the battered BEF in Flanders - Imperial Germany collapsed and Kaiser Wilhelm was forced to abdicate, seeking refuge in Holland. Following fighting in the streets, Hamburg was under the control of revolutionary forces and Prussian diplomats were placed under arrest. By night and day during fine weather on Sunday, 10th November, the RAF dropped over forty tons of bombs, spreading havoc among the demoralised retreating German road and rail transport.

Major C E M Pickthorne leading a patrol of SE5a machines of No.84 Squadron in F904, engaged a formation of enemy scouts and shot down a Fokker DVII, east of Mutage.

Another local airman, Lieut George Ebben Randall, of Third Avenue, Manor Park, on patrol with No.20 Squadron in Bristol Fighter E2429, defended a formation of DH9 bombers under attack from 11 Fokker biplanes. With the aid of his observer's Lewis gun, manned by 2nd Lieut G V Learmond, they destroyed a Fokker DVII and, half an hour later, another falling near Louerval at 11.35 hrs: it would be the last EA claimed by local airmen during the Great War.

At 23.00 hrs a wireless message from Berlin authorised German emissaries negotiating in a railway carriage on a siding behind the Allied front lines to sign an armistice agreement. At 05.00 hrs on Monday, 11th November, the terms were signed - the cease fire to become effective from 11.00 hrs.

It had been business as usual for the RAF during the last hours; twenty tons of bombs were dropped at Louvain railway junction - an ammunition train was hit and the resulting explosions caused many fires.

Back at Hainault Farm aerodrome the armistice was greeted with mixed feelings, as an order for No.44 Squadron to proceed to France for front line service was cancelled.

An air of unreality prevailed in Ilford after the ending of hostilities. Mounting excitement during the afternoon erupted on to the streets of the town and that evening crowds of singing and cheering men, women, and children converged into High Road - four years and two months of heartache and hardship were forgotten for a few hours. It was over! No more goodbyes, no more dread as a telegram boy cycled down the road; the 'War to end all wars' had finally ground to halt.

Lieut Stanley Apling, taking leave once again of Northolt aerodrome, hurried through the euphoric population of London home to Ilford and Nancy - this time by train.

More than ten thousand Ilford men served in the armed forces during the 1914-18 war; one thousand one hundred and seventy are known to have lost their lives, and a far greater number had been wounded, gassed, lost their hearing or their sight.

At Hainault Farm aerodrome on Monday, 16th December, Lieut Thomas Rowland Burns, from New Zealand, suffered fatal injuries in an accident involving a crash in F6326, a 110hp Le Rhône engined Camel. Two weeks later on 30th December, Lieut W A H Ellercamp, just after becoming airborne from Hainault Farm in Camel D6637, collided with Camel D9459 of No.78 Squadron from Suttons Farm and piloted by Lieut C D Hurndall: both were killed.

The surviving triplane built under contract from the Sopwith Company by the Ilford Aeroplane Works in 1917 can be seen at the Royal Air Force Museum, Hendon (*Ken Feline*)

Lieutenant Stanley Apling and his fiancée, Nancy, at the end of the Great War (*Stanley Apling*)

Stanley Apling gives the thumbs up in preparation for a flight to celebrate his 93rd birthday (*Stanley Apling*)

1919 and after

On 1st July, 1919, No.44 Squadron were reduced to a cadre and transferred from Hainault farm to North Weald to be disbanded on 31st December. Reformed at Wyton on 8th March, 1937, No.44 Squadron entered WW2 flying twin engined Handley Page Hampden bombers. Fate decreed that the former WW1 night fighter squadrons would be the first squadron in Bomber Command equipped with four engined Avro Lancaster heavy bombers - the hunters had become the hunted. During WW2 7 bombs, 3 parachute mines, and one flying bomb fell in the vicinity of Hainault Farm, where the remaining WW1 aeroplane sheds were occupied by an engineering firm manufacturing, among other things for the war effort, bomb loading trollies for the RAF.

No. 54 TDS at Fairlop, with HQ at Chingford, was disbanded on 7th February, 1919. Sadly at least two more fatal accidents happened before the aerodrome closed. The first involved 2nd Lieut T B Simpson, whilst performing aerobatics in Camel F9548 on Thursday, 19th December, 1918. Entering a spin from the top of a loop, like so many more before him, he did not recover control in time to level out. Engine failure claimed the last known fatal casualty of No.54 TDS when the 130 hp Clerget rotary of Avro D9844 cut out shortly after take off, injuring the pilot, Lieut R Starbuck, and killing FlSgt Russell Cound in the crash.

Unlike Hainault Farm aerodrome, Fairlop also served in WW2 - this time as an airfield for Fighter Command RAF,

occupying a site on the opposite side of Forest Road from September, 1941, until September, 1944, when it was taken over by Balloon Command RAF. Fairlop was officially demobbed on August, 1946.

In the early post-war years the deserted aerodrome became the Mecca of the many model aeroplane clubs in and around the London area until 1950.

Today the WW2 aerodrome site is better known as Fairlop Waters - the popular Essex outdoor pursuits centre.

In the aftermath of the 1914-1918 war, the Commonwealth War Graves Commission faced the mammoth task of placing permanent headstones upon the graves of the fallen. Relatives were notified and sometimes offered the wooden cross that had marked the resting place of loved ones. Herbert and Ada Beck of Mayfair Avenue, Ilford, were among the grieving parents who presented the grave cross of their son, 2nd Lieut Herbert Musgrove Beck, Royal Flying Corps, to their local church. On 27th February, 1992, the *Ilford Recorder* published a photograph of local police officer, Jim Mitchell, holding a wooden cross that had been found in the road by a night patrol car crew. PC Mitchell, who is also a lay preacher, contacted local churches in an effort to find the owner and Father John Ives of St. Clement's, Great Ilford, replied. 2nd Lieut H M Beck had once been a member of his parish. Through the church archives PC Mitchell tried to contact surviving members of the Beck family, but in vain. However, he did discover that the cross went missing when the original St Clement's Church had been demolished back in the 1970's. Plans were made with Father John to re-dedicate the cross of 2nd Lieut H M Beck to St. Clement's that today stands on the opposite side of the road. The author read of PC Jim Mitchell and his splendid effort to prevent a part of Ilford history from being thrown into the dustbin and provided service details and a photograph of the young airman. Jim Mitchell was surprised and delighted to have at last the full details of `Bertie' after weeks of enquiries.

On Sunday, 8th November, 1992, local members of Cross & Cockade International and their families joined the congregation of St. Clement's for their Remembrance Day Sunday service: they had been invited for assisting PC Mitchell with his enquiries. During the service PC Jim Mitchell, as visiting Lay Preacher, included the young flyer in his sermon and the wooden cross from the French grave of 2nd Lieut Herbert Musgrove Beck,

No.3 Squadron Royal Flying Corps, was blessed and re-dedicated. Flt/Lt John Carr, No.6 Squadron Coltishall, carried the cross and laid a wreath from the Royal British Legion. Herbert Beck had been attached to No.6 Squadron training the R.E.8 aircrew in the art of low level ground attack when his Camel spun into the ground on Tuesday morning, 22nd January, 1918. He was buried at the military cemetery of St. Pierre, Amiens. Members of No.4F Air Training Corps (Barking) were also in attendance and Trumpeter Alan Peters of the Metropolitan Police Band sounded the Last Post.

2nd Lieutenant Herbert M Beck (*Ilford War Memorial Gazette*)

An RE8 observation machine of No.59 Squadron (*Colin Ross*)